Introduction to Judaism
Part II

Professor Shai Cherry

THE TEACHING COMPANY ®

PUBLISHED BY:

THE TEACHING COMPANY
4840 Westfields Boulevard, Suite 500
Chantilly, Virginia 20151-2299
1-800-TEACH-12
Fax—703-378-3819
www.teach12.com

ISBN 1-56585-926-X

Shai Cherry, Ph.D.

Assistant Professor of Jewish Thought, Vanderbilt University

Shai Cherry (b. 1966) straddles the worlds of higher education and community education. Although it took Dr. Cherry seven years to acquire a B.A. (*magna cum Laude* and *Phi Beta Kappa*) in philosophy, politics, and economics from Claremont McKenna College, he managed to attend the Wharton School of Finance, two universities in England, the University of California at Santa Cruz, and the Hebrew University of Jerusalem. During that period, he taught junior high school and high school students at various southern California Reform temples and Conservative synagogues, as well as volunteered in Israel for 10 months on Project Otzma.

As Dr. Cherry pursued his doctorate in Jewish thought from Brandeis University (2001), he served as family educator at a Reform temple in the Boston area. He also taught Rabbinics and Modern Jewish Thought for Hebrew College. Having begun his formal Jewish education at an unorthodox *yeshiva* (seminary) in Jerusalem, the Pardes Institute, he returned on completion of his Ph.D. for another year of Talmud study at the Conservative Yeshiva.

Since 2001, Professor Cherry has taught at Vanderbilt University in Nashville, Tennessee, as the Mellon Assistant Professor of Jewish Thought. At the same time, he has served as an instructor in the Florence Melton Adult Mini-School.

Dr. Cherry's research focuses on biblical interpretation and the nexus between science and Judaism. "Three Twentieth-Century Jewish Responses to Evolutionary Theory" appeared in the 2003 volume of *Aleph: Historical Studies in Science and Judaism*. Slated to appear in 2005 is his essay "Crisis Management via Biblical Interpretation: Fundamentalism, Modern Orthodoxy and Genesis" in *Jewish Tradition and the Challenge of Evolution*. The following year will see the publication of Dr. Cherry's first book on Jewish interpretations of Torah.

The professor has received numerous awards for his work in community education and continues to teach across the United States and in Israel.

Table of Contents
Introduction to Judaism
Part II

Introduction to Judaism

Scope:

Judaism is not a book (the Hebrew Bible) or even a set of books (the Hebrew Bible plus the Talmud plus other legal, mystical, and philosophical writings), but a living religious tradition. Even to call Judaism a "religion" is not quite accurate. The Land of Israel and the People of Israel have been essential, intertwined components of Judaism for 3,000 years. Most religions, like Christianity, do not have quite the same relationship to a particular place or national group. Judaism has variously been called a culture, an ethnicity, and a civilization, all terms that struggle to include more than "just" religion. This course, *Introduction to Judaism*, presents the unfolding of the *religious* aspects of the Jewish civilization from the Hebrew Bible to today, while keeping an eye on the historical background against which those changes within Judaism have occurred.

The Hebrew Bible is Judaism's foundation text. Knowing the Hebrew Bible, however, will tell you surprisingly little about Judaism, especially in its contemporary expressions. We begin our course with a discussion of the Bible and its relationship to Judaism. We'll also discuss modern assumptions about the human authorship of the Bible and compare them to traditional assumptions that the Bible is, somehow, the word of God.

We then begin to describe the varieties of early Judaisms. Although Jewish history is not one long tale of travails, there have been several catastrophes that powerfully shaped the Jewish consciousness. Among them was the destruction of the First and Second Temples in Jerusalem by the Babylonians and Romans, respectively. In the wake of the destruction of the Second Temple, some of the groups competing for power in the Jewish world lost their power bases, while others gained from the changing circumstances. Eventually, it was Rabbinic Judaism that achieved hegemony among the vying ideologies and interest groups.

After discussing what we know about this power struggle to assume leadership in the Jewish world, we will look closely at some of the core values and practices of the Rabbis. Most of their agenda, such as the emphasis on deeds of loving kindness, has roots in the Bible. But the ways in which the Rabbis promoted other practices, such as study, repentance, and prayer, are quite innovative. In our discussion of the afterlife, for example, we will see how a relatively late and marginal idea in the Hebrew Bible became critical in the late Second Temple period.

With the destruction of the Second Temple in 70 C.E., however, celebrating God's presence in time, rather than space (as in the Jerusalem Temple), became central in Rabbinic Judaism. The next section of the course, therefore, focuses on the Jewish calendar, beginning with the Sabbath. After looking at the Rabbinic development of this biblical institution, we'll pause to focus on the broader question of the relationship between the letter of the law and its spirit. We will then continue with our journey through the Jewish year, always conscious of how the holidays, often relating to harvests in the Land of Israel, were given new dimensions and reinterpreted for a people who no longer lived in the Land.

At this point, we'll introduce the Jewish philosophers and mystics of the Middle Ages. What explains the emergence of these new expressions of Judaism? How do they differ in their understandings of the relationship between God and the world? As we make this bridge between ancient and modern Judaism, we'll focus on the issue of evil. Beginning with biblical understandings of evil and suffering, we will then move to Rabbinic responses. The Jewish philosophers and mystics of the Middle Ages resort to dramatically different styles of language to address their equally different explanations for the persistence of evil. Finally, we'll see how some modern Jewish thinkers have responded to the greatest of all Jewish catastrophes, the Holocaust. How do contemporary theodicies (explanations for evil in a world created by a good and powerful God) relate to the historical ones?

Our next five sessions will be devoted to modern expressions of Judaism. The varied faces of Judaism that we see today are all outgrowths of the historical changes of the Jewish emancipation and enlightenment of the 18th and 19th centuries. Surprisingly, we'll see that Ultra-Orthodox Judaism is just as much a product of modernity as is Reform Judaism. We'll then explain the ideologies and the reasons for the emergence of the major movements in the "middle": Modern Orthodoxy, Conservative Judaism, and Reconstructionist Judaism. We'll also discuss the modern phenomenon of atheism/secularism among Jews. (Being a Jewish atheist is not a contradiction in terms, while being a Christian atheist is.) Some secular Jews (and a few religious ones, too) chose to express their Jewish commitments through a return to the historic Land of Israel. Thus, modernity has brought with it the possibility of identifying, for the first time in nearly 2,000 years, with any, all, or none of the following: the Land of Israel, the People of Israel, and the Torah of Israel.

Our final three sessions will consider sensitive issues of contemporary interest and trace their developments from the Torah to today's different Jewish denominations. The emphasis in these lectures will be on the process of how Jewish thought and practice develops. What is the role and status of women according to Jewish law? How does Judaism understand Christianity? Is it an expression of idolatry or another path to the one God? Finally, are the Jews the Chosen People? And, if so, for what have they been chosen and by whom? Throughout these lectures, we will highlight the wide range of Jewish expressions, so that an equally legitimate name for this course might be: *Introduction to Judaisms*.

Lecture Thirteen
Minor Holidays—Then and Now

Scope:

With apologies to Cole Porter, how strange the change to major from minor! Chanukah isn't even mentioned in the Hebrew Bible, and Purim celebrates the reversal of a near-death experience for the Jewish people. Although the Rabbis were ambivalent about both holidays, they have become two of the most celebrated days in the Jewish year. We'll explain the ambivalence and suggest reasons for their persistent popularity.

Tu b'Shvat is called the New Year for the Tree. Although it has become the major holiday for "Green Judaism," it started off as the fiscal new year for taxing agriculture. We'll chart its growth. Tisha b'Av solemnly commemorates the destruction of the Temples in Jerusalem and is followed by the least known of our minor holidays, Tu b'Av, akin to a feminist version of Valentine's Day. Another minor holiday that has been recently reclaimed by women is Rosh Chodesh (New Month).

Outline

I. Chanukah (Dedication).

    A. Chanukah is the only Jewish holiday that is mentioned in neither the TaNaKH nor the Mishnah!

        1. There are two books recording the deeds of the Maccabees in the Apocrypha.

            a. The Maccabean Revolt against the Syrian Greeks, or Seleucids, was from 168 B.C.E.–165 B.C.E.

            b. The Hasmonean family, from Modi'in, eventually claimed both religious and political leadership. The family was of a priestly class but not a high-priestly class. Thus, the Hasmoneans should not have claimed the office of high priest. Because they were not of Davidic descent, they should not have claimed political leadership.

        2. The Gemara, written about 500 years after the Maccabean Revolt, introduces the story about the cruse of oil lasting for eight days (b. Shabbat 21a).

B. The holiday was extremely popular and could not be suppressed, though it seems the Rabbis tried.

   1. It's an eight-day holiday because it is patterned after the dedication of the First Temple, which coincided with the holidays of Sukkot and Shmini Atzeret (I Kings 8 and II Macc. 10).

   2. The motif of oil, bread, and fish miraculously multiplying is common in both Jewish and Christian Scriptures (II Kings 4:14, 42 and Matt. 14:16–21).

   3. On a literary level, the Maccabees represent the purity of living a lifestyle dedicated to God and God's will in the midst of the impurity of Hellenistic sexual and religious practices.

C. The popularity of the day can be traced to cross-cultural influences.

   1. The eighth day of Chanukah, when nine lights are lit in the Chanukiah, is the darkest day of the year because it always falls on the new moon following the winter solstice.

   2. In America, the tradition of gift giving for Christmas influenced Jews to emphasize the previously muted aspect of gift giving on Chanukah.

   3. In Israel, Chanukah became an important traditional holiday to celebrate the valor of the Israelites in their struggle to survive the evil designs of their neighbors.

II. Purim (Lots).

A. The book of Esther describes how Haman's plot to kill all the Judeans (not yet Jews) was frustrated by Esther and Mordechai. Haman, a descendant of King Agag of Amalek, is hanged, along with his 10 sons; the anti-Judean riffraff are killed; no plunder is taken; and Mordechai becomes second in command of the kingdom of Persia.

B. The Rabbis debate whether this text should be included in the TaNaKH.

   1. The name of God appears nowhere in the text.

   2. The book is sexually suggestive.

   3. Perhaps the Rabbis decided to include this text precisely because it moves its readers to see God's presence and providence even when God seems to be absent and the world seems to be full of chance. (The name of the holiday, *Purim*, means "lots." See Esther 3:7.) We must read between the lines of the text because God's name does not appear.

C. The celebration of turning the tables on Haman becomes an annual event. The timing of this holiday in the early spring parallels other carnival festivals that celebrate the "near death" of the winter months.

    1. The characteristically Jewish elements of the holiday include gift giving and *tzedakah* (Esther 9:22). Neither activity was mentioned in the story itself.

    2. The Talmud also says that we should overindulge so that we can no longer distinguish between cursed Haman and blessed Mordechai (b. Megillah 7b).

    3. Contemporary practice is a carnivalesque combination of Halloween costumes, gift giving, tzedakah, and drinking to excess. In Israel, plastic head bobbers and silly string are part of the festivities.

III. Tu b'Shvat.

A. In the Mishnah, this day marks the beginning of the fiscal year for purposes of tithing agriculture.

B. In the 16th century, Jewish mystics imagined God's beneficence flowing down from the heavens like an upside down tree. With roots in heaven, the mystics draw down the divine energy, or sap, so that it "fructifies" on earth. They developed a seder on Tu b'Shvat with different kinds of fruits to facilitate the drawing down of these divine blessings.

C. In the early 20th century, the Zionist movement wanted to plant trees in the Land of Israel. Tu b'Shvat became a Jewish Arbor Day, and the Jewish National Fund collected money to plant trees.

D. Several decades ago, Jewish environmentalists latched on to this day to promote traditional Jewish wisdom on the environment.

IV. Tisha b'Av.

A. This day of mourning commemorates communal destructions in Jewish history, specifically the First and Second Temples.

B. The prohibitions of Yom Kippur are also in effect for Tisha b'Av. In the evening, the book of Lamentations, describing the destruction of the First Temple, is chanted.

C. From the beginning of Av until the ninth (Tisha), there is a period of semi-mourning similar to the first 32 days of the Omer.

V. Tu b'Av.

A. Six days after Tisha b'Av, there is a Jewish combination of Valentine's and Sadie Hawkins Day, about which the Mishnah describes the young women of Jerusalem going out to the vineyards and joyously dancing with the young men (m. Ta'anit, end).

B. Although Rabbi Shimon ben Gamliel describes this day as one of incredible joy, it was not widely celebrated throughout Jewish history. Today, some Jewish couples mark the day with picnics, complete with Israeli wine.

VI. Rosh Chodesh (Head of the Month).

A. In the Bible, the celebration of the new moon involved animal sacrifices, a festive meal, and abstention from work parallel to other holidays (Num. 28:11–15, I Sam. 20:5, and Amos 8:5).

B. After the destruction of the Temple, the holiday was reduced to singing psalms in the synagogue.

C. Already in the Rabbinic period, the holiday was associated with women, most likely because of the parallel between the lunar cycle and a woman's menstrual cycle. Today, there are women's Rosh Chodesh groups in many cities across the world.

D. It is customary on the Saturday night prior to the full moon, which always falls on the 15th of the Hebrew month, to bless the waxing moon. This blessing, *Kiddush L'vana*, is done outside, in sight of the moon, and the prayers are included in all traditional prayer books.

Essential Reading:

Agus, "This Month Is for You," in *The Jewish Woman*.

Greenberg, *The Jewish Way*, pp. 217–304 and 411–420.

Klein, *A Guide to Jewish Religious Practice*, pp. 225–240 and 255–268.

Waskow, *Seasons of Our Joy*, pp. 87–132, 207–218, and 228–230.

Supplementary Reading:

Bickerman, *The Maccabees*.

Elon, Hyman, and Waskow, eds. *Trees, Earth, and Torah : A Tu b'Shvat Anthology*.

Goodman, *A Purim Anthology*, *A Hannuka Anthology*.

Questions to Consider:

1. What is it about Chanukah that allowed the holiday to survive and flourish even without initial endorsement by Rabbinic culture?

2. Tu b'Shvat went from being a fiscal new year to a semi-holiday that promotes environmental activism. What are the advantages and disadvantages of this kind of flexibility? What are the limits and who decides?

3. What do we learn from the parallel sequence of introspection/ mourning to joy in the transitions from Yom Kippur to Sukkot and from Tisha b'Av to Tu b'Av?

Lecture Thirteen—Transcript
Minor Holidays—Then and Now

We're going to conclude our unit on the Jewish calendar by looking at historically minor holidays and, with apologies to Cole Porter, how strange the change to major from minor. In most cases, the holidays that had been relatively insignificant, compared to the other holidays we've discussed so far, gained tremendously in their importance and in terms of the number of Jews celebrating those holidays in the modern period. We'll talk a little bit about the historic background of those holidays, and we suggest reasons why they might be more popular today than they had been in the past.

So let us begin with *Channukah*. Channukah is one of the best-known Jewish holidays. The word itself "*channukah*" means "dedication" and we'll explain why it has that name. Channukah is unique amongst the Jewish holidays because it is mentioned in neither the TaNaKH (the Hebrew Bible) nor in the Mishnah—and yet, it's this huge Jewish holiday. So what about the day prevented it from being mentioned in Bible? History prevented it because the events that it chronicles happened after the events that are described in the biblical corpus of books stopped. Once the Jews came back to the Land of Israel after the destruction of the First Temple, at the end of the sixth century BCE, you have the historical narrative of the Hebrew Bible stopping, but the events that we celebrate in the holiday of Channukah describe what happened in that Maccabean Revolt against the Selecuid Greeks, from 168 BCE to 165 BCE. So, chronologically, the holiday of Channukah is out of bounds of the Hebrew Bible—So, that explains why it is not in the Hebrew Bible.

But why isn't it in the Mishnah? Why isn't the holiday of Channukah mentioned anywhere in the Mishnah? Certainly by the beginning of the third century CE, hundreds of years after the events that the holiday of Channukah described, those events must have been well known, and the holiday must have been celebrated by large numbers of people, both in the Land of Israel and outside the Land of Israel. So, why wasn't it mentioned? That's the question. We'll answer that shortly.

A little more about the holiday of Channukah—we've got the internal rebellion by the Hasmoneans, or the Maccabees. The name "Maccabee" means "hammer," but it can also be an acronym for a verse in *Exodus*, the first letters of which are "m, c, b, y" *mi camocha b'elim adonai*, which, in the proper historical translation would translate into: "Who is like you amongst the gods?"—from this period in Israelite theological development in which there was still a recognition that other nations had other gods. Sometimes that verse is translated as: "Who is like you amongst the mighty?" But, "who is like you amongst the gods" *mi camocha b'elim adonai—yud hey vav hey*—that YHWH transliteration—that was the moniker of the Hasmonean family. So, they are either called the Hasmoneans or the Maccabees.

They, as we have mentioned before, were rebelling both against the Selecuid Greeks and the religious oppression they were facing from Antiochus, the Syrian ruler, as well as the more secularizing Hellenistic Jews, who were very willing to take on those cosmopolitan secular ways of the Greeks and abandon the traditions of their fathers. So, the Maccabean Revolt was both against the external enemy (the Selecuid Greeks) and the internal foes or enemies (the secularizing or Hellenistic Jews).

The family came from Modi'in, and they eventually claimed, once they were successful. It wasn't all to their credit that they were successful in pushing the Selecuid Greeks out; the Selecuid Greeks had other—bigger—fish to fry in their international empire-building strategy, so they thought it best to let the Hasmoneans win this one. So, when the Hasmoneans did win, they took control of both the secular aspects of the government, and the High Priesthood. That was a problem. Although the Hasmoneans were a priestly family, they weren't of the High-Priestly lineage, which are descendants from Aaron's grandson Phinehas. They were priests, but not High Priests. Yet they arrogated to themselves the office of the High Priesthood. Similarly, they arrogated to themselves the political leadership of the country. But that, according to the Bible, was supposed to be invested in the descendants of David. They weren't descendants of David. So, on both counts—both in terms of temporal power and in terms of sacral power—they arrogated to themselves positions that they weren't biblically entitled to.

Moreover, they became very corrupt, and by 63 BCE, one brother—because of infighting with another brother—invited Pompey and the Romans to come into the Land of Israel. So, the Rabbis weren't interested in promoting this family—because of their corruption, because they invited the Romans into the Land of Israel, and because they basically ignored the separation of powers that is outlined in the book of *Deuteronomy* between the governmental affairs of the nation and the Temple or sacred affairs of the nation.

The *Gemarrah*, which is the second part of the Talmud (remember, the Mishnah plus the *Gemarrah* equals the Talmud) in a section that was probably written about 500 years after the Maccabean Revolt, introduces the story about the cruse of oil lasting for eight days. That was the version that I learned in Hebrew school, and it's the version that is widely popular. So, a little bit like, "Virginia, I'm afraid to tell you there ain't no Santa Claus" ... We have a similar story about this cruse of oil that lasted for eight days. We know most of what we know about the war of the Maccabees from the two *Books of the Maccabees* (*Maccabees I* and *Maccabees II*), but they are not in the Hebrew Bible. They are included in a set of books called the Apocrypha, including the *Wisdom of Solomon* and *Judith*. This set of books (the Apocrypha) was included in the Catholic or Christian Bible, as part of their Old Testament, but the Jews didn't include it in the TaNaKH. So, if you remember in our very first lecture we made the distinction between the Hebrew Bible and the Old Testament, or the TaNaKH and the Old Testament. The two names don't even include the same books. They also don't include overlapping books in the same order—All the more reason to make the distinction between the Christian Old Testament and the TaNaKH. In the Christian Old Testament, there are books that are not included in the Jewish TaNaKH.

In those early eyewitness accounts or records of the Hasmonean Revolt, we don't have anything about the cruse of oil being found in the Temple and lasting for eight days when there was just enough oil to last for a single day. The first time we see that story is 500 years later in that little piece of Gemarrah. In the whole, big, wide Talmud, Channukah is only mentioned two times, both times in *Masechet Shabbat*, where it is talking about issues of lighting. As you light candles on Shabbat, you also light candles for Channukah. We'll talk about the *Channukiah* in just a moment.

The idea—the literary idea—of the cruse of oil lasting for eight days, when there had originally been only enough oil for one day, goes back to try to explain the idea that this was an eight-day holiday. The *Books of the Maccabees* tell you why it's an eight-day holiday: Because when the Maccabees, in their attempts at being good guerrilla fighters, were in the hills attacking the Seleucids, they were getting very excited in the summer months, thinking that they would be able to rout the Syrians, and rededicate the Temple that had been defiled by the Syrian Greeks, by the holiday of Sukkot, that big pilgrimage festival that is seven days plus Shmini Atzeret, at the very end of that seven-day period, which gives you the eighth day. They were looking forward to this eight-day holiday of Sukkot, but they didn't do it in time. Wars sometimes don't go exactly as the commanders plan, and sometimes they trail on, to unfortunate political consequences, longer than the leaders had anticipated. But they did finally rout the Syrian Greeks in December, or in the Hebrew month of *Kislev*. In order to compensate them for their depression and their disappointment at not being able to celebrate Sukkot at its proper time, they had an eight-day rededication ceremony to parallel the eight days of Sukkot in Shmini Atzeret. That's the historical explanation of why we have an eight-day holiday for Channukah.

But the Gemarrah comes in and talks about this little bit of oil lasting eight days. This motif of a little bit lasting for a long time and going a long way is a common biblical motif. We see it with oil. We see it with bread in the Hebrew Bible (the TaNaKH) in *II Kings,* chapter 4. It has another iteration in the New Testament, with the bread and fish that Jesus multiplies. So this idea of precious resources multiplying is a literary motif that the Rabbis took from the Hebrew Bible and applied to this oil lasting for a long time—but, on a symbolic level, it is getting at a very important truth. One of my teachers from the Pardes Institute of Jewish Studies, Baruch Feldstern, used to say that just because it's fiction doesn't mean it's false. I found that to be very powerful. There is truth in the symbolism of the story that is found in the Talmud about this little cruse of oil lasting for eight days—and that is, that from the Jewish perspective, the purity of living a lifestyle dedicated to God and God's will in the midst of this vast Greek empire that included (again from the Jewish point of view) Hellenistic practices involving sexual orgies and cultic prostitution, as well as their religious practices of idolatry, which represent the great environment of impurity, but the Hasmoneans were able to maintain that pure life style.

So, just like in the midst of the ruins of the Temple that had been defiled by the Syrian Greeks, there was one little *pach shemen*, one little cruse of oil, that was able to sustain that surviving remnant until more oil could be pressed.

I want to also talk about why the popularity of this holiday persists even until today. On the eighth day of Channukah, there are a total of eight candles in the Channukiah, plus the one in the middle that represents the servant that lights the other eight candles. So, a Channukiah has a total of nine candles or nine lights, four on each side and then one in the middle. For halachic reasons, you light the candles with the *shamas* (or the *shamash* in Hebrew—*shamas* is Yiddish). You use the central candle to light the other ones. The purpose of lighting the candles has an anthropological parallel in other cultures that have holidays of lights in the darkest season of the year. It always happens—because of the way that the lunar calendar falls out—that the eighth day of Channukah, when you light the greatest number of lights, is the darkest day of the year. Why? Because it always falls on the New Moon following the winter solstice. So, anthropologically, we see that at the darkest time of the year—what do you want to do? You want to create light.

Some people confuse the Jewish Channukiah, which has a total of nine candles or nine flames, with the *menorah* (which we find in the book of *Exodus*), which is a symbol of the Temple. It is a symbol of the Jewish people, but it only has three candlesticks on each side, and one in the middle, for a total of seven.

In America, of course, the 25th of Kislev—which is the date that Channukah begins—and the 25th of December, fall in the same season, sometimes even overlapping. So, the prominence of Channukah was raised by the centrality of Christmas in the Christian religion, and all of a sudden there became this tradition of giving lots of gifts on Channukah, one for each of the eight nights in some families. The tradition of gift giving is not historical. It is something that really developed in America. Indeed, in other countries and in Israel, if you get anything you get nuts or raisins or a candy bar, but the gift-giving quality of the day is muted.

But Channukah is still very important in Israel. Why? Because Channukah celebrates the military victory of the ancient Israelites against their surrounding neighboring enemies. That's exactly what contemporary Israelis need as a model for their own precarious military situation today.

The next holiday is *Purim*. *Purim* literally means "lots." We read about the holiday of Purim in the book of *Esther*, in the TaNaKH. The book describes how Haman's plot to kill all the Judaeans (they're not quite yet Jews) was frustrated by Esther and Mordechai. This happens in that period after the destruction of the First Temple, but before the Jews have been led back by Ezra and Nechemiah in the fifth century BCE. Haman is a descendant of King Agag of Amalek. He's an Amalekite. The Amalekites were very bad to the Israelites in the book of *Exodus* on their way out of Egypt. The Amalekites attacked those that were straggling amongst the Israelites: the weak, the women, the children. So, the Amalekites have a very bad name in the Hebrew Bible, and there is a commandment to wipe them out.

In the book of *Esther*, they are, indeed, finally all wiped out, as well as the anti-Judaean riffraff that's trying to execute a pogromme against the Judaeans all over the kingdom. No plunder is taken, and Mordechai becomes second in command in the kingdom of Persia. So, it is a story of a reversal of fortune, where the Israelites or Judaeans escaped a near-death experience, but they came out on top. That becomes the paradigm for Jewish survival when they are stateless. They have nothing to rely on except the grace of God, and their own cunning, and their own wits to ensure their survival.

Interestingly enough, the Rabbis debated whether this text should be included in the TaNaKH or not. Why did they have this debate? Because the name of God nowhere appears in the text. That's unusual. There are only two other books in the TaNaKH where the name of God does not appear: *The Song of Songs* and the book of *Ecclesiastes*. The name of God is attached onto the very end of the book of *Ecclesiastes*.

Another reason why the Rabbis debated whether *Esther* should be included in the Hebrew Bible is because the book is sexually suggestive—not exactly family reading; it is very burlesque. Ultimately, the Rabbis decided to include this text in the Hebrew Bible precisely because it forces its readers to perceive God's presence even when God seems to be absent and the world seems to be full of chance. Remember, the name "Purim" means "lots." Chance. Everything is up to chance. It's random. It's destiny. But the idea of Purim is that we need to take control of our own destiny. We need to see God between the lines when God is no longer apparently or transparently acting in Jewish history.

The celebration of turning the tables on Haman and his sons and his henchmen becomes an annual event. The timing of this holiday in the early Spring parallels other Carnival events that celebrate the "near-death" of the winter months. So, here, we have another anthropological connection. But there is something that is characteristically Jewish about Purim, as well. Here I'm reading from the ninth chapter of *Esther*:

> … the same days on which the Jews enjoyed relief from their foes and the same month which had been transformed for them from one of grief and mourning to one of festive joy. They were to observe them as days of feasting and merrymaking, and as an occasion for sending gifts to one another and presents to the poor.

That's part of the mitzvah—that's part of the commandment of how we celebrate Purim. Why? So that it's not just another day to party. These things ("sending gifts to one another and presents to the poor") have nothing to do with the story of Purim. They are tacked on as a kind of biblical moral veneer to this otherwise rather bawdy holiday tale that is celebrated even today very energetically and enthusiastically. What do I mean by that? The Talmud says that we should over-indulge so that we can no longer distinguish between cursed Haman and blessed Mordechai. That traditionally has been understood as a commandment to get so drunk that you don't know good from bad. One contemporary Jewish renewal Rabbi, Arthur Waskow, talks about getting so "mellow" that you can't distinguish between good and bad. The Talmud is not specific about the medium one uses to enter this state of a lack of differentiation between good and bad. But you get the sense that for some people, only when those distinctions become blurry or are erased does it facilitate their perception that God is acting in this world.

Contemporary practice is a carnivalesque combination of Halloween costumes, gift giving, tzedakah (giving to charity), and drinking to excess. In Israel, plastic head boppers or hammers and silly string are part of the festivities.

The next holiday is *Tu b'Shvat*. Why do I say holiday? Because I am a 21st-century Jew. Tu b'Shvat initially wasn't even a holiday. It is not mentioned in the Bible. It's mentioned in the Mishnah, as what? The beginning of the fiscal year for purposes of tithing agriculture. There was a tithe. You didn't pay with your money, you paid with your agriculture in an agrarian society. And you had to know when that fiscal year began. So it's Tu b'Shvat. *Tu* is *gematria* where every letter corresponds to a number. Nine and six are *Tu*, so together they are 15. The 15th day of the month of Shvat is the beginning of the fiscal year for the purposes of tithing agriculture. No holiday. No celebration. We don't celebrate April 15th when we have to pay our taxes. (Some people do because they no longer have to write out their forms and work on their forms.) But, there is nothing celebratory about this.

Notice: We go forward a thousand years, and in the Middle Ages, in the 16th century, Jewish mystics (we'll talk about them in a couple of lectures)—they imagine that God's blessings, God's beneficence, flowed down from the heavens like an upside-down tree—where the roots in God are in heaven, and the sap comes down the trees and "fructifies" at the very end of that on earth. They actually developed a seder, very similar to a Passover seder, with different kinds of fruits to facilitate the drawing down of these divine blessings. So, now, this day—Tu b'Shvat—is moved from being a fiscal year, to being a day that's a semi-holiday.

In the early 20th century, the Zionists who wanted to plant trees in the Land of Israel, in order to dry up the swamps in the north and in order to reforest large portions of the north that had been deforested over the centuries—they latched on to Tu b'Shvat as a holiday to promote the trees in Israel. So it became a Jewish Arbor Day, and the Jewish National Fund sent around these little blue cans or *pushkas*, and everyday, or before Shabbat, you would put coins in the *pushka*, and eventually the money would be sent through the Jewish National Fund to Israel, to plant trees in Israel. A couple of decades ago, the Jewish environmentalist movement emerged, parallel to the environmentalist movement that's going on, the general Green movement all around the world, and they latched onto Tu b'Shvat, not exclusively to promote the idea of Jews and the connection with trees, but to promote traditional Jewish wisdom on the environment.

So, I love Tu b'Shvat because it shows you the development of a day that moved from a fiscal new year for purposes of tithing, to this mystical idea of drawing down divine blessing, to a Jewish Arbor Day, to a Jewish environmentalist day. Tu b'Shvat.

The next holiday is *Tisha b'Av*. *Tisha* is the ninth; it actually means "ninth," the ninth of the month of *Av*. This is the collective day of mourning for the Jewish people. It commemorates the destructions of the First Temple in 586 BCE and the Second Temple by the Romans in the year 70 CE. The prohibitions of Yom Kippur are also in effect for Tisha b'Av. In the evening, the book of *Lamentations*, which describes the destruction of the First Temple, is chanted in a very dirge-like melody. In Israel, there are several prayer groups that meet at the Haas Promenade, which overlooks the Old City, and so, as the sun sets and we move into Tisha b'Av, these congregants take candles and chant the book of *Lamentations*, overlooking the new, rebuilt city of Jerusalem. It's a very powerful experience.

From the beginning of Av (the month of Av) until the ninth (Tisha), there is a period of semi-mourning similar to the first 32 days of the Omer (that period between Passover and LaG b'Omer*)*.

The next holiday, which happens just six days after Tisha b'Av, is *Tu b'Av*. Tu b'Av is not well known at all in this country, unfortunately. It's a combination of Valentine's and Sadie Hawkins where the Mishnah describes the young women of Jerusalem going out to the vineyards and joyously dancing with the young men. This might be a sanitized Rabbinic version of what actually happened—but, in any case, the Mishnah describes this day as one of incredible joy, although, once the Temple was destroyed, it wasn't widely celebrated. Today, there are some Jewish couples that are giving it resurgence, and they celebrate the day with picnics, complete with Israeli wine—and now you can choose from wine from the West Bank, or the Golan Heights, or Israel proper, depending on your politics.

Rosh Chodesh is the last holiday I want to talk about. Literally, *Rosh Chodesh* means "the head of the month." Like *Rosh Hashanah* is "the head of the year," *Rosh Chodesh* is the head of the month. In the Bible, the celebration of the New Moon involved animal sacrifices, a festive meal, and abstention from work, parallel to the other holidays. So, it was really a semi-holiday. Once the Temple was destroyed in 70 CE, the holiday was reduced to the singing of a handful of psalms in the synagogue. That's more or less what it remained until the modern period.

Already in the Rabbinic period, the holiday was associated with women. Why? Most likely because of the parallel between the lunar cycle and a woman's menstrual cycle. So today, as a result of the forces of feminism, there are Rosh Chodesh groups that have popped up in major cities all over the world, where women get together—and I don't know exactly what they do because I can't go; it's restricted to women—but they celebrate the New Moon. There is an additional custom, for women not to engage in household chores on this day. Sometimes Rosh Chodesh (sometimes the New Moon) is celebrated for one day; sometimes it is celebrated for two days. My wife does no washing whenever it's Rosh Chodesh, so that is entirely my responsibility.

There is also a blessing that happens, not at the time of the New Moon, but at the time of the greatest waxing of the moon. So, it is customary on the Saturday night prior to the full moon—and the full moon always falls on the 15th, and the 15th is *Tu*, so that's why we have Tu b'Av and Tu b'Shvat and Purim happening on the 15th in most places—to bless the New Moon. The full moon is when the spirits are out, so we need to bring godliness into the world in order to combat those evil spirits (on an anthropological level, in any case). So after Saturday night's *havdalah* service, which ushers out the Sabbath queen, it is customary to go outside and literally howl at the moon, by blessing the waxing moon. This blessing is called the *Kiddush L'vana,* and it's done in sight of the moon. All the prayers are included in the traditional prayer book, but it captures the idea that just as the moon waxes and wanes, so too does our relationship with God, as well as our fortunes, and we should always be trying to move towards the waxing side—the side of increased joy, of increased dedication, and increased love. The moon gets bigger and bigger, even though we know there are cycles in life that will overtake us at certain points in our lives.

This idea of cycles of life is a good opportunity for me to try to wrap up this unit on the Jewish calendar. The Greeks had a view of history that was entirely cyclical. So, if you remember the myth of Demeter and Persephone in order to explain the seasons, and when Demeter and Persephone were separated, that's when the flowers withered, and it explained the death, the mourning, of the natural cycles.

What Judaism does is to bring an historical understanding to the natural cycle. So, we still celebrate Rosh Hashanah every year (that's the cyclical part), but Rosh Hashanah represents creation. We've got Passover that represents liberation. We've got Sukkot that represents that journey in the wilderness toward the Promised Land—toward redemption, and we've got Shavuot, which represents the revelation of God's will.

Jews, when they are referring to events that happened in their own past, they don't talk about Winter, Spring, Summer, or Fall. They are not plugged into the seasons. They'll say, "Oh, just before Channukah," or "Just after Pesach." It's the holidays that orient a Jew in time. Abraham Joshua Heschel wrote in his book, *The Sabbath*: "Time is like a wasteland. It has grandeur, but no beauty."

What the Jewish calendar tries to do is to give beauty to time by having these outposts in what otherwise would be a wasteland of time, in order to promote the idea that history is going somewhere. There is a movement and there is a direction to history—and, ultimately, history is redemptive, unlike Greek thought.

Now that we've taken a look at certain concepts of the Rabbis in terms of their belief system, their practice, and their holidays, we want to move into the Middle Ages, which we've touched on in other lectures up until now, and look at the very different Judaisms that emerge in the Middle Ages.

Lecture Fourteen
Medieval Jewish Philosophy—Maimonides

Scope:

Beginning in the 9th century, the Jews living in Arab lands came under the influence of Greek philosophy. The writings of Aristotle and Plato, among others, were translated into Arabic and challenged the traditional religious sensibilities of both Jews and Muslims. Aristotle, in particular, posed a threat because of his prestige as the philosopher par excellence and his depiction of a transcendent, unchanging, and uncaring god. Although medieval Jewish philosophy emerges with Isaac Israeli and Sa'adia Gaon, Moses Maimonides (1138–1204) represents the most significant response to Aristotelian thought. We will look at his *Guide of the Perplexed* (1190) on such issues as the creation of the world, prayer, and the reasons for the commandments.

Outline

I. Beginnings of Jewish philosophy.

    A. Philo of Alexandria (20 B.C.E.–40 C.E.) began the process of understanding Judaism allegorically and philosophically. His writings were influential in early Christianity but unknown to the Jewish community until the 19th century.

    B. Under the influence of Islam, Jews began incorporating philosophical argumentation in their presentations of Judaism. Sa'adia Gaon (882–942) was among the earliest Jewish philosophers.

        1. Jewish philosophy was, in large part, responding to the intellectual challenge of Aristotle, who held that God is totally transcendent, unchanging, and uncaring.

        2. Biblical verses and traditional religious notions in tension with Aristotelian thought were the focus of attention by Jewish philosophers.

II. Moses Maimonides (1138–1204).

    A. Maimonides was born in southern Spain but immigrated to Cairo because of Islamic oppression.

    B. He wrote medical works, a commentary on the Mishnah, and the *Mishneh Torah* (1180), a comprehensive law code.

C. Maimonides wrote *Guide of the Perplexed* in 1190 to address the tensions between Judaism and Aristotelian philosophy.

III. Creation of the world.

    A. Aristotle assumed that the world was eternal.

    B. Genesis 1 and the Rabbis generally offered a more Platonic version of creation, whereby God fashioned the universe as we know it from pre-existing material.

    C. By the Middle Ages, the philosophical stakes became clear. If one agrees with Aristotle's version of the eternity of the world and the impossibility of divine intervention in the movement of the cosmos, then miracles become impossible.

    D. Maimonides argued that Aristotle did not prove that the universe was eternal; therefore, we are free to disagree with what has not been conclusively proven.

    E. Maimonides then argues that creation *ex nihilo* (*yesh m'ayin*) should be accepted, even without conclusive proof, on the strength of prophecy (see *Guide* II:16).

IV. Prayer.

    A. The god of Aristotle is both uninterested in human prayer and incapable of responding. A personal relationship with such a god is quite difficult.

    B. Although Maimonides maintains that prayer is a mitzvah, he also understands that it is a concession to human psychology.

        1. "A sudden transition from one opposite to another is impossible" (*Guide* III:32). The Israelites in Egypt were steeped in the idolatrous practices of the Egyptians. These practices included animal sacrifices.

        2. As a gracious ruse, or noble lie, God allowed the Israelites to continue in those idolatrous practices, but now with the correct address. Maimonides's point is that those practices are of no use to God.

        3. Maimonides then draws the comparison to prayer that is of value only for the pray-er to feel connected to God. But, like Aristotle, Maimonides believes that God is totally transcendent and uninterested and unmoved by prayer.

V. Reasons for the commandments.

    A. Although there was dispute among the Rabbis about the reasons for the commandments, one school of thought held that the commandments were given to refine or purify humanity.

    B. Maimonides agreed with this position (*Guide* III:27).

        1. The most important function of the commandments is to promote truth.

            a. This is accomplished through inculcating true beliefs about God and the world.

            b. It is also necessary to distance us from wrong, pagan beliefs about God and the world.

        2. Although less important than the attainment of truth, one must first attain physical safety and political security in order to enjoy the conditions to pursue philosophy.

            a. Commandments abolish wrongdoing among people.

            b. Commandments promote noble, moral qualities.

Essential Reading:

Agus, "Medieval Jewish Philosophy," in *Contemporary Jewish Religious Thought*, pp. 573–579.

Fox, "Creation or Eternity" and "Prayer and the Religious Life," in *Interpreting Maimonides*.

Maimonides, *Guide of the Perplexed*, Book III:25–33.

Supplementary Reading:

Samuelson, "Medieval Jewish Philosophy," in *Back to the Sources*, pp. 261–303.

Tirosh-Samuelson, "The Bible in the Jewish Philosophical Tradition," in *The Jewish Study Bible*, pp. 1948–1975.

Weiss, Roslyn. "From Freedom to Formalism: Maimonides on Prayer," in *CCAR Journal* (Fall 1997).

Questions to Consider:

1. The medieval debate on creation parallels the contemporary debate on evolution. How do you think Maimonides would respond to Darwinism?

2. If one understands prayer as does Maimonides, why continue to pray, as opposed to meditating in silence?

3. Some scholars have linked Jewish laxity in the performance of commandments to the philosophical approach of explaining the function of the commandments. Can you think of any current examples of this phenomenon?

Medieval Jewish Philosophy—Maimonides

We're now going to move into the Middle Ages, and we're going to be having two lectures: the first on Jewish philosophy, and the second on Jewish mysticism. What I'm going to be doing is introducing the towering figure of Jewish philosophy in the Middle Ages—Moses Maimonides—and comparing Maimonides on three different points to the school or the trend of Jewish mysticism in the Middle Ages. So, not only will we get a taste of Jewish philosophy and Jewish mysticism, we'll see how they compare on these three central issues. So we are beginning with Jewish philosophy.

Jewish philosophy doesn't spring up in full form in the Middle Ages. You already have an inkling of the attempts to bring together philosophical ideas and the biblical tradition with a man by the name of Philo of Alexandria, who lived from 20 BCE to 40 CE. Philo tries to read Judaism allegorically and philosophically while still maintaining allegiance to traditional Rabbinic law. His writings are very influential for early Christianity, but they are almost entirely unknown to the Jewish community until the 19th century. So, although Philo is of great interest to Jewish intellectual historians, as we talk about his influence on the Jewish community—from the Rabbinic period to the Middle Ages—it is nil. So we're not really going to look at Philo at all.

Under the influence of Islam, which really spread over much of the world in the 7th century, Jews began incorporating philosophical argumentation into their presentations of Judaism. Amongst the very earliest Jewish philosophers are Isaac Israeli and Sa'adia Gaon in the early part of the tenth century. They write in relatively simple ways; not that reading them is simple, but in a simple way of reconciling philosophical ideas and religious truths. The better philosophers understood that the way of bringing together philosophy and religion was indeed much more difficult than Sa'adia and, on the Islamic side, the *kalam* (the religious philosophers of Islam) presented.

Moses Maimonides was the greatest, earliest philosopher in the Jewish tradition. He was debating, or he was contending, with an idea of God that was the inheritance of Aristotle. Aristotle, of course, is an ancient Greek philosopher. Aristotle's understanding of God is one that is totally transcendent—not connected to the earth at all. God is unchanging. God is eternal, and God is uncaring. God does not care at all for the wishes, the ambitions, the dreams, and desires of creation—of human beings in particular. There were biblical verses and traditional religious notions that were in strong tension with Aristotelian thought. In the Bible, God is portrayed anthropomorphically—as having the form of a human body. God's nostrils flare. God stretches out his hand. God sees. These kinds of anthropomorphisms were understood by the philosophical tradition as figurative readings. They should not be understood literally. God has no body.

Indeed, Moses Maimonides spends the first part of his *magnum opus*, the *Guide of the Perplexed*, which he wrote in 1190, showing you how all those anthropomorphic and anthropopathic (attributing feelings to God) terms in the Hebrew Bible should not be understood literally, but should be understood figuratively. He, indeed, said that if you understand them literally, you are an idolater. He had very strong words of condemnation for that kind of literalist reading. There were others in the Jewish community who thought, "You're not an idolater. And, Maimonides, there are people who are bigger and better and smarter than you that have understood it literally, and they weren't idolaters."

That provides me with an opportunity to say that Jewish philosophy was widespread among the elite. But the elites are the elites, and not everybody was reading the *Guide of the Perplexed*. Indeed, Maimonides says in his introduction that if he is writing for one in 10,000 he will be satisfied to educate them and to bring them out of their perplexities as to how traditional philosophy understands the world and how traditional religion or Judaism understands the world.

Moses Maimonides was born in Cordoba, Spain, in 1138. He died in Old Cairo, or Fustat, Egypt, in 1204. His father was a religious judge in Cordoba. Around the time Moses Maimonides was ten years old, in 1148, there was a change of regime in southern Spain, and a more-tolerant version of Islam was replaced by a less-tolerant version of Islam with the Almohad invasion of southern Spain. At that point, the Maimonides family had to leave or face persecution. So they immediately left. There was a mother and father and two brothers (Moses and David). They first went to Fez, Morocco, and then they traveled all over northern Africa, and then they made it up to Palestine, and then Moses Maimonides settled outside of Cairo in a community called Fustat.

Maimonides wasn't just a philosopher. He was also a physician. He wrote many medical works. He was the doctor to the Egyptian sultan. He wrote a commentary on the Mishnah, which he completed by the age of 23, which is a fact that makes all graduate students quake in their chairs. In 1180, he wrote the perhaps easiest-to-read code of Jewish law called the *Mishneh Torah*. *Mishneh Torah* literally means "the second Torah." In his introduction, he writes:

> If you have the Torah and the *Mishneh Torah* [his book], those are all the Jewish books you need. Now go do something important with your time. Go study Aristotelian physics and metaphysics.

Maimonides was not a particularly humble man, we learn from the introduction to the Mishneh Torah, nor was he successful because generation after generation of Jewish students have taken the Mishneh Torah and tried to find its sources in the Talmud, in the Bible, and in previous legal literature, so they haven't gone to Aristotle's physics and metaphysics. So, in that goal, Maimonides was unsuccessful.

Maimonides writes the Mishneh Torah in 1180. Ten years later, in 1190, he writes the *Guide of the Perplexed*, precisely to address the tensions between Rabbinic Judaism and Aristotelian philosophy.

The first of the three issues that we are going to take a look at is the debate around the creation of the world. Aristotle's position is clear: Aristotle maintains that the world is eternal—eternal this way, eternal that way, eternal in the past, and eternal in the future. It will never change. It has never come into being. It will never decay or corrupt. What we see is what we get. That is not the position that the Hebrew Bible takes in *Genesis* (*Genesis* 1 in any case), or Plato. Plato, who came a generation before Aristotle, writes in the *Timaeus* that the *demiurge*, or the craftsman, takes elements that are already on the scene and fashions them into the world that we know. That is basically the description of creation that we get in *Genesis* 1. When the curtain goes up on the drama of creation, according to *Genesis* 1, there are all kinds of elements swirling around in a disorderly fashion. It's like a wasteland—a swirling, howling, chaotic wasteland on stage. What God does is impose order on disorder, or impose harmony or a universe out of chaos—out of disorder.

The Rabbis who inherited this biblical material were familiar with Aristotle, although Aristotle was never quoted by name in the Talmud or any of Rabbinic literature; but, they didn't really understand the stakes involved. Maimonides understands the stakes involved in the description of the universe according to Aristotle versus the description of the universe even according to Plato and *Genesis* 1. We'll see that Maimonides offers another understanding of creation altogether. This is what Maimonides has to say in the *Guide of the Perplexed*:

> The belief in eternity the way Aristotle sees it—that is, the belief according to which the world exists in virtue of necessity, that no nature changes at all, and that the customary course of events cannot be modified with regard to anything—destroys the law in its principle, necessarily gives the lie to every miracle, and reduces to inanity all the hopes and threats that the law has held out.

Wow. What Maimonides is saying is that, if you believe in Aristotle, that everything happens by necessity, that the world is the way it is and events in the terrestrial realm on earth are governed by the supernal realms, by the movement of the stars, and there is no change in the order of nature—then, that means miracles can't possibly ever happen. And if miracles can't possibly ever happen, then the rewards and the punishments that are offered in the Torah as ways of keeping the Israelites in line are a lie.

So, Maimonides understands that if you believe in eternity as the vision or the perspective of the way the world—not the way the world came into being—but the nature of reality, then the Torah must be false. So how does Maimonides handle this?

First of all, he says that Aristotle didn't prove that the universe was eternal. He just asserted it. Therefore, we are free to disagree with what has not been conclusively proven. Maimonides says, "Look. If the scientists prove without a shadow of a doubt that the world is eternal, then we have to deal with it and face the consequences and take a cold bath as to what that means for our reality. But Aristotle didn't prove it. He just asserted it. Maimonides then argues that creation *ex nihilo* (in Hebrew *yesh m'ayin*)—"something from nothing"—should be accepted, even without conclusive proof. Maimonides didn't think there was conclusive proof for creation out of nothing, but he said that we should accept it because it's possible, and on the strength of prophecy. This is what the prophet Isaiah describes, and it is what at least one voice in the Talmudic tradition also understood to be the origins of the earth—that God created everything—"Poof!"—out of nothing. In other words, when the curtain goes up on the stage of creation, there is nothing on stage. Then God creates the disordered swirling mass, and from that disordered swirling mass, God imposes order.

So we really have three different models of creation. We have Aristotle; we have Plato and *Genesis* 1, that talk about pre-existent elements that God then imposes order on; and then we have this third model that Maimonides champions and becomes doctrine or Jewish doctrine in the Middle Ages, it is one of *creatio ex nihilo*, *yesh m'ayin*—creation out of nothing. And that allows God to do whatever God wants with the material that God had made.

So if God wants to program in miracles, or if God wants to monkey around with creation, God can do so because God is the author of creation. And as the author, God can manipulate the text or creation as God sees fit. So, creatio ex nihilo allows for miracles and it allows for divine intervention in a way that Aristotelian necessity does not.

Let's take a look at the second issue here, which is prayer. The God of Aristotle is both uninterested in human prayer and incapable of responding to human prayer. The God of the philosopher is not an interventionist deity. A personal relationship with such a God, therefore, is quite difficult. Why pray to such a God? What are you hoping to get out of the exercise? Maimonides maintains, along with the Rabbinic tradition, that prayer is a mitzvah. It's a commandment, but he also understands that prayer is a concession to human psychology. So here's how it works:

Maimonides says in the *Guide of the Perplexed* that: "A sudden transition from one opposite to another is impossible."

People can't go from understanding everything about the world this way to understanding everything about the world in a completely different way. They need time to adjust. He says this in the context of the Israelites being freed from slavery. In Egypt, they were steeped in idolatrous practices—those practices of the Egyptians. Those practices included animal sacrifices. So Maimonides says that when God brought the Israelites out of Egypt into the desert, the only way the Israelites knew to worship God was through these animal sacrifices. So, as a gracious ruse, or noble lie (different translations of that Platonic idea of a noble lie), God allowed the Israelites to continue in this idolatrous practice of sacrificing animals, but now with the right address. In other words, the only thing that changed was the address; so that way, the Israelites could still feel like what they were doing was efficacious. What they were doing was still worshiping God, even though that's not the most noble, most authentic, way of worshiping God, because God doesn't need it.

Maimonides, like Aristotle, doesn't believe that God needs those animal sacrifices. Rather, we need to feel like we're doing something to communicate with God. Then, what Maimonides does is he draws the comparison to prayer, which is of value only for the pray-er, so that we can feel connected to God—just like the ancient Israelites maintained this noble lie or this gracious ruse of sacrificing animals to God, like the idolatrous Egyptians.

Does prayer have any impact on God? No. Did the animal sacrifices have any impact on God? No. But it is a concession to human psychology. Here, Maimonides is writing like a contemporary psychologist of religion, or sociologist of religion, and he's probably right in the sense that there is a kind of cognitive dissonance when one goes from worshiping one way to radically changing the mode of worship. So, Maimonides understands that the animal sacrifices and prayer are a kind of gracious ruse.

The last issue that we are going to look at is a huge genre of Jewish literature called *ta'amei hamitzvot*, or the Reasons for the Commandments. Everybody always asks me, "So why is it that we are supposed to separate milk from meat?" There is only one true answer to that question, and that is, "We don't know." The Bible doesn't say why we are supposed to separate milk from meat as part of the dietary codes of *kashrut*, or keeping kosher. But, nevertheless, we know that we've got this commandment. There have been all kinds of suggestions, including one by Maimonides that is plausible about why we separate milk from meat, but as we learned in the very first lecture, the contemporary scholar Jack Sasson at Vanderbilt says the prohibition isn't about separating milk and meat at all. It's about separating fat and meat, from the same animal. "You shall not seethe a kid in its mother's fat." So all of these explanations of the commandment for separating milk and meat were actually providing explanations for a commandment that doesn't exist (at least, according to Professor Sasson).

There are a few explanations within the Hebrew Bible as to why we should follow certain commandments. We should honor our mother and father. Why? So that we should live long on the land. Do what they tell you to do, and then you'll have a long tenure on the land. That was the biblical version of immortality. Your name will be present in that place. In the Rabbinic period, there were disputes among the Rabbis as to whether the commandments had reasons—if they were to refine humanity; if they didn't have any reason at all, but it was just a decree of the king; or if they had reasons but it's not our job to look into them because you get into trouble when you think you understand the reason for a commandment.

The explanation that Maimonides liked the best was that all of the commandments were given to refine or purify humanity—the Hebrew is *letzaref*. It comes from the field of metallurgy—what you do to a metal when you burn it down and you refine it, where you purify the metal—*letzaref*. We'll come back to that in the next lecture.

The most important function of the commandments is to promote truth. That's part of the refining of humanity. This is accomplished by inculcating true beliefs about God and the world. So, for instance, in *Deuteronomy* 6:4, it says: "Hear O Israel, the LORD our God, the LORD is one."

There is a truth that is instilled by that verse—that there is only one God, that God is one divine unity. But, Maimonides continues, there are also portions of the Hebrew Bible that were written in order to distance us from wrong pagan beliefs about God and the world. In *Deuteronomy* 11, for instance, it says that if we are obedient to God's will, we will have rain in our season, but if we are disobedient to God's will, we will have drought, famine, and disaster. In an agrarian society, rain equals prosperity; drought equals death. So what does Maimonides say about that? He says, "Look. If you look at what the other pagan religions were involved with that surrounded the ancient Israelites, they believed that if you worshiped these deities (these idols) that you would get rain in the season. So, as a gracious ruse, God said, 'Okay. Same thing. You worship God (you follow God's will) and you will get rain in your season, but [and here's the zinger] if you worship them—if you fall back on the idolatrous practices of your surrounding pagan neighbors—not only will you not get rain immediately, but you will be punished with drought.'"

Ah. Maimonides doesn't believe this is true. It's not that you're going to be punished with drought, but the Torah included that warning as a way of distancing us from false or pagan beliefs, so that it would be an extra disincentive to falling back to the idolatrous ways that we have known as slaves in Egypt.

So, some things in the Bible are true. Some things are false. But they are written with the purpose of distancing us from these pagan beliefs. Refining our intellect is the most important part of the commandments in the Torah, for Maimonides.

But a second reason for the commandments, for Maimonides, which has to happen before (so it's chronologically before you can start intellectualizing about the correct nature of God and the world), is the attainment of physical safety and political security because without physical safety and political security you can't enjoy the conditions that are necessary to pursue philosophical truths. So, in this category, you've got commandments about abolishing wrongdoing among people—so no thievery, no murder, no adultery, things like that. You've also got commandments that promote noble, moral qualities such as honor your parents, love your neighbor as yourself. These ideas combine to flesh out what Maimonides understands are the reasons for the commandments: that they are designed to help us attain intellectual truths, and they are designed to promote political stability and physical safety. That's it, for Maimonides.

It's all about us. The reason for the commandments—to refine humanity. They have nothing to do with God. Why don't they have anything to do with God? Because in the Aristotelian/Maimonidean world view, God is autarchic. What does that mean? God is self-sufficient. God needs nothing. God really cares nothing about God's creation. This idea is so antithetical to Judaism that Maimonides sometimes has to write in a way that is cryptic or esoteric, so it is sometimes difficult to really understand what Maimonides is driving at because he'll lie. He will say two different things in different places in the *Guide of the Perplexed*, and what's more is that he tells you that he is going to lie, in his introduction. So, since he tells you that he is going to lie, you are looking for these lies all the way through the book, and scholars have historically disagreed about where Maimonides is lying and where Maimonides is telling the truth. So, starting already in the 13th century, there wasn't agreement among Jewish scholars as to what Maimonides meant.

Indeed, those scholars that understood Maimonides to be as heretical in his thinking as some contemporary scholars, they banned the reading of Maimonides, and some even burned the *Guide of the Perplexed*. He was not a universally loved figure for his philosophical contributions. Even today, in the traditional world, Maimonides is studied in the orthodox *yeshivas*—the book that he wrote on the law code, Mishneh Torah. You'll rarely find people studying his philosophical work, *Guide of the Perplexed*; that has really been relegated to academic study. So, at the universities, people look at the *Guide of the Perplexed*, and they show how it has influenced Saint Thomas Aquinas, who lived several decades later, in the 13th century, and how it synthesized Islamic thought and how it brought together certain elements of *kalam* that Maimonides had a very low view of. Maimonides also had a very low view of Sa'adia Gaon, for that matter, and the philosophers that came before him, and interpreted the Rabbinic tradition in a new way, with very creative readings. Much in the spirit of how the Rabbis offered new creative readings of Torah, Maimonides offers new creative readings of the Bible and Rabbinic literature in order to make them gel with certain tenets of Aristotelian philosophy.

As we move into Jewish mysticism in the Middle Ages, we are going to take a look at these three aspects—of creation, of prayer, and of the reason for the commandments—and we will see a very different kind of response to Maimonides. It is sometimes argued that Jewish philosophy and Maimonides, in particular, was responsible for the emergence of Jewish mysticism because without that rationalization of the religion, Jewish mysticism wouldn't have swung its pendulum to the opposite extreme (as we will see in the next lecture) of looking at the world and God's relationship to the world as not primarily anthropocentric, having human beings in the middle. Remember, for Maimonides everything that the Torah has to say is for the benefit of human beings, but what we find in Jewish mysticism is this radically *chutzpahdech* or audacious view that the Torah is coming to teach us how we can best serve God's needs.

Unlike Aristotle, for Jewish mysticism, God is totally dependent on human activity—and to be fair, it's not just human activity, but it is male Jewish mystics performing commandments with the right intention, with the right *kavannah*. So, what we see as we make this shift from Jewish philosophy to Jewish mysticism is the shift from anthropocentrism—with human beings in the middle, but the Torah is to serve our interests and to refine humanity—to theocentrism, where God is the core and the reason behind which all Jewish ritual and ethical activity is commanded.

Lecture Fifteen
Medieval Jewish Mysticism—Kabbalah

Scope:

The Kabbalah is a vocabulary of dynamic symbols that many Jewish medieval mystics used to describe their understanding of God and God's relationship to the world. The Kabbalah is a literary combination of neo-Platonic philosophy and ancient Near Eastern mythology. It accepts but devalues Aristotelian thought through a poetry that distinguishes between that aspect of God that is transcendent and about which we can know nothing (*Ein sof*) and another aspect of God that is in continuous relation to the world (*s'firot*). This relationship between God and the world is in a state of constant flux depending on human actions. We will explore the same issues that we looked at with Maimonides to see the very different responses offered by the mystics.

Outline

I. Early Jewish mysticism.

   A. One characteristic of mysticism is the desire for an unmediated experience of God. Biblical Judaism mediated one's relationship to God through the priest. Rabbinic Judaism mediates that relationship through the *halachah*.

   B. But the Bible does contain several episodes of individuals directly experiencing God (see Exod. 24:9–11 and Ez. 1 and 10).

   C. Although there is relatively little mysticism in Rabbinic literature, other genres of literature during the Rabbinic period recount voyages through the heavens to meet God. This literature is called *merkavah* ("chariot") and *heichalot* ("palaces").

   D. Rabbinic Judaism tended to discourage mystical experimentation.

II. Kabbalah.

   A. The word *Kabbalah* designates "that which was received." The medieval claim was that these works were transmitted during the Rabbinic period but were just now being committed to writing.

B. What distinguishes the Kabbalah from other varieties of Jewish mysticism is a specific vocabulary of dynamic symbols to express God's relationship within God's self and to the world.

C. The earliest works of Kabbalah are the *Bahir* (late 12th century) and the *Zohar* (late 13th century). Both texts emerge from the Spanish Jewish community. They combine poetry and mythology.

III. Creation of God and the world.

A. Maimonides held that God was totally transcendent and unknowable in his essence. The Kabbalists agreed that there was an aspect of God beyond all human comprehension. They designated that transcendent aspect of God as *Ein sof*, or infinitude.

B. Unlike Maimonides, however, the Kabbalists held that there is another aspect to God that humans could understand and relate to. It is through this aspect of God that the divine is immanent and acts in the world.

C. Jewish medieval philosophers used the term *yesh m'ayin* ("something from nothing") to designate creation out of nothing. The Kabbalists understood that creation proceeded from the Divine Nothing, where *ayin* refers to that aspect of God about which we can know nothing. In other words, creation is not distinct from God but emanates from God's very self and, therefore, creation pulsates with divine energy.

D. The God that is mentioned in the first verse of *Genesis* was brought into existence through the emanation of the *s'firot* from the *Ein sof*.

    1. Each *s'firah* of the 10 *s'firot* represents a station in the unfolding of divinity in the process of divine self-revelation and the creation of the cosmos. Through meditation, the mystic can climb back up the ladder of the *s'firot*.

    2. This model of emanation is derived from neo-Platonic philosophy.

    3. The final *s'firah*, which links the supernal world with our physical world, is called, alternatively, the *Shchinah*, the divine presence, and *Knesset Yisrael*, the community of Israel. Each of the *s'firot* has many names.

    4. Conceptually, there are similarities between the *Shchinah* and the role of the Virgin Mary in medieval Christian piety.

  E. Because the physical world reflects divine emanation, we can learn something about God's inner life through understanding the relationships in the natural world. We can understand God because we are a part of divine reality.

IV. Prayer.

  A. One mystic from 13th-century Spain, Moses Nachmanides, was angered by Maimonides's suggestion that God did not really need sacrifices or prayer.

    1. Nachmanides points out that sacrifices, far from being a concession to the Israelites who were steeped in the idolatrous practices of their neighbors, were one of the first acts in the Torah. Cain and Abel offered sacrifices to God.

    2. Nachmanides argues that sacrifices and, by extension, prayer serve a "supernal need."

  B. Unlike the Aristotelian/Maimonidean God, the God of Kabbalists has needs that only human beings (or male Jewish mystics with the proper *kavannah*) can fulfill.

    1. As a result of Adam's transgression, evil enters the world and God's powers for good are diminished. Every transgression against God's will weakens God and empowers the forces of the *sitra achra*, the other side, which are parasites that feed off human transgressions.

    2. Conversely, when commandments are performed with the proper kavannah, God is strengthened. Sacrifices and prayer strengthen God and the godly forces in the world.

V. Reasons for the commandments.

  A. The commandments are not to refine or purify (*letzaref*) humans, as they are for Maimonides, but to join together (also *letzaref*) the male and female *s'firot* to allow divine energy to flow through the *s'firotic* system and, eventually, overflow into this world.

    1. Primarily, the commandments are for God's benefit.

2. A felicitous byproduct of the smooth flow of the s'firotic system is that the *shefa*, or divine blessing, overflows into our world through the *Shchinah*.

B. Another mystical understanding of the reasons for the commandments is to join (*letzaref*) us to God. They're not functional as much as relational.

C. The Kabbalistic system is audaciously anthropocentric. The fate of God and the world is in the hands of humans.

Essential Reading:

Fine, "Kabbalistic Texts," in *Back to the Sources*, pp. 305–359.

Idel, "Mysticism," in *Contemporary Jewish Religious Thought*, pp. 643–655.

Matt, "The Mystic and the Mizwot," in *Jewish Spirituality*, Vol. I, pp. 367–404.

Scholem, *Kabbalah*, pp. 88–116 and 128–144.

Supplementary Reading:

Dan, *Ancient Jewish Mysticism*.

Green, "Shekhinah, the Virgin Mary, and the Song of Songs," in *AJS Review* 26:1, 1–52.

Idel, *Kabbalah: New Perspectives*.

Matt, "Ayin: The Concept of Nothingness in Jewish Mysticism," in *Essential Papers on Kabbalah*, pp. 67–108.

Tishby, *Wisdom of the Zohar*, pp. 230–246, 269–308, 371–388, 423–430, 549–560, 867–908, 941–974, 1155–1172.

Questions to Consider:

1. What's the difference between God being in creation and God being creation?

2. Why do most organized religions discourage mysticism?

3. Why would the Kabbalists design a myth that places God's fate in our hands?

Lecture Fifteen—Transcript
Medieval Jewish Mysticism—Kabbalah

Just as medieval Jewish philosophy didn't emerge fully-grown in the 10th, or 11th, or 12th centuries, neither did Jewish mysticism. We have precursors to Jewish mysticism already in the Hebrew Bible. One salient characteristic of mysticism—whether it's Jewish mysticism, or Christian mysticism, or Islamic mysticism—is the desire for an unmediated experience of God.

Today, very frequently, you hear facile comparisons of Christianity and Judaism, such as "In Judaism, there is no priestly intermediary, while at least in Catholicism, there is somebody that gets in the way between your relationship with God." That is not a fair critique. In Biblical Judaism or the Israelite religion, there, indeed, was a priestly intermediary, and when that priest no longer served his function in the Temple, what replaced the function of having that intermediary was the halachah, was Jewish law. So, Rabbinic Judaism mediates the individual Jew's relationship with God, through the halachic structure, and some people are uncomfortable with that, and they chafe at having that relationship with God mediated by any structure, and they seek divine intimacy and divine immediacy.

Within the Hebrew Bible, itself, we have examples of people having visions of God. We see this in the book of *Exodus*, as well as in *Ezekiel*. The first chapter and the tenth chapter describe Ezekiel's vision of the divine chariots coming down from the heavens and appearing before him in tremendous splendor.

In the Rabbinic period, there are genres of mystical literature that are outside of Rabbinic literature. They are unauthorized texts, if you will. They fall into two distinctive categories. The first is *Heichalot* literature. "Heichalot" means "palaces" or "castles." Here, the mystic describes his experience penetrating different layers of the castle on his route to the inner sanctum of the castle, where the throne of God is located. There is another genre of literature during this Rabbinic period called *Merkavot* literature. "*Merkavot*" are the chariots that harken back to Ezekiel's chariot vision. There, the mystic or the visionary describes the process of ascending through the seven heavens on this chariot to get to God—closer and closer to God.

Rabbinic Judaism tended to discourage mystical experimentation. The most famous Rabbinic passage dealing with this issue involves

Rabbi Akiva and three other Rabbis, who, when going into the *pardes*—which is probably a code word for mystical experience or mystical speculation—one of them converted, one of them died, and one of them went crazy. Only Rabbi Akiva went in in peace and went out in peace. So we have the sense that the Rabbis are discouraging this kind of mystical speculation.

What we don't have in the Rabbinic period is *Kabbalah*. Kabbalah is a product of the Jewish Middle Ages that combines a mystical explanation, or mystical visions of their approach to God, with a certain vocabulary that describes different aspects of God, and those aspects of God are constantly changing depending on human action. Remember, in the last lecture, we talked about one of the differences between Aristotelian/Maimonidean philosophy and Jewish mysticism is that for the Maimonideans and Aristotelians, God doesn't change. But for the mystical tradition, God is always changing, and depending on human actions or the actions of Jewish mystics, who performed commandments with the proper kavannah (with the right mystical intention), there are changes within the energy flows of the godhead.

Let's try to unpack that a little bit. I want to make the point again that you don't have Kabbalah—this language used to describe the energy flows within God's self—until the Middle Ages. Although you have mysticism in the Bible and mysticism in the Rabbinic period, Kabbalah doesn't really emerge as its own distinctive literary genre until the Middle Ages. The very first *Kabbalistic* book that experiments with kabbalistic vocabulary and imagery is the *Bahir*, coming out of Spain in the late 12th century. But the bible of Jewish mysticism is the *Zohar* (which means "splendor" or "radiance") that we see coming out of Spain in the last decades of the 13th century. Both of these books—the *Bahir* and the *Zohar*—come out of Spain, where we know from certain historical documents that religious observance was lax.

I mentioned in the last lecture that there is a danger in trying to explain the reasons behind the commandments. Let me give you a contemporary example. Some people today (and in the past as well) have thought that the reason why pork is prohibited in the Hebrew Bible is because of the danger of trichinosis—those little microscopic worms that get you real sick. Maybe. But now, today, the USDA supervises meat, and we have irradiation techniques that are supposed to kill all trichinosis. So, if trichinosis is no longer a problem, then bring on the pork chops. What's the problem with pork chops if the original problem was the danger of trichinosis? So, now you've gotten rid of that original danger, so you violate the biblical commandments and eat the pork. The problem is that the Bible itself doesn't tell us that the reason why pork is prohibited is because it makes you sick. There is no medical explanation offered in the Torah. Maybe it's an entirely different explanation.

So, the rationalists (like Maimonides and his ilk) come around and say that all of the mitzvot in the Torah are for our benefit, in order to refine humanity, and let me give you some examples of that, as Maimonides does in his *Guide for the Perplexed*. A Jew in Spain in the 12th and 13th centuries might think that, "Okay. Now that I know what the reason for the commandment is, I don't need to do the commandment because I'll know to avoid that particular concern that the Torah has." It seems as though that phenomenon was occurring in Spain, as evidenced by certain historical documents we have suggesting that there was religious laxity. So, in the background to what I'm going to be talking about today, we'll see a promotion of the importance of following the commandments—not in order to refine humanity, but because God needs you to do those things for God's own benefit. There is no better way to promote ritual observance and traditional halachic practice than to say it's not for your need, it's for God's need—and who doesn't want to help God out. "We get by with a little help from our friends."

Let's take a look at the creation of God and the world. Let's review. Maimonides held that God was totally transcendent and unknowable in his essence. Indeed, this generated in the Jewish world what is called "negative theology." You can't say anything positive about God and God's essence. You can't say, "God knows," because when we say, "God knows," we think about our own knowledge. God doesn't know like we know. God's knowledge is of a totally different kind. What you can say is that God is not ignorant, using a negative. Negative theology is not that theology is bad or God is bad, but using negatives to describe the essence of God because you can't say anything positive about God.

The Kabbalists agreed that there was an aspect of God beyond all human comprehension—something about which we can know nothing, we can say nothing, we have not an inkling. They designated that transcendent aspect of God as *Ein Sof*—without end, or Infinity, or Infinitude—*Ein Sof*. There is that aspect. But, unlike Maimonides, the Kabbalists held that there is another aspect to God that humans can understand and relate to, unlike the Maimonidean God. It is through this aspect of God that the divine is immanent (meaning dwelling within the world) and intervenes or acts in the world. This is really the innovation—the radical innovation—of the Kabbalists and how they apply their language (their Kabbalistic language) of the *s'firot*.

Jewish medieval philosophers used the term *yesh m'ayin* (something from nothing) to designate creation out of nothing in terms of the explanation for the world. Remember that was what Maimonides said. We should believe it even though we can't prove it. *Yesh m'ayin*, creation from nothing. The Kabbalists reread the entire Jewish tradition, including Maimonides, but the Talmud and the Bible as well, and they understood that creation proceeded from nothing—the divine nothing—where "ayin" in that phrase "yesh m'ayin" refers to that aspect of God about which we can know nothing or say nothing. So, it's not that creation out of nothing as God [snaps his fingers] creating on the stage of creation, but yesh m'ayin is God creating out of God's self, out of that aspect of God that we know nothing, or can say nothing, or have no comprehension of. God emanates from God's self, and therefore creation pulsates with divine energy. Everything that is emanated from God is part of God. Maimonides would have nothing to do with such a paganistic, pantheistic idea that there is somehow divine energy in the world. Remember, for Maimonides the divine is totally transcendent.

The way that the emanation process happens is described very elusively in the *Zohar*, this book of Jewish mysticism. There is the Ein Sof. Then, if we look at the process of emanation in visual terms, there is a kind of cascading overflow, like a *ma'ayan*, like a fountain, that continuously flows over and over and over itself. This image is borrowed from Neo-Platonic philosophy. We talked about Aristotelian philosophy with Maimonides, and now we introduce Neo-Platonic philosophy, where the divine overflows in its desire to share itself. It has no envy. It wants to overflow and share divinity, but at each stage, or at each level of overflow, the divine energy becomes more and more coarse, in Neo-Platonic philosophy. So, in Jewish mysticism, this image of this fountain that continuously overflows is mapped onto the s'firot.

There are 10 *s'firot*. What is a *sefirah*? It's related linguistically to the idea of a number or a numeral, but it's a station in the divine self-revelation. Each sefirah in the unfolding of the divinity has a series of names. Sometimes they are biblical characters like Abraham, Moses, and David. Other times they are aspects of personality like mercy, anger, justice, and compassion. Other times they are symbols of nature: the sun, the moon, and the ocean. But all of them try to get at the interaction within the godhead that's reflected in our world with these energy exchanges between Jacob, and Joshua, and Moses, and Aaron—or between the sun, and the moon, and the earth. So, the s'firot represents a station—each sefirah represents a station—in the unfolding of divinity in the process of divine revelation and the creation of the cosmos. Through meditation, the mystic can climb back up the ladder of the s'firots in order to have this kind of visionary, mystical experience.

The final sefirah, which links the supernal world (the upper world) with our physical world, is called the *Shchinah*, or the divine presence; it's also called the *Knesset Yisrael* (as I said, each sefirah has many different names)—Knesset Yisrael—the community of Israel. Conceptually it seems as though the Shchinah is feminized in the Kabbalah—the word "Shchinah" exists in Rabbinic literature as the indwelling presence of God. Grammatically, it is a feminine noun, but it doesn't have any feminine characteristics in Rabbinic literature. Every noun is either masculine or feminine. With the Kabbalah, the Shchinah becomes feminized. It becomes the doorway through which the divine energy of the s'firot—the *shefa*, this divine overflow—enters the material world.

It seems as though, according to Professor Arthur Greene, my own teacher, that there are conceptual parallels between the image of the Virgin Mary in medieval Christian piety from the 12th century, and how the Kabbalah develops the notion of the Shchinah in the 13th century and later on—this feminine presence in both has a connection to the upper worlds. Mary in 12th-century devotional piety is the consort of God, as well as that that brings Christ into the world, for Christ's blessings. The Shchinah also has this dual relationship with the masculine forces in the supernal worlds and the masculine mystic in the lower, material worlds.

Let me go through now the *Zohar*'s understanding of the very first verse of *Genesis* 1, to give you an idea of how it rereads the Bible while simultaneously explaining this process of emanation. So, remember your first verse of *Genesis* 1: "When God began to create ..."—that's the new Jewish Publication Society translation. The King James translation is: "In the beginning, God created ..." In Hebrew, we've got three words: "*Beresheit bara Elohim* ..." "Beresheit"—"in the beginning," or "at the beginning," "bara" (created) "Elohim—one of the names that the Hebrew Bible uses for God. So, here's how the *Zohar* rereads those first three words of *Genesis*:

"*Beresheit*"—"at the beginning," or "in the beginning." The *beth*— that "b" sound in "*beresheit*" can also mean "through," and "*resheit*" ("beginning") is the name of one of the s'firot. So, through that sefirah of "beginning" which is the second sefirah—nothingness. The Ein Sof. "Ayin"—that which we can't say anything about, that which we know nothing about—and since we don't know anything about it it's not written in the Torah itself. So you can imagine it being in brackets. So, through the sefirah of resheit (of beginning) blank— nothing—the divine nothing—bara (created) Elohim.

In other words, the *Zohar* rereads those first three words of *Genesis* 1 and moves or shifts Elohim (God) from being the subject of the verse (the one that is doing the creating) to being the object of the verse (that which is created). Is this the *pshat*? Is this the contextual meaning? Is this the simple sense of the Bible? Of course not, we know that grammatically. But the *Zohar* is rereading through these mystical lenses, the entire biblical tradition. So, Elohim was created or emanated. Elohim is the name of another sefirah, farther down the s'firotic ladder. So, through this supernal or upper sefirah, one of the later s'firot was created or was emanated.

Let's take a step back. Nice rereading. Very creative. What do we do with it? It's the *Zohar*'s way of saying that there is an aspect of reality and of the divine about which the Bible is totally silent because (accepting this Maimonidean distinction) there is a part of God that we don't know anything about. Don't think that you can get to the whole truth from just the Bible. You need the Kabbalah. And what does Kabbalah literally mean? "That which is received," or "that which was received." *L'kabel* is "to receive." So, it is this mystical lore that was received (so the medieval mystics say) already in the first and second centuries by people like Rabbi Akiva, the lore that was passed down orally, and only now is emerging because of the need—some scholars might say because of the need to combat the rationalism of Jewish philosophy.

Also what comes out of this process of divine emanation is that the physical world is a reflection of the supernal worlds. So, we can learn something about God's inner life through understanding the relationships in the natural world, and we can understand God because we are part of divine reality—very different than the Maimonidean explanation.

Let's move on to prayer. One mystic from 12th-century Spain is Moses Nachmanides. Like Moses Maimonides, Nachmanides was a physician. He was in the northern part of Spain, in Gerona, which is just north of Barcelona today. (It was also just north of Barcelona in the 12th century, when Nachmanides lived.) He was a communal leader. He wrote on the Talmud. He wrote a biblical commentary, and he was a sparring partner, periodically, with Maimonides. In his commentary on the story of Cain and Abel in *Genesis* 4, Nachmanides points out that sacrifices—far from being a concession to the Israelites who were steeped in the idolatrous practices of their neighbors—were one of the first acts in the Torah. Cain and Abel offer sacrifices to God. Nachmanides uses very sharp language to say, basically, "This should shut Maimonides's mouth." Very sharp language is used by Nachmanides because there is a lot at stake. If you make the jump from animal sacrifices to prayer, one could read Maimonides as saying, "Ideal prayer is sitting in silence and meditating." One could read Maimonides like that.

But Nachmanides wants to say, "No." The prayer, like sacrifice, is not a concession to religious psychology, but it actually serves a *Tzorech givoha*—a supernal need. Just like God needed (on some level) the animal sacrifices, God needs, or God benefits from, our prayer when offered by a male Jewish mystic with the proper kavannah, with the proper intention. I think I will stop issuing that caveat every time I say it, but you should add it yourself. So, unlike the Aristotelian/Maimonidean God, the God of the Kabbalists has needs that only human beings can fulfil—a very different understanding.

As a result of Adam's transgression in the Garden of Eden, evil enters the world and God's powers for good are diminished. What does that mean? In the conception that the *Zohar* has of the world and of evil, every transgression against God's will weakens God and empowers the forces of the *sitra achra*. "Sitra achra" is an Aramaic term for "the other side." What that means is that evil is a parasite that feeds off human transgressions.

We're going to spend the next lecture and the following lecture discussing the problem of evil, but I wanted to provide a preface to the problem of evil because it explains what God needs and why God needs us to perform the commandments, as well as why God needs us to shy away from any kinds of transgressions. Because when we commit transgressions, we empower those evil forces on the other side (on the *sitra achra*). But when commandments are performed with the proper kavannah, God is strengthened. Sacrifices and prayer strengthen God and the godly forces in the world.

Reasons for the commandments in Jewish mysticism. Remember I said that in the Rabbinic world, one reason offered to why we should engage in the commandments is to refine or purify (letzaref) humanity. Maimonides picks up on that. Now it turns out that this word, "letzaref," also means "to join." Remember that I said that it comes from the language of metallurgy. So it has to do with refining, smelting, and joining one metal to another. But the same word, or the same root (*tzadee, resh, peh—letzaref*), brings together these two meanings—to purify and also to join. So, the Kabbalists reread that Maimonidean and Rabbinic tradition of purifying humanity as joining together the male and female aspects of the godhead.

There are many different ways to think about the s'firot. The left side is evil and justice, and the right side is mercy and compassion. That's one way. Another way that the Kabbalists understood the relationship between the s'firot is the balance of masculine and feminine energy. The ninth sefirah represents the phallus. The tenth sefirah—which is the Shchinah, or that feminine aspect—represents the womb, represents that door. You can almost think about it as a vagina, in terms of giving forth to the world the blessings of God. Because the Shchinah, that tenth sefirah, is the portal through which the divine blessings overflow. That's shefa, which I was talking about earlier.

So, the commandments are primarily for God's benefit, to unite the male and female aspects of the godhead, so that the pump can be primed—so that everything is in harmony and everything is in balance. But a byproduct—a felicitous byproduct, I will admit, but a byproduct—of the male and female coupling in the godhead is that you have this kind of union, and the flow then overflows to the recipients in the material world. So it is not as though the mystics are engaged in the commandments in order to get something out of it, nakedly. The mystics are engaged in the commandments and are recommending and promoting the value of engaging in the commandments to help God out because God needs it.

But, for your trouble, for your time, we're going to throw in a bonus. The bonus is that when the male and female aspects of God come together, that divine overflow—that shefa—then trickles down and blesses the worldly inhabitants, and the Jews in particular. So it's not quite naked bribery, as a sacrifice in some idolatrous practices might be, or as sacrifice in Greek religion was ("We're going to sacrifice our daughters so that we have favorable winds for our ships to sail off to battle."). The initial impetus for the execution of the commandments is for God's benefit, not for our benefit.

Another mystical understanding of the reasons for the commandments is to join (again, it's this word letzaref)—not to refine us, and not to join the male and female aspects of God—but to join us to God. I particularly like this explanation because it's not functional as much as relational. So that when you wear a shirt that doesn't combine wool and linen, and doesn't violate the biblical prohibition of *shatnes* that we find in *Leviticus*, it's not that it's helping God out; it's not that it's making me a better person. It's just a ritual that I do that binds me to God—that connects me in some way to God and raises my consciousness. I am part of this relationship.

The Kabbalistic system is audaciously anthropocentric. Earlier I had said that the Kabbalah is theocentric, which is true. It just depends on what we are talking about. It is theocentric in the sense that all of the mitzvot that one engages in are for God's sake—God in search of man, God in need of human beings. Another way to look at it is to flip it on its side, that God doesn't control all the shots; God is not calling all the shots. The human being (the male mystic) has the fate of God and the world in his hands. It's a very powerful idea, that the Jews (as their control of the physical and political world diminishes) create a thought system that enhances their control of the metaphysical realm. This has been suggested by scholars: that, as the political and physical power of the Jews diminish in Spain, their control of the metaphysical realms increases as a way of compensating for their loss in the political world.

Let's take a look now at what we have covered in these last two sessions. It's a great example of religious syncretism—of borrowing from Aristotelianism (as Maimonides did), and borrowing from Neo-Platonism (as the Kabbalists did), and also borrowing from the majority culture of Christianity by using the image of the Virgin Mary to help develop the feminine aspect of that final sefirah known as the Shchinah. Judaism has always been influenced by its majority cultures. So here, with medieval Jewish philosophy and medieval Jewish mysticism, we have great examples of religious syncretism, borrowing from the philosophical traditions, as well as the majority religious tradition of Christianity.

Our next two sessions will focus on the problem of evil. After seeing biblical and Rabbinic attempts to grapple with this greatest challenge to faith, we'll see how the Judaisms of the Middle Ages responded.

Lecture Sixteen
Evil and Suffering—Biblical and Rabbinic

Scope:

There is no more wrenching question than that of evil. Why do the innocent suffer? And why do those who so richly deserve punishment seem to get away, sometimes literally, with murder? The Hebrew Bible offers a variety of theodicies from Genesis through Job. Although the dominant explanation for suffering in the Torah is that we get what we deserve, Job allows for the possibility that there is no connection between our behavior and our rewards or punishments. The Rabbis developed the biblical material that they inherited, sometimes making explicit certain biblical theodicies, such as *measure for measure*, and sometimes introducing novel (and radical) explanations for the existence of evil. We will focus on individual suffering as well as communal catastrophe.

Outline

I. Individual and communal responsibility on the horizontal plane.

    A. There are no rewards for the individual who follows specific laws of the Torah. The collective reward, that the people Israel will live long in their land, redounds to the benefit of each person (see Deut. 11:21).

    B. In contrast, there are punishments for individuals who transgress the laws. But the punishment can also extend to the entire community. For instance, when Israel disobeys God's will, drought and famine will be the results (see Deut. 11:13–17).

    C. In the Rabbinic period, some Rabbis argued that Jerusalem was destroyed because certain communal leaders acted with *sinat hinam*, gratuitous nastiness (see b. Gittin 55b/56a).

II. Inter-generational reward and punishment.

    A. "For I the Lord your God am an impassioned God, visiting the guilt of the parents upon the children, upon the third and upon the fourth generations of those who reject Me, but showing kindness to the thousandth generation of those who love Me and keep My commandments" (Exod. 20: 5–6).

B. Ezekiel rejected this theology. Each person is held accountable only for his or her own actions (Ezek. 18:2–4).

III. Eschatological explanations.

    A. In the Rabbinic period, notions of heaven and hell were used to explain why the righteous suffer in this world and why the wicked prosper. The righteous are punished here for the few misdeeds they commit. The wicked are rewarded here for their few good deeds.

    B. Alternatively, there is simply no connection to the happenings in this world and our behavior. We will be rewarded or punished in the coming world for our deeds in this world.

IV. This world makes sense.

    A. Good things happen to good people. "God rewards each person according to his deeds" (Ps. 62:13).

    B. This theology, on a communal level, is enshrined in the liturgy: "We were exiled from our Land because of our sins." Though harsh, this theology promotes introspection.

    C. Often, the specific reward or punishment we receive is identifiably related to the deed. This is called *measure for measure*.

        1. The Egyptians lost their males in the last plague and in the Sea of Reeds because they had sought to kill all the Israelite males by throwing them in the Nile.

        2. Shifra and Puah, the Hebrew midwives who defied Pharaoh's order to kill the Israelite boys, were rewarded by God with children (Exod. 1:15–22).

V. The world makes no sense.

    A. The world really does make sense to God, but our finite intellects can't understand the grand plan (see Job 38–39).

    B. Rabbi Yakov said that there are no rewards for the commandments in this world. The next world will make sense, but this world does not.

Essential Reading:

Hartman, "Suffering," in *Contemporary Jewish Religious Thought*, pp. 939–946.

Rubinstein, "Evil," in *Contemporary Jewish Religious Thought*, pp. 203–210.

Schechter, *Aspects of Rabbinic Theology*, pp. 170–198.

Sherwin, "Theodicy," in *Contemporary Jewish Religious Thought*, pp. 959–970.

Supplementary Reading:

Hartman, *A Living Covenant*, chapters 8 and 9.

Urbach, *The Sages*, pp. 420–523.

Questions to Consider:

1. David Hartman writes: "Rabbinic Judaism foreswore systematic theology, not because the rabbis could not think in a coherent, philosophical way, but because systematic theology could not do justice to the vitality and complexity of experience." What does the plurality of theodicies tell you about Judaism?

2. Rabbinic and medieval Jews generally understood the suffering servant of Isaiah (51–53) as Israel suffering for the world's sins. Christians understand the suffering servant as a prophecy of Jesus (Php. 2). How does this notion of vicarious atonement fit into our discussion?

3. How could anyone ever think that this world makes sense and that people receive their just desserts?

Lecture Sixteen—Transcript
Evil and Suffering—Biblical and Rabbinic

Why do the righteous suffer and the wicked prosper? These questions have been at the heart of religious traditions and philosophical traditions for thousands and thousands of years. I want to make the disclaimer at the beginning of this two-part investigation into the nature of evil and suffering in Judaism that there is no answer. By that, I mean there is no single answer to the question. The reason why I waited to introduce the discussion of evil and suffering until this point in the lecture is so that we could map our discussion onto developments within medieval Judaism, and then bring it up to the present in terms of modern Jewish responses— specifically, modern Jewish responses to the *Shoah,* or to what is also called the Holocaust. The first lecture in this two-lecture series is going to focus on biblical and Rabbinic responses to evil and suffering.

There are a variety of responses within the biblical literature itself. So let's begin by taking a look at individual and communal responsibility on the horizontal plane. What do I mean by the horizontal plane? That the individual—any individual—is located within a community. Judaism is a religion that is part and parcel of a whole Jewish civilization, or Judaean civilization, or Israelite civilization. So to separate the religion from its cultural, national roots that we see in the Bible somehow distorts the religiosity that is presented in the Hebrew Bible. So first, let's begin there.

There are no rewards for the individual who follows specific laws of the Torah, no such thing as an individual reward. There is a collective reward: that is, the people Israel will live long in the Land of Israel, and that redounds to the benefit of each and every person. In contrast, there are punishments for individuals who transgress the laws, but the punishment can also extend to the entire community. For instance, as I mentioned a few lectures ago, when Israel disobeys God's will, there will be drought and famine. I'm now reading from *Deuteronomy* 11, verses 13 through 17.

> If then, you obey the commandments that I enjoin upon you this day, loving the LORD your God and serving Him with all your heart and soul, I will grant the rain for your land in [its] season … Take care not to be lured away to serve other gods and bow to them. For the LORD's anger will flare up

against you, and He will shut up the skies so that there will be no rain … and you will soon perish from the good land the LORD is assigning to you.

In other words, the communal punishment is exile. Exile is a motif in the Hebrew Bible. Adam and Eve are exiled from the Garden of Eden. The Jewish people are exiled from the Land of Israel. This process of exile and return, exile and return—redemption—is a leitmotif of the Hebrew Bible, getting back to the land that represents salvation—represents redemption in the biblical mindset.

In the Rabbinic period, some Rabbis argued that Jerusalem and the Temple were destroyed because certain communal leaders acted with *sinat hinam*. Sinat hinam, I think, is best translated as "gratuitous nastiness," being nasty for no good reason. The story that is told in *Tractate Gittin* is of a party or a banquet, and the host of the party sends out a series of invitations, and the messenger actually makes a mistake. Instead of sending it to John Doe, he sends the invitation to Doe John or Don Jones. When Don Jones gets the invitation he is very surprised because he knows the host, and they don't get along too well. So he's wondering why the host invited him, after all. When Don Jones shows up at the banquet, the host doesn't understand what's happened, and orders his servants to kick Don Jones out of the party. Well, that's not very nice, and it would humiliate Don Jones. So, Don Jones negotiates with the host and says, "Let's not embarrass me. I'll stay for just a little while. I'll pay for what I eat. Just don't throw me out." This host, who happens to be a Rabbi, doesn't take "No" for an answer, and he kicks Don Jones out. Don Jones is upset and seeks revenge, and through an interesting combination of events, he manages to get the Rabbinic host and the friends of the host (the other Rabbis of the time) to refuse to accept an offering from the Roman government because there is a flaw in the animal that the Romans give the host to be sacrificed; the Romans are insulted by this. This, according to the Talmud, kicks off the war between the Romans and the Jews: the Great Revolt, from the year 66 to 70, that culminated in the destruction of Jerusalem and the Temple.

The end of the story is less important than the beginning of the story. The Rabbis are saying here that it is not anything that could have been that was destined or fated. It was the individual actions of these Rabbis as the result of *sinat hinam* (gratuitous nastiness) that led to the events—that the Temple was destroyed as well as Jerusalem. People ask, "Where was God?" on September 11th, 2001. If we ask that same question about the destruction of the Temple in Jerusalem, "Where was God?" God doesn't appear in the story. In other words, one of the events that is as central to the Rabbinic religion and the Rabbinic mindset as the destruction of the Temple, the story that presents that destruction doesn't feature God as a player. It's all about how human beings inflict wounds on themselves through senseless hatred or gratuitous nastiness that culminate in these communal catastrophes.

That's one kind of evil—an evil that's visited upon an entire generation, the horizontal plane. But there's also a kind of evil or suffering that the Bible describes as being visited upon not a generation, but inter-generationally, or vertically, if I can use that image. So let's go to the Decalogue for an example of that kind of punishment. I'm reading from *Exodus*, chapter 20, verses 5 and 6.

> For I the LORD your God am an impassioned God, visiting the guilt of the parents upon the children, upon the third and upon the fourth generations of those who reject Me, but showing kindness to the thousandth generation of those who love Me and keep My commandments.

So you see that there is a lack of symmetry between the punishing side and the rewarding side. Punishment only happens for three or four generations, but the lovingkindness, that continues on for 1,000 generations. That kind of theology—where the children inherit or where the children are visited by God as a result of the sins of the parents, and grandparents, and great-grandparents—didn't survive the Hebrew Bible uncontested. Already in the book of *Deuteronomy* and then in the prophets (in *Ezekiel*) there is a rejection of that kind of theology. Each person is held accountable only for his or her own actions—not for what somebody else in the community did, and certainly not for what their great-grandmother did.

So we see different voices trying to grapple with and trying to understand why evil happens. And in the process of that grappling, some of the theodicies (I'll explain that word in a second), some of the theodicies that are presented are explicitly rejected already within the biblical literature.

So what is a theodicy? *"Theo"*—"God"; *"dic"* as in "judicial." "Theodicy" means justifying God's ways. If we want to hold on to (and most of us do want to hold on to) God's goodness and God's power, how can we explain the existence of evil in the world? Maybe God's not all good. Or maybe God's not all-powerful. But if we want to hold on to those two things, then what can we offer as an explanation of the evil that seems to be ever-present before our eyes?

There is one other kind of explanation for evil, that doesn't involve a kind of communal suffering or an inter-generational suffering—what I'm calling an eschatological explanation. "Eschatology" means "the end of days," or the next world, or the afterlife. This is what I'm referring to. Not in the Bible, but in the Rabbinic period, notions of heaven and hell were used to explain why the righteous suffer in this world, and why the wicked prosper. The righteous are punished. They are punished here for the very few bad deeds that they commit. No one is totally righteous, so they must have done some small peccadillo, some small transgression. So let them be punished in this world, so that they can be rewarded in the world that is eternally long—in the world to come. Similarly, the wicked are rewarded here for that one old lady that they helped to cross the street. But they'll be punished for the rest of their wicked deeds in a world that is very, very long.

In another version of the eschatological explanation, there is simply no connection between what happens in this world and our behavior. Things happen in this world by chance, by circumstance, by God. We don't know. It's only in the afterlife that we will get our comeuppance. We will either be rewarded for our good deeds, or we will suffer for our misdeeds.

Perhaps the most common theodicy in the Hebrew Bible (what I would call the normative theodicy of the Hebrew Bible) is that this world makes sense, and that good things happen to good people, and bad things happen to bad people. *Psalm* 62 says this very nicely. God rewards each person according to his deeds. This theology or this theodicy is enshrined in the Jewish liturgy. So for the holidays, we read in the Jewish prayer book: "We were exiled from our land because of our sins."

In other words, we sinned and, as a response, we were exiled. Notice, this is a different theodicy than the story I explained about the host who invited the wrong person (Don Jones). God wasn't involved in that story explicitly, but Rabbinic theology is comforted (and indeed, I think it is comforting to think) that all of our actions have an equal and appropriate reaction by God. So, the righteous are rewarded, and the wicked are punished. So, if there was a punishment in the form of exile from the Land of Israel, then that must mean that the Jews transgressed. The Jews sinned.

Often the specific reward or punishment that we receive is identifiably related to the deed. This is called *measure for measure*. This was an idea of the Rabbis even before Shakespeare got a hold of it. So, let me give you an example of "measure for measure." Absalom was very vain about his hair, and he had a long mane of hair (this biblical character). So, he was hanged by his hair. Samson was led astray by his eyes, by being seduced by Delilah. So, his punishment was his eyes being gouged out. The Egyptians lost all of their males in the last plague and in the Sea of Reeds. Why? Because they had sought to kill all of the Israelite males by throwing them in the Nile. So, that's action that one commits influences the reward or punishment that one receives. That's called "measure for measure." Although the term "measure for measure" isn't spelled out in the Bible, the Rabbis use the term *midah kneged midah* as a way of understanding what happens in the Hebrew Bible as well as in our world.

Sometimes it can have very nice exegetical results as well. There is a particular story at the beginning of *Exodus*. It involves Shifra and Puah, two Hebrew midwives. We're not sure if they are midwives of the Hebrews (in other words, Egyptian midwives of the Hebrews), or if they are actually Israelite midwives. Their names are Shifra and Puah, and there is a midwifery society in Israel called the Shifra and Puah Society. They disobeyed the Pharaoh's command to throw all of the male children into the Nile, and the text says they were rewarded with houses. God rewarded them with houses. So what does that mean that they were rewarded with houses? Does it mean that God, as a carpenter, built them row houses or a nice development in a better neighborhood? Or is the word "house" being used here like "the house of Shifra," and "the house of Puah"? "The house of David," as a metaphor for their family. It must be used as a metaphor for the entire family if we have an understanding that the Bible works in this kind of measure-for-measure way. Shifra and Puah saved the children of the Israelites, so they were rewarded; they were blessed with having children of their own. So, God blessed them by providing a home—not in terms of a physical structure, but in terms of children.

This theology of measure-for-measure and of everyone receiving what they deserve is sometimes harsh. We go back to the example of the Jews being exiled from the land for their sins. So some contemporary psychologists might say, "Isn't this an example of blaming the victim?" Maybe it all had to do with Romans and power politics and didn't have anything to do, historically, with Jewish actions. Historically, that may or may not be the case. We imagine that there was certainly Jewish involvement in the revolt that led to the exile and the destruction of the Temple.

But on a spiritual level, what this kind of theology does is promote introspection. It is empowering (in a way) to blame the victim because it means that the victim in the future can do something differently to change his fate or her fate—so that, no longer am I destined or fated to be exiled from Spain in 1492 or whatever the negative consequence might be. But if we understand that we get back what we put out, then it's going to make us extra conscientious to put out into the world good things, and blessings, and behaving nicely, because for those people who need that kind of extrinsic reward system, they will imagine that as a result of their good deeds and good actions, they will be appropriately and proportionately compensated by God for their actions. So, although historically we were exiled for our sins, perhaps in the future we will be blessed and we will be restored for our good deeds.

That's an example of the world making sense. Already in the Bible, perhaps one of the most famous books of the TaNaKH describes a world that doesn't make sense. At least it doesn't make sense to the creatures of the world. Of course, I am referring to the book of *Job*. Job is a righteous man, and yet he has all kinds of catastrophes and calamities visited upon him to test his faith. At the end of the book, a voice resounds out of the whirlwind, and says the following. God speaks to Job, in chapter 39, verses 26 through 28:

> Is it by your wisdom that the hawk grows pinions,
> Spreads his wings to the south?
> Does the eagle soar at your command,
> Building his nest high,
> Dwelling in the rock …?

In other words, there is a logic and a rationale to the way the world works, but you are merely a finite creature, with no chance to be able to comprehend the depths of wisdom that were involved in my creation.

And so, rather than being so (and here I'll use the word a little differently) anthropocentric in thinking that you're at the center of the universe, understand your place as a cog—not in a machine—but a cog in the divine drama. God is still in charge in this Jobian model, but God's justice and God's goodness are not transparent to human beings.

The Rabbis developed that thought into something far more unsettling. I've already mentioned this theodicy when I touched on eschatological explanations. In the Talmud we have Rabbi Yakov (Rabbi Jacob) saying that there is no reward for commandments in this world. It's a simple-enough line, but what it means is that this world doesn't make sense. There is no connection in this world between what we do and what we get. Everything awaits the afterlife, for Rabbi Yakov.

This is a little different than Job. Job is saying the world makes sense to God. It is only you that can't figure it out. This might be saying— this at a minimum says—that the world doesn't make sense. It might even be saying that the world doesn't make sense even to God. Even to God, the world that God created operates in such a way that things that shouldn't be, happen. As a result of giving God's creatures free will, we do things that God disapproves of, but God pulls back and restrains God's self from intervening because the price of intervention would come at the cost of free will for human beings, God's creatures, and God is unwilling to pay that price.

This set of explanations—or theodicies—for evil and suffering is not exhaustive, nor is it sufficient. You can see that there is a multiplicity of responses that might fit different occasions of evil, that might fit different personalities or temperaments in terms of how they respond to evil—or they might best reflect how someone sees evil as a young man, or as a mature adult, or as an elderly sage. Judaism doesn't force anyone to see the presence of evil in the world in a certain way. It offers a variety of explanations for a condition that seems to be inevitable.

Why do I say that it seems to be inevitable? In those first chapters of *Genesis*, from *Genesis* 1 to *Genesis* 11, primeval history, as Professor Levine called it in her The Teaching Company's *Introduction to the Old Testament* series, you've got the story of Cain and Abel, which we have mentioned already. Cain and Abel is a very disturbing story because Cain offers the first sacrifice. That sacrifice is not accepted. Abel plays copycat with his brother, and he offers a sacrifice. Cain's is not described as being nearly of the same quality as Abel's sacrifice. Cain's sacrifice, therefore (seemingly), is not accepted. So what would you expect? You would expect that God's favor would shine upon Abel, and God would punish Cain. That's what you would expect. But what happens? Cain kills Abel in a jealous rage, and Cain gets away with murder. So even though God had accepted Abel's sacrifice, that acceptance didn't afford Abel any kind of divine protection.

More troublingly, not only does Cain get away with murder, but he is protected by God. Cain complains to God and says, "Look, anybody who sees me is going to kill me. You need to give me some form of protection, so that, if you're not going to kill me, nobody else is going to kill me either." So, Cain gets away with murder, and God gives him some kind of a mark or sign. It's not a stigma. Go back and read *Genesis* chapter 4. It's a sign of protection—that anyone who kills Cain will be avenged seven-fold. How can this be? How can Cain get away with murder and receive a kind of divine sanction and protection, and *Hevel* [Abel] (who was favored by God) be killed?

This bothered the early interpreters—the Christian Fathers, and the Rabbis of the Talmud, and the Midrash. The only way that the Rabbis of the Talmud could reconcile what they were reading is to say, "Ah. We have an easy explanation for this. It must be that after Cain's murder of his brother Abel, Cain did teshuvah. Cain repented. That's why God didn't kill him and that's why God protected him." Does the text say that Cain did teshuvah? Not exactly, but both the Church Fathers who have this understanding and the Rabbis of the Midrash who have this understanding read the text in such a way (in such a midrashic fashion) in order to have some kind of explanation for why Cain wasn't killed as punishment for having murdered his brother.

Fast forward 2,000 years. Elie Wiesel. Elie Wiesel in an examination of this story says, "Perhaps God wanted to show us, the readers, or Cain and Abel already at the very beginning of history, that history is inevitably unjust." And so we have this story to demonstrate the lack of justice in this world. Elie Wiesel is a figure who has survived the horrors of Auschwitz, and perhaps he is more finely attuned to injustice than some others. But, nevertheless, we have this continuing interpretation and reinterpretation of the biblical text, whereby this very troubling story of Cain and Abel, which, I don't imagine, troubled you quite as much before I presented at least one reading of the text. But it bothered some of the interpreters. And, so, whether you're willing to add a conversation or an event in the middle of the text, like: "Oh, well, *Kayin* [Cain] must have done teshuvah. *Kayin* [Cain] must have repented for his deeds," or, to take the approach that Elie Wiesel took and say, "No. We're going to leave the text as it is, and it's going to teach us a lesson about the inherent injustice of the world that is blessed with human free will." No matter which approach you take, somehow you have to deal with the existence of evil.

So, what we have done in the first session is to chart out different ways that the Bible and the Rabbis grappled with the inevitability of evil. And, as we move into the second lecture on evil, we will take a look at how the philosophers and the mystics of the Middle Ages dealt with that question, as well as have a discussion of the Holocaust (the *Shoah*) and different Jewish responses to the Shoah.

Lecture Seventeen
Evil and Suffering—Medieval and Modern

Scope:

Is evil real, or is it merely the absence of good? The Jewish philosophers of the Middle Ages who followed Aristotle maintained that evil is merely an absence of good, while those who are associated with the mystical movements offer an entirely different explanation for the reality and pervasive power of evil. For the mystics, evil has its roots in divinity itself. We'll track this debate by looking at Maimonides's *Guide for the Perplexed* (1190), the classic work of Jewish mysticism called the *Zohar* (late 13th century), and Lurianic Kabbalah (mid-16th century). The lecture will conclude with a discussion of the *Shoah* (Holocaust) and a review of several responses by contemporary Jewish thinkers.

Outline

I. The philosophical Maimonides—evil as the absence of good.

    A. All of God's actions are purely good for the universe as a whole. Our finite intellect is often unable to penetrate divine wisdom (*Guide of the Perplexed*, III:10).

    B. Maimonides's *Guide* lists three types of evil that befall humans (*Guide*, III:12).

        1. Evils that befall us because we are flesh and blood are the most infrequent. Maimonides argues that in order for there to be generation and increase, there must be passing away.

        2. More common are those evils that people inflict on one another.

        3. Most common are self-inflicted wounds.

II. The mysticism of the *Zohar*—evil is real but parasitic.

    A. There are two problems to understanding evil as real.

        1. If evil is real, does that mean God, the source of all reality, is evil?

        2. If God is not the source of evil, does that mean that there is another power in the world that is the source of evil?

B. For the *Zohar*, evil is real but not autonomous.

    1. Adam's transgression in the Garden threw the finely tuned balance of divine mercy and justice off kilter.

    2. Cosmic evil is activated by human evil, which, in the *Zohar*'s creation myth, originates from justice not being tempered by mercy. Evil emerges as creation unfolds.

    3. Every act of disobedience to God's will empowers the metaphysical forces arrayed against us. We bring on evil ourselves, and a parasitic synergy exists that serves to make our punishments disproportionate to our deeds.

III. Isaac Luria—*tsimtsum* and the breaking of the vessels.

    A. *Tsimtsum* is the opening scene in Luria's drama of creation. It is a withdrawal or contraction of the divine in order to "make room" for that which is other than infinite.

    B. The process of *tsimtsum* did not create a total vacuum. As when one pours oil from a bottle, there remains a residue. In Luria's myth, this residue contained the roots of the demonic.

    C. When God emanates divine light in the form of vessels back into the empty space, these roots of the demonic create instability, and the vessels shatter.

    D. The mission of *tikkun*, repair, requires us to be engaged in ethical and ritual acts to repair the shattered vessels.

    E. In Luria's myth, the roots of evil are a necessary precondition of creation. Evil is built into the structure of the cosmos.

IV. *Shoah*—not Holocaust.

    A. *Holocaust* means a wholly burnt offering to God to atone for sins. This term was coined by Christian theologians to describe the Shoah.

    B. *Shoah* is Hebrew for "catastrophe" and is used to refer to the destruction of European Jewry.

        1. Approximately six million Jews were systematically murdered from 1939–1945 in Nazi-controlled Europe.

        2. That figure represents two-thirds of European Jewry, one-third of world Jewry and roughly 1.5 million children.

V. Religious responses to the Shoah.

    A. A few Ultra-Orthodox Jews maintain that the Jews were punished communally for their crimes.

        1. Zionism arrogated to itself the creation of the State of Israel before the coming of the Messiah.

        2. Reform Judaism, which emerged in Germany, rejected the binding authority of the Torah and halachah.

    B. God has hidden his face.

        1. Since the destruction of the Second Temple, the Jews are in a state of hapless aimlessness as a result of the hiding of God's face (Deut. 31:18).

        2. God's hiding is not punitive but fundamental to who God is (Isa. 45:15). This is what allows for free will and human responsibility.

    C. God is exercising self-restraint as a parent must to allow the children to mature and assume responsibility.

        1. "Who is mighty? One who exercises self-restraint" (m. Avot 4:1).

        2. There are conceptual parallels between the Rabbinic notion of divine self-restraint and the Lurianic notion of divine withdrawal. Both insist on God's presence and suffering with his creatures but lean against divine intervention.

    D. God lacks omnipotence. The work of God is accomplished, today, through human hands.

Essential Reading:

Berkovits, *Faith after the Holocaust*.

Friedlander, *Out of the Whirlwind*.

Greenberg, *The Jewish Way,* "The Shattered Paradigm."

Rosenberg, *Good and Evil in Jewish Thought*.

Rubinstein, "Evil," in *Contemporary Jewish Religious Thought*, pp. 203–210.

Scholem, *Kabbalah*, pp. 122–128, and *On the Mystical Shape of the Godhead*, pp. 56–87.

Sherwin, "Theodicy," in *Contemporary Jewish Religious Thought*, pp. 959–970.

Supplementary Reading:

Rosenberg and Heuman, *Theological and Halakhic Reflections on the Holocaust.*

Roth and Berenbaum, *Holocaust.*

Questions to Consider:

1. What does the variety of explanations for evil in traditional Judaism tell you about Judaism?

2. Palaeontologists tell us that the vast majority of species to have ever existed on the planet are now extinct. Do any of the theodicies designed to account for evil in Jewish history accommodate the apparent evils in natural history?

3. Is the Shoah essentially different than other catastrophes that have punctuated Jewish history, such as the destruction of the Temples or the Spanish exile in 1492?

4. Although the traditional theodicy of recompense according to deed might promote introspection, doesn't it also blame the victim? Is this viable after the Shoah?

Lecture Seventeen—Transcript
Evil and Suffering—Medieval and Modern

We're continuing our discussion of evil, and we're moving into the medieval period. We're going to be looking at Maimonides's response, as well as *The Zohar*'s, and then a later group of Jewish mystics who were associated with Isaac Luria in Tsfat (Safed) in the Land of Israel in the 16th century. Then, finally, we will talk about the Shoah (the Holocaust) and some religious responses to the Holocaust.

As we begin to reflect philosophically about the nature of evil, Maimonides tells us we must come to the understanding that evil is not real. Evil is only appearance. I'm not sure if Maimonides ever had to tell someone who was experiencing suffering that evil is not real, but this is what he writes. (I should say, as a biographical note, that Maimonides was no stranger to suffering. His younger brother David drowned in a ship accident, and from what the historical records indicate, Maimonides was crushed by this and didn't leave his house for a period of a year. So he was no stranger to depression.)

Nevertheless, Maimonides says that evil is the absence of good, that there is no reality to evil itself. Imagine a bagel. Is the hole in the bagel real? Or is it just the absence of the bagel? It is the absence of the dough in that circular form that you bite into with cream cheese and lox. So, just like the hole in the bagel is not real, evil is not real, it is just the absence of good. For Maimonides, as for Job (there are certain Jobian echoes here), all of God's actions are purely good for the universe as a whole. But our finite intellect is often unable to penetrate the divine wisdom. I want to read for you a quote from Maimonides's *Guide for the Perplexed*, because you will get a feel for Maimonides's personality:

> Often it occurs to the imagination of the multitude that there are more evils in the world than there are good things. The reason for this whole mistake lies in the fact that this ignoramus and those like him among the multitude consider that which exists only with reference to a human individual. Every ignoramus imagines that all that exists exists with a view to his individual sake. It is as if there were nothing that exists except him. And if something happens to him that is contrary to what he wishes, he makes the trenchant

judgement that all that exists is an evil. However, if man considered and represented to himself that which exists and knew the smallness of his part in it, the truth would become clear and manifest to him.

So, Maimonides doesn't have much patience with those individuals (those "ignoramuses") who understand that they are the center of the universe. Indeed, Maimonides was not anthropocentric. He did not believe that the universe was made for human beings, in this sense. We are just one part of God's creation. Once we understand the glory and magnitude of God's creation (which is why we should study Aristotelian physics), we will understand our small part in it.

But, nevertheless, Maimonides does recognize that there is suffering in the world. So how does he explain that suffering? Maimonides breaks it down into three types. There are evils that befall human beings because we are made of flesh and blood, but flesh and blood is necessary in order for there to be generation and increase—so, there must be passing away. This, Maimonides says, is the most infrequent kind of evil. So, evils that fall into this category would be something like cancer. We've got to be made of flesh and blood in order to reproduce, but if we are made of flesh and blood, then we also decrease and we die away. We pass on. This is obvious to Maimonides. But as a result of being flesh and blood, certain things can go wrong with our flesh, and—more than that—we are then susceptible to earthquakes, fires, tidal waves, and being victims of ship accidents on the high seas. But Maimonides says that that is the most infrequent kind of evil that befalls human beings.

More common are those evils that people inflict on one another, and, of course, here we are talking about murder, we're talking about war, we're talking also about psychological evils, or cheating (cheating in business or cheating in marital relations)—those kinds of evils as well.

But, according to Maimonides, the most common evils that human beings experience are self-inflicted wounds. I'm not sure if he's speaking from personal experience or not, but it's interesting to do an inventory of the evils that we have experienced, and ask ourselves if most of those evils have been the result of self-inflicted wounds. For Maimonides and the Aristotelian tradition, evil is not real. Evil is only apparent. It is the absence of good.

As we move on to Jewish mysticism, the mystics can't deny the reality of evil. It is too pressing to them to deny it. But, nevertheless, that raises a problem. When you admit the reality of evil, does that mean that God, who is the source of all reality, is evil? Or, alternatively, if God is not the source of evil, does that mean that there is another power in the world that is the source of evil? In a monotheistic tradition, you can't admit other, independent powers that perpetrate evil in the world—that is gnosticism, the belief in two separate deities, a god of good and a god of bad, or Zoroastrianism. These were religions that Judaism polemicized against. In *Isaiah*, we have the prophet saying that God created both good and bad, in contradistinction to the religious culture that the prophet was living within, in Persia—this idea of dualism, of two different gods, a god of good and a god of evil.

So how does *The Zohar* do it? It is ingenious. *The Zohar* says that God is real. That is true. *The Zohar* says that evil is real, but it is not autonomous. Evil is parasitic on human transgression. Okay, so how does this work?

Adam's transgression in the Garden of Eden threw off this finely tuned symmetrical balance within the godhead. If we think back to the s'firot, I said that one way to picture the s'firot is the male and female energies being in synch. Another way to imagine the s'firot is the right side (the side of mercy) and the left side (the side of judgment) being in balance. According to the myth of *The Zohar*, when that finely tuned balance of mercy and justice gets thrown off kilter, justice becomes inflamed and breaks away from mercy, and evil is created. So up until that moment in the Garden of Eden, mercy and justice were in balance. They were in synch. They were finely tuned. As a result of human transgression, the aspect of divine justice was inflamed and broke off from divine mercy, and justice (and here is the psychological truth behind the myth)—that justice, untempered or unbalanced by mercy, can become evil. That's what happens in the mythological world of *The Zohar*. That justice, untempered by mercy, becomes evil, and what does it do? It creates this whole other universe of evil forces that is exactly parallel and symmetric to the forces of good. This is called the *sitra achra*, which is Aramaic for "the other side." If you think about George Lucas's *Star Wars*, he understood this kind of theology very well, because Luke Skywalker and Darth Vader are not opposing, autonomous forces of good and evil. They are good and evil, but they are drawing from the same

"Force." "The Force" is the force, but Darth Vader is the dark side of the Force. This is not Gnosticism. George Lucas is not a Gnostic in this sense. Just like in *Star Wars*, you've got The Force and the Dark Side, in Jewish mysticism you've got—well, there's no name. Just like The Force, you've got God and godliness in this sphere-otic world, and the sitra achra, or the other side.

And what is so audaciously anthropocentric in this sense is that whatever human beings do (and remember, we're really not talking about human beings for *The Zohar*; we're talking about male mystics who are engaged in the commandments with the proper kavannah, or the proper intention)—whatever they do, whether it is a transgression or a commandment, they can either empower the godly forces (the good forces) or the demonic evil forces in the sitra achra. Then, what happens is something like trickle-down economics. As a result of doing good or doing bad, it primes the pump, and it begins a process (a synergistic process) whereby the time good or bad acts filter down through these different worlds and demons into our world, the effects are disproportionate to whatever good or bad the individual did. So, that's how we can explain (or that's how the mystics in Spain could explain) the beginning of anti-Semitic riots in 1391, for instance.

It must have been something that the Jews did, whether intentionally or unintentionally, because (this is interesting) transgressions don't require malicious intent. In American law, for the highest degree of punishment you need *mens rae*—you need criminal intent. In Jewish mysticism (the mysticism of *The Zohar*), in order to get the full benefit of God's blessings, you need to engage in a commandment with the proper intention. But, if you commit a transgression, it doesn't matter if you were intending to commit the transgression or not, or if you were intending to commit the transgression for a good reason or not. The classic example of this is nocturnal emissions. You're not intending to commit this act, but, nevertheless, according to *The Zohar*, it unleashes all kinds of malevolent forces in the world.

So, cosmic evil is activated by human evil, which in *The Zohar's* creation myth originates from justice not being tempered by mercy. Evil emerges as creation unfolds. It wasn't necessary that there be evil in this creation myth, in this theodicy, in this explanation of evil—but, it was precipitated by human disobedience. And every act of disobedience to God's will empowers those metaphysical forces arrayed against us. We bring on evil ourselves, and there is this parasitic synergy that serves to make our punishments disproportionate to our deeds. That's what we see in *The Zohar* in 13th-century Spain.

Now let's talk about the next major development of Jewish mysticism, in the Land of Israel, in this gorgeous mountain community called Tsfat or Safed, as it is usually translated in English. The author of this mythical worldview is Isaac Luria, the "holy lion," Ari Hakodesh. He describes a very different process of creation and of the origins of evil.

The first scene in Isaac Luria's drama of creation is one of *tsimtsum*, or divine withdrawal. Abraham Joshua Heschel translates this as "divine restraint." Luria understands that the entire universe—I shouldn't really be talking about space, but let's say all is filled with God—everything is divine. So, in order for God to create something that is not divine, God needs to withdraw, or pull back, into this space and then into that vacuum. God can then send in divine energy in order to create the material world. So, the first act of creation (and, indeed, according to Isaac Luria, the first act of every creation— every creative act) begins with pulling back, with holding back, with self-restraint. Before you can put something out into the world, you need to hold yourself back. It's an interesting idea about the creative process since tsimtsum begins this process. But, just like pouring oil out of a jug leaves a thin residue on the surface of the inside, when God withdrew from that vacuum, it wasn't a total vacuum. There was a kind of divine residue in that space, and in that residue, were the roots of the demonic. They were the dregs—the roots of the demonic. So, when God sent back in divine energy in the form of vessels that were supposed to contain that divine energy, the balance and the symmetry of those divine vessels were upset by the existence of these shards—or these roots—of the demonic, and the vessels shattered. It is our job in the world to repair the vessels. In Hebrew, the way to explain that process of repair is *tikkun*. There is a liberal Jewish magazine called *Tikkun*, and on the back cover it says, "to heal, mend, repair the world."

Originally, in the Lurianic Kabbalah, the idea of tikkun wasn't to heal, mend, or repair the world, but it was to heal, mend, and repair those shattered vessels—that now, in the mythological explanation when Jews engage in the commandments, what they are doing is helping to pick up those shards of glass and to restore those vessels. And, of course, every act, every transgression the Jews engage in, further disintegrates those vessels, and they undo the work that had been done in trying to restore cosmic and divine harmony. Then, of course, the messianic culmination is when everyone succeeds in completely restoring those shattered vessels.

If we go back to the Bible's account of creation, you will remember that I said the Bible has a kind of Platonic understanding of the nature of creation. So that, when the curtain opens up on creation, there's already this kind of swirling mass of things on stage. So, it could be that that swirling mass, that *tohu v'vohu* in Hebrew, chaos and confusion, wild and waste, unformed and void, according to the different translations—Isaac Luria could be explaining how that unformed mass of chaos got there. It's not that it's not divine. It is divine. But it's this kind of demonic dregs from the tsimtsum, from the divine withdrawal, that then God and human beings together in partnership are going to try to impose some order and some harmony on to restore that initial cosmic harmony.

For Isaac Luria, unlike for *The Zohar*, evil is built into the very structure of the world. There couldn't be creation without these demonic dregs, these demonic elements—this metaphysical evil to already foul up the great recipe, to foul up the cosmos. For *The Zohar*, evil is parasitic on human actions. But Isaac Luria, in the 16th century—after the Spanish exile, after the Jews were exiled from Spain in 1492 as a product of King Ferdinand and Queen Isabella's consolidation of Spain on the Iberian Peninsula. They no longer wanted to have a Jewish presence. They had finally gotten rid of the Muslim presence, and they had pushed the Muslims back across the Straits of Gibraltar, to North Africa. Similarly, they wanted to have a uniform religious presence of Catholicism within Spain, so the Jews were exiled.

So, what Isaac Luria does, is have God exiled. God no longer is in the universe. So, the political conditions of exile may very well have informed Isaac Luria's understanding of this myth of tsimtsum, of divine withdrawal or divine exile, and it would have given him a much more recent taste of the reality of evil and suffering than perhaps was the case with Maimonides and the philosophical tradition. I don't want to be too psycho-biographical about this, but we do have Isaac Luria writing in the decades after the expulsion from Spain. So, the reality of evil was, perhaps, so present for him that Luria created a myth that understood evil to be part and parcel of the very creation of the cosmos.

We are now going to move from theory to reality. Beginning in 1939, we have a six-year process (from 1939 to 1945) of the Holocaust—or, in Hebrew, we describe it as the *Shoah*. "Shoah" means "catastrophe." The reason why Jews do not use the term Holocaust is because the word itself means a wholly burnt offering to God in order to atone for sins. The term "Holocaust" itself was coined by Christian theologians to describe the Shoah. Jews do not understand what happened in Nazi Europe between 1939 and 1945 as any kind of sacrifice to God to atone for sins, although there might be some Jews that wouldn't disagree entirely with that description. But the Hebrew term "Shoah" means "catastrophe," and that is generally the term that is used in the American Jewish community, certainly, as well as in Israel, to describe these events that resulted in the death—the systematic death, the systematic murder—of 6 million Jews. That was two out of every three Jews on continental Europe— one out of every three Jews in the world. It included roughly 1.5 million children.

You can read volumes from histories and biographies about the Holocaust. What I am more interested in doing now than going into the details of the Shoah, is to look at certain religious responses to the Shoah. Perhaps the religious responses that have the most continuity with the biblical theodicies that we saw in the last lecture are those by the Ultra-Orthodox. We'll talk about the Ultra-Orthodox in a couple of lectures, but just to give you a visual image, the Ultra-Orthodox today are identifiable because of their black hats and black coats. They wear distinctive clothing to separate them from the rest of the societies in which they live. They understood that Jews were punished communally for their crimes. This kind of theodicy has two different versions. One crime that this particular group of Ultra-Orthodoxy understands the Jews were communally punished for was Zionism, that Zionism arrogated to itself the creation of the State of Israel before the coming of the Messiah. According to this understanding, which, in my opinion, is not a good reading of Rabbinic sources, but according to this understanding, the Messiah should first come and usher in the messianic era by creating a State of Israel, or re-establishing the Third Jewish Commonwealth. So, the Messiah's presence needs to precede the State, according to this reading. I don't think that's an accurate reading of the Rabbinic sources, but that's their reading.

An interesting biographical note: I am teaching at Vanderbilt University from Nashville, Tennessee, and one Rabbi during the Shoah, whose name is Isachar Solomon Tiechtel, who had, before World War II, been sympathetic to this Ultra-Orthodox group and what their belief system was, and who thought that Zionism was a bad idea—during the war, he comes to write a book called *Em HaBanim Semeicha, The Joyful Mother of Children*, in which he says that he had thought that Zionism was a terrible tragedy, but now he understands that the real tragedy was by not going to Israel (going to Palestine, at that time) and supporting the Zionist movement because the full extent of the Holocaust could never have been possible had there been fewer Jews in Nazi Europe. So, he comes to offer in the middle of World War II, this Ultra-Orthodox Rabbi comes to offer a kind of Zionist program and is sympathetic to the aims of Zionism. His grandson is Yitzchok Tiechtel, who is a Rabbi in Nashville, Tennessee—the Rabbi of one of these Ultra-Orthodox groups in the Hasidic world, called *Chabad*. So he is our Chabad Rabbi.

Another understanding of the nature of the sin that caused God to punish the Jews communally with the Holocaust was Reform Judaism. Reform Judaism emerged in Germany, where the Nazi leadership also emerged. What did Reform Judaism do that was so bad? They rejected the binding authority of Torah and the halachah. They accepted biblical criticism that God didn't write the Bible, that the Bible is not a product of divine dictation, and that the halachah is not binding on every Jew. So, you do have a relatively minor population (even today, within the Jewish world) who understands that the Holocaust was divine punishment for our sins.

Another explanation for the Holocaust that goes back to the Bible is that God has hidden his face. This theodicy also comes in two different forms. The first form suggests that since the destruction of the Second Temple by the Romans in the year 70, the Jews are in a state of hapless aimlessness, as a result of the hiding of God's face. For our sins we were exiled, and once we were exiled, God hid God's face—so, we are subject to nature, subject to history. We are without divine protection. We are vulnerable. That's one understanding. And, as a result of our vulnerability without a State, the Holocaust could happen. The Shoah could happen.

Another understanding of the hiding of God's face is that the Shoah was not punitive because the hiding of God's face is constitutional; it is fundamental to who God is. Let me read you a quote from *Isaiah* 45:15. Isaiah, already in the Bible, says: "You are indeed a God who concealed himself." So, one contemporary Jewish thinker, Eleazar Birkovits, talks about God as needing to hide God's face in order not to overwhelm us and interfere with our own free will, which allows for human responsibility. If we are supposed to choose the good and not to choose the evil, then we need to have the free will to do that, and God's presence needs to be somehow masked from us.

A third explanation or theodicy for the Shoah goes back, not to the Bible, but to the Rabbinic period. We find these statements in the Talmud (in the Mishnah, in particular). There is a wonderful question that is asked in the Mishnah: *mi zeh gibor*, "Who is mighty?" In the Hebrew Bible, a *gibbor* is kind of a macho guy—somebody who is strong, and muscular, and can defeat people in hand-to-hand combat on the field of battle. So that's what a reader in the Rabbinic period who is familiar with the Bible would immediately think: "Who is somebody that is strong—that can bench press 220?" (That's strong.)

But the Rabbinic answer is "One who exercises self-restraint," one who is in control of their emotions and their passions, not one who has eliminated them. We need to have our emotions. We need to have our passions. But we can't let them get the best of us. So who is the mightiest? God. "God is omnipotent," the Rabbis would certainly say, and how do we know God is omnipotent? Because God can control God's own anger. So, even though God wanted to lash out at the Romans for persecuting the Jews and destroying the Temple, God demonstrated that divine self-restraint by not doing that. You really see here how changes in the politics inform changes in theology, and then those changes in theology changed anthropology—just like God demonstrates self-restraint, so too should we demonstrate self-restraint so that we can imitate God. *Imitatio dei.*

There are conceptual parallels between this Rabbinic notion of divine self-restraint and the Lurianic notion of divine withdrawal (tsimtsum or divine self-restraint). Both insist on God's presence and suffering with His creatures, but they lean against divine intervention.

©2004 The Teaching Company.

Another understanding, which is very modern, is that God lacks omnipotence. In this idea of divine self-restraint, God doesn't lack omnipotence—God just demonstrates self-restraint. But in the modern period, there have been Jews that said, "No. We can no longer hold on to the idea that God is all-good and all-powerful. In the face of such evil, we have to give up the idea that God is all-powerful. God is still all-good, but God needs our help. The work of God is accomplished, today, through human hands.

What's new in this post-Shoah theodicy is the abandonment of mythological language to describe God's lack of omnipotence because I think that this idea of divine self-restraint that the Rabbis offered, or even Isaac Luria's tsimtsum (divine self-withdrawal)—functionally it means the same thing—that God is incapable of intervening, which is exactly what bothers so many people about the nature of the Shoah. Where was God? God was right here. God was with us. God was suffering with us. Nevertheless, God was incapable of intervening. So, I think what's new in this modern period is a demythologization—taking the mythical language out of the Kabbalah, and a democratization of divine service.

It's no longer just the male Jewish mystics with the proper intention who can help God in divine service. Everyone can do God's work.

Of course, there's another response to the Holocaust, to the Shoah, but that's not new: to say that God is dead, that there is no God. Atheism is not a new response, nor is it particularly religious.

This emphasis in the modern period on what the individual can do—on the power that we can give to enhance God's own power—moves us into modernity and the whole enlightenment project of emphasizing the worth of the individual and the unlimited road of progress. So, this is an appropriate segue for us to move into a discussion of Jews in modernity.

Lecture Eighteen
Emancipation, Enlightenment, and Reform

Scope:

Traditional Jewish life began to break down in Western Europe toward the end of the 18th century. The emancipation of Western European Jewry extended political rights and educational opportunities to members of the Jewish community with the expectation that the Jews would acculturate into their new national settings. Many Jews were eager to accept the invitation to leave their autonomous Jewish communities but were reluctant to abandon all ties to their ancestral faith.

As Jews began receiving secular education, a small group of German Jews began to study Jewish texts and Jewish history using the critical methods of academic scholarship. Some of these "enlightened" Jews used the conclusions of the academic study of Judaism to legitimize the reforms to Judaism that they were espousing. The ideology of Reform Judaism thus emerged in the German context of emancipation and enlightenment, although Reform found its most fertile soil in America.

Outline

I. Emancipation.
    A. Throughout the Middle Ages, Jews lived in self-governing corporations as guests of their host countries.
    B. Although falling short of political equality, the Edict of Tolerance in 1782 was designed to "make the Jewish nation useful and serviceable to the State, mainly through better education and enlightenment of its youth as well as by directing them to the sciences, the arts and the crafts."
    C. In Europe, Jews were first recognized as citizens of the country in which they lived as a result of the French Revolution (1790).
    D. There was an expectation amongst the Gentiles that citizenship would lead to "civic amelioration." In other words, without persecution and segregation, the Jews would acculturate and lose their ethnic particularity.

E. As citizens, Jews were no longer expected to yearn to return to the Land of Israel or consider themselves in exile.

F. Being Jewish became optional because Judaism became, for the first time, "just" a religion.

II. Jewish enlightenment (Haskalah).

    A. Among a small band of Europeans Jews, at first in France and Germany in the early 19th century, there was an eager embrace of the fruits of emancipation. Chief among those was a secular education.

        1. European languages and literature were studied.

        2. The natural sciences also became slightly more popular as academic subjects.

        3. In the traditional Jewish curriculum, less time was devoted to Talmud and more to Bible and ethics.

    B. The *maskilim* (proponents of the Haskalah) encouraged certain reforms throughout the Jewish community.

        1. The Jewish labor pool, concentrated in commerce and finance, should be diversified and include agriculture and crafts.

        2. The language used for synagogue sermons should be the vernacular, rather than Yiddish.

        3. Synagogues should also have greater decorum, similar to Protestant services.

    C. By the middle of the 19th century, the Haskalah had moved to Eastern Europe and Russia. In each community, the Haskalah had different characteristics and a different internal dynamic.

III. Reform Judaism.

    A. A small number of modest reforms in the first two decades of the 19th century preceded an ideological program of Reform.

        1. Order and decorum should prevail in the synagogue.

        2. Sermons should be edifying, rather than legalistic, and should be delivered in the vernacular.

        3. Some synagogues shortened services and introduced an organ.

    B. In 1818, a synagogue in Hamburg put into effect liturgical changes reflecting the presuppositions of emancipation.

<ol start="1">
<li>The traditional blessing for the return to Israel was eliminated. Judaism was now exclusively understood to be a faith without the ethnic or national elements.</li>
<li>The traditional blessing for the rebuilding of the Temple in Jerusalem and the reinstitution of animal sacrifices was similarly deleted from the prayer books. Even today, many Reform houses of worship are called "temples" because they no longer look toward rebuilding the Jerusalem Temple.</li>
</ol>

C. No longer did these Jews consider themselves to be living in exile as a punishment for earlier sins. Now, rehabilitating an image from Isaiah, the Jews were a "light unto the nations," spreading the good works commanded by ethical monotheism (see Isa. 42:6, 49:6, and 51:4).

D. Early scholars in the Reform movement, such as Abraham Geiger, stressed that historical development was a constant characteristic in Judaism and that Reform Judaism was simply being faithful to that tradition of progressive change.

E. By far, the most radical innovation by the early Reform movement in Germany was its claim that the traditional commandments were no longer obligatory.

<ol start="1">
<li>Immanuel Kant (1724–1804) charged that Judaism was "heteronomous," denying the individual the freedom to choose his own modes of piety.</li>
<li>Reform Judaism responds to this charge by allowing individuals to choose which commandments to observe based on which are most spiritually edifying.</li>
<li>Although traditional dress, laws of family purity, and dietary restrictions were often rejected, circumcision was almost always preserved for the newborn boys in the community.</li>
</ol>

Essential Reading:

Hyman, "Emancipation," in *Contemporary Jewish Religious Thought*, pp. 165–170.

Katz, *Out of the Ghetto*.

Meyer, "Reform Judaism," in *Contemporary Jewish Religious Thought*, pp. 767–772.

Seltzer, "Enlightenment," in *Contemporary Jewish Religious Thought*, pp. 171–175.

Supplementary Reading:

Feiner, *The Jewish Enlightenment*.

Meyer, *Response to Modernity*, pp. 3–224.

Petuchowski, "History of Reform Judaism," in *Studies in Modern Theology*, pp. 223–282.

Questions to Consider:

1. Why might Jews have been skeptical of the aims of emancipation?

2. Many of the 19th-century maskilim looked at Maimonides as their hero. In what ways were the maskilim similar to and different from Maimonides?

3. Throughout the 19th century, many of the children and grandchildren of the pioneering maskilim and Reformers abandoned Judaism and sometimes converted to Christianity. What may be some of the factors to explain that phenomenon?

Lecture Eighteen—Transcript
Emancipation, Enlightenment, and Reform

With this lecture we move into the modern period. Specifically, we're going to be looking at issues of emancipation, enlightenment, and the beginnings of Reform Judaism in Germany in the 19th century. But before we get there, we should spend a moment and try to understand what the political situation was like for Jews in the Middle Ages.

Throughout the Middle Ages, Jews lived in self-governing, autonomous corporations as guests of their host countries. In other words, a sovereign, for whatever reason, usually having to do with economics, would invite a Jewish community in and would be very specific about the kinds of vocations (the kinds of employment) that Jews could engage in in that community. Sometimes they adhered to the letter of the law and sometimes they didn't, but usually these economic incentives brought Jews to new communities. The taxes that were collected weren't collected by each individual Jew, but it was the responsibility of the *kehilah*, the self-governing authority, to collect taxes from the individuals, and then to pay the sovereign. There wasn't any expectation that the Jews had some kind of right to be living in that country. They were guests of the host country, and when the host decided that they were no longer welcome, then the guests were asked to leave. This happened periodically through Jewish history. It actually contributed to Jews going into more mobile businesses and not investing in real estate. Of course, there were also laws that prevented Jews from owning real estate very often, but Jews had a reputation (and it is a truthful reputation) for being involved in banking, in money lending—things that are easily portable so that you can pick it up. In the event that your host asks you to leave or demands that you leave, or the social situation becomes unbearable, you can pick up and take off. So, the Jews lived at the sufferance of the ruler of that society.

As we move into the modern period, you've got different ideas of government. People like John Locke are thinking about the natural rights of individuals and their relationship to the government, and this begins to filter down into the sovereigns' attitude toward the Jewish community, at the close of the 18th century. Although falling far short of political equality, the Edict of Tolerance in 1782 was designed:

It is our goal to make the Jewish nation useful and serviceable to the State, mainly through better education and enlightenment of its youth, as well as by directing them to the sciences, the arts and the crafts.

So, there are changes (there are winds of change) happening in central Europe. The Edict of Tolerance was by the Hapsburg Emperor Joseph II in 1782. This involved the government wanting to educate the Jews through a secular education. Up until this point Jews had only had a Jewish education, and they were in particular trades. But, here, you can really see what the Edict of Tolerance wants to do is to expand the kinds of trades that Jews go into, to make them more like the other citizens of the State. It doesn't give them full rights, it doesn't give them voting rights, but it is one of the first moves.

The first real extension of political liberty and political rights to the Jewish community was a result of the French Revolution in 1789, so that—by the year 1790—Jews were recognized as citizens of the country in which they lived. They were expected to be first and foremost Frenchmen, and only secondly members of the Jewish religion. So, they were supposed to have more in common with the French Catholic—not necessarily next door because in most of this period Jews still lived in ghettos. The word "ghetto" is Italian. It probably means an iron foundry. That's where the first ghetto in Venice, Italy, was at the beginning of the 16th century. Whether the ghetto was imposed by the government, or whether it was something that Jews chose to live in—in their own neighborhoods voluntarily— that was the norm in Europe for the entire Middle Ages. Jews didn't break out of the Jewish neighborhood, or the ghetto, until the 19th century at the very earliest.

So, there was an expectation among the gentiles that by extending civil rights, the Jews would acculturate. That doesn't mean that they would assimilate and give up their Jewishness, or their religiosity, but it means that they would dress like their neighbors and speak like their neighbors, and not continue to speak Yiddish—which was the general language of European Jewry. Yiddish is a combination of street German and Hebrew (a few Hebrew words thrown in). So, the vernacular of France or, later, Germany would come to crowd out those distinctively Jewish languages. In other places, they spoke

Ladino—which is a combination of Spanish and Hebrew, although, just like Yiddish, mostly Spanish.

The hope was that Judaism would become just another confession, just another religious faith. So you could have the Heugenots (the French Protestants) and the French Catholics and the French Jews, and what would unite them all would be their Frenchness, their commitment to France as a nation, and their loyalties to France as a nation—which also meant the idea of going back to Israel to reestablish the Third Jewish Commonwealth would no longer claim their loyalties. Up until this point, the Jews—no matter where they lived (whether it was in Europe, Asia, or North Africa)—they understood themselves to be part of a single nation.

So, this radical project of emancipation, to bring the Jews into the nations in which they lived, really required a whole shift in how the Jews perceived themselves and how the gentiles perceived the Jews. The hope was that they would acculturate and lose their ethnic particularity.

At this point, I want to introduce a Torah—the hasidic reading of a particular line from the Pesach haggadah, from that script that Jews read once or twice a year, around Passover. The line from the Passover haggadah is as follows: "In each generation, they rise up to destroy us, but God saves us from their hand."

The word for "destroy us" is *kaloteinu*. In the context of the Passover haggadah, we are recounting that even though it was the Egyptians that we are talking about in this Passover haggadah, trying to destroy us, and then the Israelites successfully leaving—in a different generation it might be the Romans, and in a different generation it might be the Nazis. Of course, this hasidic Torah was written in the 18th century, before the Nazis came to power—but the idea of being persecuted, that seems to be something that the Rabbis wanted to include in the haggadah. Fair enough. Although it is a part of Jewish history, it's not the entirety of Jewish history, but the Rabbis felt as though that at this moment in the Passover seder, it's worthwhile focusing on that aspect of Jewish history: persecution. And what the hasidic Rabbi does is reread that word "*kaloteinu*," which means, "to destroy us." "*Kaloteinu*" can also mean, "to betroth us." The word *kalah* is "bride." *Kalot* are "brides." So, the hasidic Rabbi goes on to say, "In this generation, what the nations want to do is to betroth us; they want to marry us," and then the continuation of that line from the haggadah is that God saves us from their hand. So, the hasidic Rabbi says that they are extending their hand to us in marriage: "They're the groom, we're the bride. Come; let's marry. Let's be one. We'll move into the same house and have the same customs and have the same traditions."

This is not just a Rabbinic pun. This is the hasidic Rabbi's way of saying, "Beware because now the way in which our enemies want to destroy us is by marrying us, by making us just like them, by bringing us into their house." This is, indeed, the project of emancipation. To solve the Jewish problem by making the Jews a people just like any other people, by having their ethnic identity being reduced to a religious identity so that they no longer consider themselves to be in exile from Israel and longing to get back to Israel, but, rather, they are good members of whatever nation-state they happen to be residing in at the time.

Several decades after this process of emancipation really begins, we have another phenomenon called the *Haskalah*—the Jewish Enlightenment. The European Enlightenment begins a hundred years earlier—but within the Jewish community, the Haskalah begins with a small band of European Jews, at first in France and Germany in the early 19th century, and then extending to eastern Europe toward the second half of the 19th century. These *maskilim* (from the word "haskalah"), these "enlightened ones"—they were ready to embrace the fruits of modernity. If the gates of the university were thrown open to them, they wanted to learn natural science, mathematics, foreign languages and foreign literatures, history, archaeology, anthropology, and sociology. They wanted those things that they hadn't been able to learn in the traditional Jewish curriculum, which—for the most part—was Talmud, Talmud, Talmud; and then Talmud commentaries, Talmud commentaries, Talmud commentaries. All of a sudden, this new world of knowledge was available to them, and they were very aggressive in pursuing that new world, or that new universe of knowledge.

European languages and literatures were studied. Natural sciences became more popular as academic subjects. Even within the Jewish curriculum itself there were changes—less time was devoted to Talmud and Talmud commentaries, and more time was devoted to the Bible and to Jewish ethics. After all, the Rabbis, now that there was more interaction between Jews and gentiles, the Rabbis didn't want the Jewish community to be perceived as in any way being less ethically sensitive than their gentile neighbors.

The maskilim (the proponents of the Haskalah) encouraged certain reforms throughout the Jewish community. Among them were the same reforms that Joseph II, the Hapsburg Emperor, also promulgated in his Edict of Tolerance—namely, to move the Jewish labor pool into different areas. While they had been concentrated in commerce and finance, the Jewish labor pool should be diversified and include agriculture as well as crafts.

Other reforms that the maskilim were promoting involved having sermons in synagogue services. Normally, although this is somewhat surprising to contemporary Jews, normally, traditionally, up until the 19th century, there were only sermons by a Rabbinic figure twice a year: around Passover and the Sabbath between Rosh Hashannah and Yom Kippur. Otherwise, people would go to the synagogue and they would *daven* (they would pray) the daily prayers or the holiday prayers, and then go home and eat. But, in order to model themselves after Protestant churches in Germany, where the pastor would give an edifying sermon in good German, these maskilim also demanded that their Rabbis start giving sermons—and not about traditional legalistic things, about the halachah and what you can do and what you can't do on the Sabbath—but, about spiritually edifying matters to raise up our spiritual level and our awareness of God's presence in our world. And, the sermons should be done, not in Yiddish, the traditional language of Jews, but in the vernacular—in this case, in high German.

Also, synagogues should have greater decorum. This word "decorum" will come up again when we talk about the Reform movement. In traditional synagogues, you've got kids running back and forth, you've got people talking during services, even today. All the more so, several hundred years ago, from what I have been told and from what I have read, the Protestant services were much more "buttoned-up." They didn't have the children talking, and there certainly weren't animals running around. (I don't know if there were animals running around in Jewish services.) But you get the idea that a Jewish service was not well orchestrated in the sense of having everyone in their place at the right time, and everyone else being silent. There was more of a free flow in traditional Jewish services, but in order to emulate the Protestant model of worship, decorum was promoted.

By the middle of the 19th century, the Haskalah had moved to eastern Europe and Russia, and we begin to see not so much changes in the synagogue, but we begin to see changes in how those maskilim understand Judaism, the history of Jewish practice, and the history of Jewish thought. Rather than go into how the Haskalah unfolded, in each country in Europe at different times in the 19th century, let me just emphasize that the Haskalah had a different set of characteristics, and a different internal dynamic depending on whether we're looking at France, Germany, Hungary, or the Pale of Settlements in Ukraine and White Russia, and then farther east into Russia itself.

So, it really depends on the internal dynamics to understand that process of Haskalah (of Enlightenment) in each individual community.

Amongst the maskilim in Germany, there was also a desire to use these new understandings as a result of their secular education, and to use them in order to press for certain reforms within Judaism itself—not just about the service, not just about having more decorum, but also changing certain traditions and modifying their understanding of the halachah (of traditional Jewish law). These changes began in the synagogue, as I've described. It very often happens that changes on the ground precede the more ideological justifications for those changes. By the time that we get to the 1820s, we really have a small group of "enlightened" Jews who will eventually become the early leaders of the Reform movement.

So, one of the things that they started out by saying was that order and decorum should, indeed, prevail in the synagogue. They also emphasized that sermons should be edifying, rather than legalistic, and be delivered in the vernacular.

But they said more than that. They said synagogue services are too long. There are too many words. An average Saturday morning service can last two-and-a-half to three hours. So these reformers said, "You know what? Let's shorten the service." The only way to shorten the service is by taking out large chunks of things that had traditionally been said. That upset those who were more traditional in the congregation, and it greatly upset those who were more traditional but not part of the congregation. The Reformers also knew about what was going on in the Protestant churches; they wanted to introduce music—specifically, organ music. Music hadn't been part of the Jewish worship ceremony since the destruction of the Temple in the year 70. That's not entirely true. Already in the late Middle Ages, we see certain kinds of musical devices being used, but because music had been such an integral part of the Temple service while the Temple was still standing, it was felt as inappropriate for there to be music during this interim period before the Temple is rebuilt.

But, we also now begin to have the ideological consequences of emancipation. The Reform Jews (or this early group) started saying, "Wait a second. If we are German Jews, and we are not looking forward to the reestablishment of the State of Israel and the rebuilding of the Temple, then what difference does it make whether or not we have music? We are no longer honoring the loss of the Temple by not playing music because we are not looking forward to the rebuilding of the Temple." So, one of the things that happens is that music is introduced.

And the houses of worship of these early Reform communities are called "Temples." Today, if you drive in any major city, you will see that there are some Jewish houses of worship called "Temple Beth-El," or "Temple Beth-An," and there are other Jewish houses of worship called "Congregation Yehuda," or "Congregation Eilat," and then there are some called "Synagogue Beth-El" and "Synagogue Beth-An." There is actually a difference between a "temple" and a "synagogue." Almost all of the Temples that you'll bump into are Reform institutions because they are not looking forward to the Temple being rebuilt in Jerusalem and the re-institution of animal sacrifices. Although, the truth is, I don't think that too many Jews are actually looking forward to the re-institution of animal sacrifices in the Temple. But, nevertheless, it is part of Reform ideology that they are not looking forward to that Temple being rebuilt and the re-institution of animal sacrifices—so, they call their houses of worship "Temples." In the more traditional communities, or the more traditional congregations, they tend to not use that word "Temple" because they continue to pay at least lip service to the idea that eventually, in some messianic future, there will be a Temple rebuilt—whether that Temple is understood as bricks and mortar, or as the Temple of God in your soul; that's up to the interpretive capacities of each individual worshiper.

But, the thrust of the early reforms was to really be ideologically consistent—that since we are good Germans, we no longer feel that we are in exile. We are not looking forward to going back to Israel and re-establishing the Temple; that that should be reflected in our liturgy. So, they deleted those traditional blessings that talked about going back to Israel—that talked about re-establishing the Temple—and also that line about being exiled for our sins. They didn't feel that they were in exile anymore. So how did they go about addressing their presence in what is now called the Diaspora? They've been "dispersed" rather than "exiled." What they did was, they rehabilitated an image from the book of *Isaiah (Isaiah* 49:6):

> For God has said, 'Is it too little that you should be my servant? And that I raised up the tribes of Jacob and restored the survivors of Israel? I will also make you a light unto the nations, that my salvation may reach the ends of the earth.'

This idea of being a "light unto the nations" becomes the Reform mission, and it is their explanation for why there is a dispersion—not that we are in exile anymore, but what our job is, is to demonstrate ethical monotheism in all the lands that we have been dispersed to. Why? In order to serve as an example to the nations of the world as to how people should behave. The principles of ethical monotheism should characterize our behavior and influence our non-Jewish neighbors. It has nothing to do with proselytizing or with making our non-Jewish neighbors convert to Judaism, but, rather, influencing their behavior—not necessarily their religious affiliation.

In the prayer book of the Berlin Reform Association, we have the following line:

> You have called us, O Lord, to found the kingdom of truth and love on the whole earth. And for this did you disperse us, [that language of Diaspora—dispersion] so that the sparks of your light might fly to all nations to dispel the darkness of delusion from the farthest corners of the globe.

So, you get the sense now that history is being re-written. We are no longer exiled as the result of a divine punishment, but in order to spread God's light; that is the Reform mission. The author of that statement in the prayer book of the Berlin Reform Association was probably Samuel Holdheim. He wrote it in the mid-19th century. He's an interesting figure in early Reform Judaism because Samuel Holdheim was a radical. He advocated a couple of reforms in order to be ideologically consistent—that Judaism is "just" a religion, and it doesn't have an ethnic or national component. One of the things he suggested to do was to move Shabbat to Sunday, and, indeed, in the United States there were a handful of Reform Temples in the latter half of the 19th century that also had Sabbath-like services on Sunday. But Reform in general did not agree to Samuel Holdheim's idea that Shabbat should be moved to Sunday. Shabbat is Saturday, and that's where it was going to stay, even though it was a nuisance. It's much easier to have your Sabbath celebration and your day of rest when the majority of the population has their day of rest. What are you going to do if you are a storeowner or an employee? Are you going to take off Saturday, and then the store is closed on Sunday? So, as a way of making the celebration of Sabbath easier for people, Holdheim suggested that the day be shifted to Sunday. That was not widely accepted.

Also, and very radically, he promoted the idea that the *brit milah*, or the circumcision of male babies on the eighth day, should be abolished. It's got nothing to do with religiosity. It doesn't increase our awareness of God in the world. It's a mark of ethnic identification, and because Judaism is no longer about ethnicity or nationality, we should get rid of the *brit milah*. But again, that was not widely accepted. Only a very few people stopped circumcising their sons on the eighth day.

Other early scholars in the Reform movement were less radical than Samuel Holdheim. One of the more famous founders of early Reform Judaism in Germany was Abraham Geiger. What he did as a scholar was to demonstrate that Jewish law, Jewish practice, and Jewish thought has always changed—from the Bible, to the Rabbinic period, to the medieval period, and to the early modern period. He did that work as a scholar, but with the ideological axe to grind that what Reform Judaism is doing is being faithful to this idea of the progress and the development of Jewish law, and they're not doing anything radically different than what the Rabbis of the Talmud did in their day. So, this was scholarship in the service of Reform Judaism. So, there is really an overlap between the maskilim (adherents of the Enlightenment) and the founders of Reform Judaism, whereby we are being faithful, not to the content of the

Judaism that we have inherited, but we are being faithful to the process of Judaism, which always tried to grapple with issues of modernity, that has always tried to accommodate the historical and sociological circumstances that Jews find themselves in. That's exactly what people like Abraham Geiger were trying to do for the German-Jewish community in the mid-19th century.

But, by far, the most radical innovation of early Reform Judaism was its claim that the traditional commandments were no longer obligatory. This claim comes out of their commitment to scholarship and the relatively new ideas of biblical criticism—the idea that God was not the author of the Pentateuch (of the Torah); that "divine dictation" does not describe how the books that we have before us of *Genesis* through *Deuteronomy* came into existence. Rather, human beings inspired by God were trying to put into words what they understood God's will to be, and they wrote the five books of Moses—different human beings, over hundreds of years, and human beings are fallible.

Human beings are historically rooted, and they need to be viewed against the historical background from which they emerged. So, none of the laws in the Hebrew Bible are binding on us because they are eternal laws of God. Reform Judaism accepts biblical criticism and rejects the idea that the laws are binding. This was the first real break. It was okay to modify this and to change that in terms of the synagogue service. But to say that halachah, the traditional Jewish law, is no longer binding—that really is a quantum leap, and it establishes what, for traditional Judaism, is a heresy: the idea that the Torah is not the word of God, and the idea that the traditional laws are not binding. So, Reform Judaism really threw down the gauntlet at that point, in the mid-19th century. They justified their conclusions with academic scholarship, but (as we will see in the next lecture) the more traditional scholars and the more traditional Rabbis did not accept the conclusions of biblical criticism and of the scholars.

This rejection of traditional Jewish law was also a response to the famous German philosopher Immanuel Kant, who criticized Judaism as "heteronomous"—the idea that individuals weren't doing what they were motivated to do themselves out of autonomy, but they were doing what came down from God, or what came down from the Rabbis. So, Reform Judaism really emphasized the individual and the individual's autonomy to engage in those traditional forms and modes of worship that spoke to them—that increased their piety, their devotional posture; that was spiritually edifying—but the emphasis, like with the Haskalah (the Enlightenment), was on the individual.

Amongst the commandments (the traditional commandments) that almost all Reform Jews completely abandoned were traditional dress (they wanted to acculturate and look like other Germans and other Frenchmen); the laws of family purity (whereby certain times of the month during a woman's menstruation cycle, a man and his wife do not engage in sexual relations); and dietary restrictions (so that Jews might not necessarily be eating ham, but they would feel more comfortable eating in their gentile neighbors' homes or in a restaurant that wasn't under Rabbinic supervision). So, these kinds of ritual laws were widely rejected within the early Reform community, but circumcision was almost always preserved (as I mentioned) for the newborn boys in that community. That resistance signalled that even the most acculturated Jew felt instinctively that Judaism was more than just a religious faith. Our next lecture will examine the reaction to Reform by the traditionalists.

Lecture Nineteen
Orthodox Judaisms

Scope:

As a response to emancipation, enlightenment, and Reform Judaism, several varieties of Orthodox Judaism emerged in the 19th century. That's right—Orthodoxy is just as much a product of modernity as is Reform! While Modern Orthodoxy struggled to balance traditional Judaism and an open posture toward Western European culture, Ultra-Orthodoxy rejected secular studies, Western dress, and European languages.

The story is different in Eastern Europe, where the reforms that Judaism underwent were not about halachic practice but about devotional posture. The Hassidic movement focused on how one is best able to maintain a relationship with God. Although each Orthodox group responded differently to modernity, what unites the Modern Orthodox, the Ultra-Orthodox, and the Chassidic Jews is their commitment to traditional halachah.

Outline

I. Neo-Orthodoxy/Modern Orthodoxy.

    A. Rabbi Samson Raphael Hirsch (1808–1888) is widely considered the founder of this branch of Orthodoxy, which strives to combine elements of tradition and modernity.

    B. In 1836, Hirsch wrote a book in the form of a series of letters, ostensibly to a young man having difficulty with traditional Judaism, as a way of reaching out to the entire generation of newly emancipated Jews.

        1. The Torah, given by God, is a "generator of spiritual life within us. … We must read with a wakeful eye and ear, and with a mind tuned to the deeper sense and to the more profound meaning which lie beneath the surface" (Hirsch, Letter 2).

        2. "It is our duty to join ourselves as closely as possible to the state which receives us into its midst, to promote its welfare and not to consider our own well-being as in any way separate from that of the state to which we belong. This close connection with states everywhere is not at all in contradiction to the spirit of Judaism, for the independent national life of Israel was never the essence or purpose of our existence as a nation, but only a means of fulfilling our spiritual mission" (Hirsch, Letter 16).

C. In 1853, Hirsch opened up a Jewish school in Frankfurt, Germany, that combined Jewish and secular studies.

  1. He was competing for students with the Reform-leaning day school that had opened earlier.

  2. One of the founders of German Reform, Abraham Geiger, was an acquaintance of Hirsch and also held a pulpit in Frankfurt. Hirsch was dedicated to defending Orthodoxy against Reform.

D. Hirsch's motto was "*Torah im derech eretz*," or "Torah with the ways of the world."

  1. It was fine to adopt the dress and language of the country.

  2. Synagogue behavior should evidence decorum.

  3. Sermons could be in the vernacular.

  4. Choral singing was acceptable in the prayer service.

  5. All these changes were also espoused by Reform Judaism. But Hirsch maintained Hebrew and the traditional prayers.

II. Ultra-Orthodoxy.

  A. In Central Europe, particularly in Hungary, there were Jews who rejected any synagogue reforms or acculturation to the non-Jewish environment. The figurehead for such a rejection of modernity was Rabbi Moses Sofer (1762–1839).

  B. The trend toward religious conservatism was followed by Rabbi Akiva Yosef Schlesinger (1837–1922). If Reform served as the primary adversary for the Modern Orthodox, it was the Modern Orthodox who were the targets of the Ultra-Orthodox.

  1. No synagogue reforms were to be tolerated, be they liturgical, homiletical, or architectural.

  2. Stringent rulings, previously applicable for only the most pious, became the community norm.

  3. Schlesinger employed *aggadah*, in which exaggerated statements are often found unrestricted by group consensus, to invent a new halachah.

a. He argued that secular studies are prohibited even if they are necessary for one's occupation. (He eventually modified that position.)

b. The role of the non-Jews is to interact with the world, whereas the role of the Jew is to devote himself exclusively to Torah.

c. Acculturation, which the Neo-Orthodox embrace, is a Trojan horse that will turn Judaism into a religious confession and repudiate the centrality of the Jewish people, who must remain *shalem*, "whole."

d. Pronouncements included those concerning *SHemot* ("names"; we must keep traditional names and not become Toms, Dicks and Harrys), *lashon* ("language"; we must preserve Hebrew and Yiddish and not learn the vernacular of the states in which we live), and *malbush* ("clothing"; we must retain our distinctive dress and not conform to the styles and fads of European fashion).

III. Eastern European Orthodoxy.

A. Hassidism was the reform or renewal movement of Eastern Europe that promoted individual piety and devotional posture while maintaining halachic commitment.

1. The figure associated with the founding of Hassidism is Israel Ba'al Shem Tov, the "good master of the name" (1700–1760).

2. One of the essential claims of Hassidism is that religious virtue is not a monopoly of those most learned in the Talmud and traditional Jewish literature. Love for and devotion to God can be expressed beyond Talmud Torah.

3. Hassidism was a popular movement that greatly simplified the Kabbalah, while still preaching divine immanence, and appealed to the masses of Eastern Europe.

4. Although for the first three generations of Hassidism, leadership was in the hands of charismatic individuals called *tzaddikim*, by the 19th century, leadership became largely dynastic.

5. Each *tzaddik* imprinted his own personality on his Hassidim. Some, such as the Ba'al Shem Tov, emphasized divine service through joy, song, and dance. Others, like the Kotsker, demanded soul searching and purity of intention.

B. The Mitnagdim (opponents of Hassidism) were skeptical of this new mystical movement, especially given that it contained a handful of halachic innovations and challenged the supremacy of Talmud.

1. The last popular mystical movement, that of the false Messiah Shabbatei Tsvi, was still an open wound.

2. Initially, there were mutual recriminations between these groups, but they eventually perceived that they were better served as allies against their common foes.

C. Today, we use the term *Haredi* (quakers) to include what we have called the Hungarian Ultra-Orthodox, the Eastern European Hassidim and their opponents, the Mitnagdim.

1. Easily recognizable by their black garb, the Haredim tend to live in a few cities in the United States, the United Kingdom, continental Europe, and Israel.

2. Among the most famous sects in Haredi Judaism are the Lubavitch (also known as Chabad), the Ger, and the Bratslav.

IV. What unites all these groups is their commitment to the divinity of the Torah and the binding quality of halachah.

Essential Reading:

Ben-Amos, "Israel ben Eliezer, the Baal Shem Tov," in *Judaism in Practice*, pp. 488–512.

Green, "Teachings of the Hasidic Masters," in *Back to the Sources*, pp. 361–401.

Green, "Hasidism," in *Contemporary Jewish Religious Thought*, pp. 317–324.

Rosenbloom, *Tradition in an Age of Reform*.

Silber, "The Emergence of Ultra-Orthodoxy," in *The Uses of Tradition*, pp. 23–84.

Supplementary Reading:

Buber, *Hasidism and Modern Man* and *Tales of the Hasidim*.

Heschel, *Passion for Truth*.

Hirsch, *Nineteen Letters*.

Questions to Consider:

1. Samson Raphael Hirsch, responding to Reform, argues that we need to reform Jews, not Judaism. Is that possible for any religion, or is it just a rhetorical flourish?

2. Many contemporary Orthodox Jews own television sets but use them only as monitors hooked up to their VCRs and DVDs. What statement does that make about their posture toward acculturation? Is hardware/technology value-free?

3. Hassidism's emphasis on devotional posture, being conscious of God's presence at all times and in all things, was a powerful idea for the masses. How can one promote such a consciousness? Would one necessarily want to?

Lecture Nineteen—Transcript
Orthodox Judaisms

It surprises many of my students that I teach about Reform Judaism before I teach about Orthodoxy, and some of my Reform students ask me why. The answer is that Orthodoxy is a response to Reform Judaism, at least the modern Orthodoxy that we know. Sometimes, my Reform students have this image problem, that Reform Judaism is somehow inauthentic or illegitimate because it's new and it's not good old-fashioned religion. What I try to communicate to them is, there is no good old-fashioned religion, if what you mean by that is the kind of Judaism that existed before emancipation and before enlightenment in the 18th century. Emancipation and enlightenment changes everything. So, we're going to start this lecture on Orthodoxies in Judaism by looking at Modern Orthodoxy.

And again, I want to emphasize that Modern Orthodoxy developed in Germany. Why? Because that's the same place where Reform developed. The idea is that Reform Judaism generates—amongst other things—this reaction by some of the traditionalists that becomes known as Neo-Orthodoxy, or Modern Orthodoxy. The figurehead, as the founder of this movement, is Rabbi Samson Raphael Hirsch, whose dates are 1808 to 1888. He strove to combine elements of tradition, as well as bring in new, modern elements. So, Modern Orthodoxy is very much a self-conscious condemnation of what we have seen in the last lecture from emancipation and enlightenment and Reform, as well as a firm commitment to traditional halachah. This becomes known as Orthodoxy.

The book that really put Samson Raphael Hirsch on the map as the spokesman for this new generation of emancipated Jews—trying to figure out what their relationship should be between Judaism and German, ethnic national identity—was written by Samson Raphael Hirsch in the 1830s. It's called *The Nineteen Letters of Ben Uziel*. He writes this book as a series of letters to this young man who seems to be confused. He is using a literary form that Maimonides used at the very beginning of the *Guide for the Perplexed*, where his epistolatory dedication is Maimonides writing to one of his students, who he can no longer see face-to-face. He has moved far away, and Maimonides is saying, "I am writing this book to you to help you navigate through these very perplexing times."

So, what Samson Raphael Hirsch is doing, hundreds of years later, is using a similar kind of mechanism as a nod to Maimonides, that we are also living in very perplexing times, and here is my attempt to navigate between tradition and modernity. So I'm going to read a couple of quotes from the different letters of *The Nineteen Letters* that Samson Raphael Hirsch wrote. "The Torah given by God."

Already "The Torah given by God"—no biblical criticism, no authors of the Torah, no human authorship; the Torah was given by God. When we say "given by God" that's a little bit different from "written by God," but, nevertheless, Modern Orthodoxy insists on some model of divine authorship of the Torah, and it rejects biblical criticism.

> The Torah given by God is a generator of spiritual life within us. … We must read with a wakeful eye and ear, and with a mind tuned to the deeper sense and to the more profound meaning, which lie beneath the surface.

So, this is part of the project of general religion in Germany—the Protestant emphasis on individual spirituality. You can see that he doesn't want Modern Orthodoxy to be beat out by Reform as a religion that strives to enhance the individual's relationship with God. So he uses the language of spirituality, a language that had also been promoted by a famous German theologian, Frederick Schleiermacher, in the decades before Samson Raphael Hirsch wrote his book. Another quotation from Hirsch's book:

> It is our duty to join ourselves as closely as possible to the state which receives us into its midst, to promote its welfare, and not to consider our own well-being as in any way separate from that of the state to which we belong. This close connection with states everywhere is not at all in contradiction to the spirit of Judaism. For the independent national life of Israel was never the essence or purpose of our existence as a nation, but only a means of fulfilling our spiritual mission.

This quote is packed with the same kinds of sentiments that we find in Reform Judaism. Right? "We are good German citizens. We need to be loyal to the state. There shouldn't be any fear or concern of dual loyalties. We are good Germans. We are not really—the essence of Judaism is not about going to Israel."

What Modern Orthodoxy won't do—what Samson Raphael Hirsch won't do—is to change the traditional prayers by eliminating that blessing in the *Amidah* (in the central, core prayer), which talks about going to Israel and reestablishing a Jewish presence and rebuilding a Jewish Temple. He won't change the formulation of the prayer, but he'll say that that's not the essence. What the essence is is this mission—the same kind of mission that we saw with Abraham Geiger and with Samuel Holdheim, in the early Reform founders, of a mission that involves being outside of the Land of Israel, and spreading ethical monotheism all across the globe. So, even though he's not changing the halachah, he's certainly changing his language—no longer talking about exile, but also about being in dispersion. There is a spiritual mission here that Hirsch wants to promote.

In 1853, Hirsch opened up a Jewish day school in Frankfurt, Germany, that combined Jewish and secular studies. He was competing with another school that had been opened up earlier by the Reform movement, that also combined Jewish and secular studies, but it was much more about secular studies than Jewish studies. Really, the school that Samson Raphael Hirsch opened up in 1853 is the model for the contemporary Modern Orthodox day school—where half of the day is Jewish studies, often taught in Hebrew, and half of the day (and these are longer days, by the way, than we normally have in the American public school system)—the second half of the day—is devoted to the language of the state, literature, math, history, and sciences—a regular general studies curriculum. This, to this day, characterizes the Modern Orthodox school systems.

One of the founders of Reform Judaism, Abraham Geiger (who we mentioned in the last lecture), was an acquaintance of Samson Raphael Hirsch. They had met as college students. Geiger finished college, while Hirsch didn't complete the curriculum. They were together in Frankfurt, Germany—each having a separate pulpit. So there's a kind of rivalry between these two, and Hirsch is trying to get students to come to his new school, and he's very much interested in defending Orthodoxy against Reform. Back to one of Hirsch's *Letters*, he writes:

> The only object of such reform [and he uses that word, "reform"], however, must be the fulfillment of Judaism by

Jews in our time. The fulfillment of the eternal idea in harmony with the conditions set by the time. Merely to seek greater ease and comfort in life through the destruction of the eternal code set up for all time by the God of eternity, is not, and never can be, the reform which we need. Judaism seeks to lift us up to its own plane. We must never attempt to drag it down to our own level.

What Samson Raphael Hirsch is saying to Abraham Geiger and the rest of his Reform compatriots is that what we need to do is to reform Jews, not reform Judaism. So you see this rivalry in both the letters that Hirsch writes in this book *The Nineteen Letters of Ben Uziel*, as well as Hirsch's biblical commentary, which he starts writing in the 1860s and finishes in the 1870s, where he actually translates the Pentateuch into German and then gives a very spiritual and symbolic reading of the text. He draws on the traditional sources as well, but his interest is in promoting a kind of spiritual edification. He does that through his own biblical commentary.

Today, when we think about Modern Orthodox Jews, we might think of the most famous Modern Orthodox Jew in America, which is Joe Lieberman. Joe Lieberman is someone who wears a knitted *kepah*, and he has a secular education, and the rest of his dress is like everyone else's dress. His English is very good. His Hebrew is also very good. But he is someone who has acculturated into American culture while still maintaining fidelity to traditional Jewish law. This kind of dual citizenship in both the culture in which you live, as well as Judaism, is reflected in Samson Raphael Hirsch's motto for the school he opened up, which is "*Torah im derech eretz*," or "Torah with the ways of the world."

Also, he had several principles. It is fine to adopt the dress and the language of the country in which you live. Synagogue behavior should evidence decorum. He also wanted to promote the kinds of reforms (with a small "r") that the Reform movement was advocating in terms of having a less-boisterous prayer service. Sermons should be in the vernacular. Choral singing in the synagogue was acceptable (not musical instruments; that's against tradition). But choral singing, that's okay. So, you can see what Samson Raphael Hirsch and the whole Modern Orthodox movement is really trying to do is to change Judaism when it doesn't come into a direct collision with the halachah. If it is just custom, and if there is room within the halachah to make these changes, that's usually fine. But we run into much greater problems when we're talking about changes that are antithetical to what the halachah has traditionally been.

In addition, one of the differences between Reform and Modern Orthodoxy is the commitment that Modern Orthodoxy has to Hebrew in the traditional prayer service.

The traditional prayer service is going to stay the same. It's not going to be modified, and it's not going to be translated into the vernacular. Although the sermon of the Rabbi should be in the vernacular, traditional prayers were said in Hebrew, and they will continue to be said in Hebrew.

A very different kind of Orthodox response to Reform Judaism was that of what becomes called the Ultra-Orthodox. In a discussion of the Ultra-Orthodox, we move from western Europe (Germany and France) to central Europe—in particular, Hungary. There were Jews in Hungary that rejected any synagogue reforms whatsoever, or acculturation to the non-Jewish environment. The figurehead for such a movement was Rabbi Moses Sofer, whose dates are 1762 to 1839, just to give you an idea of where he falls. He coined the phrase that "change is forbidden by the Torah." He said that a lot. "Change is forbidden by the Torah." That was the theory. In practice, he was quite flexible, and when it came to finding ways to allow Jews to move more successfully in their society and in the cultures in which they were now living, Rabbi Sofer (or, as he was known, Chatam Sofer) was quite successful at molding the halachah (I don't want to say "manipulating the halachah"), but molding the halachah in order to allow Jews greater access to the outside world.

This trend toward religious conservatism was followed by Rabbi Akiva Yosef Schlesinger. He actually lived from 1837 to 1922, so we now move into the 20th century. He was very clear that if Reform served as the primary adversary for Modern Orthodox, Reform was off the map for Ultra-Orthodoxy. They weren't even worthy of being argued against. It was the Modern Orthodox folks who were the targets of the Ultra-Orthodox. They saw this whole enterprise of the emancipation and the enlightenment as a Trojan horse—the Hasidic Torah that I mentioned earlier, about "in every generation our enemies rising up to destroy us," but you can read "destroy us" as "betroth us"—the idea that God will save us from their hand in marriage, only by keeping us close to the traditional ways and not accepting any forms of acculturation. So, no synagogue reforms were to be tolerated—whether they were liturgical, or whether they were homiletical, or even architectural. We begin to see architectural changes within the Modern Orthodox community, and certainly within the Reform community in the 19th century as well. But everything needs to stay as it was. He frequently quoted his teacher in these subjects, the Chatam Sofer, "Change is forbidden by the Torah."

Moreover, when it came to halachah, what Rabbi Schlesinger did was to take the wide gamut of rulings on any given issue, and say that only the most stringent rulings that—in the past—had only been applicable to the most pious in the community, now it was the most stringent rulings that became the norm for the entire community. This really separated those who were dedicated to this kind of piety from those who were willing to accommodate modernity and acculturate to varying degrees.

Furthermore, Schlesinger employed *aggadah*, which are often exaggerated statements that aren't restricted by group consensus. He used the playful creativity of the Talmudic Rabbis in order to create a new halachah. I will give you an example of this in just a moment. He argued that secular studies are prohibited, even if they are necessary for one's occupation. Later on, he modified his position on that, but at least in theory, what the Jews should be doing is studying Torah. There is nothing wrong with studying secular subjects. That is the role, though, of the Gentiles, not of the Jews. What Schlesinger worked out is a kind of division of labor. The Jew should devote himself exclusively to Torah study, and the gentile has access to— and should engage in—secular studies, whether it's science, math, medicine, literature, or history. All those other subjects, that's in the jurisdiction of the gentiles, but the Jews should remain committed to an exclusive Torah life.

Acculturation, which the Neo-Orthodox embrace—for the Ultra-Orthodox is a Trojan horse that will turn Judaism into a religious confession—just a religion—and repudiate the centrality of the Jewish people (the idea of ethnicity and nationality), who, for the Ultra-Orthodox, must remain *shalem*. "Shalem" means "whole." What Schlesinger does is a play on this word "shalem." It is spelled "Sh"—"La"—"M," or *shin, lamed, mem*, are the Hebrew letters. He uses a Rabbinic midrash to suggest that what we need to do in order to remain whole or to remain intact is to preserve our *SHemot*—our names; our *Lashon*, or language; and our *Malbush*—our dress. Shalem: SHemot, Lashon, and Malbush—names, language, and dress. So, here is how he unpacks that idea.

In the latter part of the 19th century and the early part of the 20th century, Jews are taking on the first names of their neighbors. So we've got Toms, Dicks, and Harrys. There shouldn't be any Toms, Dicks, and Harrys according to Schlesinger. We should remain with traditional names. So we should be Mendel and Fievel and Rifkeleah—the traditional Jewish names. Furthermore, Lashon: We shouldn't be learning their language, the vernacular of whatever place the Jews were living. We should be committed to speaking Yiddish, and then for prayers, to Hebrew. And finally, Malbush: We should remain dressing the way that we have (in his imagination) always dressed, and often times, in black hats and black coats—that's what the Polish nobility wore in the 17th and 18th centuries. So, to imitate the Polish nobility, the Jews would also dress like that. Now, in the late 19th century, the Polish nobility were no longer wearing such things, but this conservative element of the Jewish world continued to wear those things. And, according to this philosophy, they should continue to wear those things—even in the heat of the Israeli summer, which gets into the triple digits Fahrenheit. But you see people walking around Israel with the black hats and the black garb; at least they are thin suits. It doesn't have to be black wool; it's just that the color has to be black.

So, for the Ultra-Orthodox, in order to remain whole—to remain intact—against this onslaught of modernity and the new temptations to acculturate and to join gentile culture, what needs to happen is that Jews need to preserve those elements of their peoplehood. And it is ironic that, in the next lecture, we're going to see a different response to modernity, that also emphasizes retaining this aspect of Jewish peoplehood—Zionism—that is as irreligious (not just unreligious, but irreligious) and impious as you can imagine. So, on one side of the peoplehood spectrum you've got the Ultra-Orthodox, who don't want to change anything from the Torah—and on the other side of the peoplehood spectrum (as we'll see in the next lecture), we've got the Zionists, who aren't at all committed to leading a Torah life, to say the least.

As we move farther east to the area of the Pale of Settlements—where most American Jews, the vast majority of American Jews, trace their ancestry to—we're talking about White Russia, Ukraine, the area around Odessa, and also Russia. There is a new kind of Judaism that is emerging that is also a Reform movement, or a Jewish renewal movement. I'm talking about Hassidism. I explain Hassidism as eastern Europe's Reform movement. The big difference between western Europe's Reform movement and eastern Europe's Reform movement with Hassidism, is that in eastern Europe the Hassidim remained committed to halachah. But in both renewal movements, there is concern with trying to promote individual piety and what my teacher Art Greene (one of the leading scholars in Hassidism) calls "devotional posture," whereby every action that a Jew makes throughout the day is a way of connecting with God and worshipping God. It's no longer only about what traditionally had been the mode of piety, which was study. There's nothing wrong with study. But there are ways in addition to study that one can express one's piety, one's devotional commitment to God. And, through raising our consciousness, that God is to be found outside of the Talmud and outside of Talmudic commentaries, this new renewal movement—which swept over eastern Europe—allowed people who were not scholars to feel as though they were engaging in pious activity, like the scholars of the community.

As I said, Hassidism swept eastern Europe. It was a mass movement. The Kabbalah and Jewish philosophy—those were elitist movements. So, what Hassidism does is to greatly simplify the Kabbalah and to spread these teachings on a popular level through individual teachers who were really sent out on foot or by carriage all over eastern Europe to preach (they are itinerant preachers)—to preach these new understandings of Hassidism.

The figure who is associated as the founder of Hassidism is Israel Ba'al Shem Tov, the good master of the name, who was born in 1700 and died in 1760. He, according to legend, did not have a traditional Jewish education in the sense of going to a yeshiva, going to a place of intense Talmudic training. He was not illiterate, but he was unenchanted by traditional study. He found his way outside of the beth midrash, the traditional house of study, to his appreciation of God through nature. And indeed, according to legend, he lived for years and years in the Carpathian Mountains. It was only as a mature man, in his forties, that he revealed himself to be this great Jewish teacher. What's so interesting is that amongst his earliest crowd of students were great Talmudic giants. So one wonders what these great Talmudic figures thought they could learn from the Ba'al Shem Tov. Clearly, it is a way of being in the world that enhances your ability, that raises your consciousness, to perceive God in all of creation, and not be so narrowly confined to the traditional mode of Jewish piety, which is Talmud study.

Although for the first three generations of Hassidism, leadership was in the hands of charismatic individuals, by the end of that third generation, leadership within the Hassidic world largely became dynastic. So, one of the sons would take over from the father, and in some cases, several of the sons—although they would have to go to different cities around eastern Europe.

Each *tzaddik* (a "tzaddik" is the leader) of the Hassidic group imprinted his own personality on his Hassidism. Some, like the Ba'al Shem Tov, emphasized divine service through joy, song, and dance. Others, like the Kotsker Rebbe, demanded soul searching and purity of intention. One scholar of Hassidism says that the only commonality between different Hassidim, who have different *tzaddikim* (different leaders), is that every Hassidim has its tzaddik. That's the only commonality. But what one tzaddik demands of his Hassidim could be totally different from what another tzaddik demands from his Hassidim.

Let me talk for a second about these terms (*tzaddik* and *Hassid*). A "tzaddik" literally means "a righteous one." "Hassid" means "piety" or "pietism." There is one tzaddik for every group of Hassidim. But, remember, I told you that what Hassidic does is to greatly simplify the Kabbalah. The ninth sefirah was also called in traditional Kabbalah, the "tzaddik"—the Righteous One. Another name for the tenth sefirah was Knesset Yisrael (the community of Israel). The ninth, which was the male, and the tenth, which was the female, need to be in union for this optimal divine flow to then grace the material world. So with the Hassidic rereading of these s'firot, the tzaddik becomes linked to the community of Israel, which is represented by the Hassidim, and they need to be connected. So no longer will the individual Hassid try to have a relationship to God that transcends the tzaddik. I call this "vicarious communion" or "vicarious cleaving." The individual Hassid can cleave to the tzaddik, and the tzaddik then cleaves to God, and it is through that way (through that mechanism) that the individual Hassid has his religious experiences.

The tzaddik also becomes the object, not of adoration, but the object of pilgrimage. It used to be, in biblical times, that you would make pilgrimage to the Temple in Jerusalem. But now, in the 19th century, the individual Hassid would make a pilgrimage to the court of his tzaddik. So, we see (in the Hassidic community, anyway) the importance of Jerusalem being displaced by the centrality of that individual charismatic figure (at the beginning of Hassidism) the tzaddik.

Not everyone thought that Hassidism was a good idea. There were opponents to Hassidism called the *Mitnagdim*. "Mitnagdim" literally means "opponents." They were skeptical of this new mystical movement for two reasons, primarily. It did contain a handful of halachic innovations (very minor halachic innovations), and it challenged the supremacy of Talmud study. They were traditionalists (the Mitnagdim), and they thought that the exclusive route to Jewish piety was through Talmud Torah.

There is also some concern and skepticism, and some wariness, that this popular mystical movement might have some echoes of a previous popular, mystical movement that went wrong. I am talking about the movement of Shabbatei Tsvi, who was the false Messia in the 17th century—and we're not so far after the 17th century that the memory of Shabbatei Tsvi is completely gone. Shabbatei Tsvi brought this mass movement of mystical elements and became a false Messiah. He converted to Islam. Thousands and thousands of Jews were left stranded and hopeless. So, the Mitnagdim didn't want anything like that to happen again. So, they really tried to dampen the popularity of Hassidism. There were mutual recriminations between these groups. There were excommunications of one Rabbi from another. But, eventually, they perceived that they were better served as allies against their common foes, the Modern Orthodox and certainly the Reformed.

Today, in contemporary language, we use the term *Haredi* (which means "quakers"—somebody who quakes with the fear of God) to include what we have called in this lecture the Hungarian Ultra-Orthodox, the eastern-European Hassidim as well as their opponents, the Mitnagdim. The Haredim are easily recognizable by their black garb, and the Haredim tend to live in a few cities in the U.S., the

U.K., continental Europe, and Israel. Amongst the most famous sects within Haredi Judaism are the Lubavitch (also known as *Chabad*), the Ger, and the Bratslavers. What unites all of these groups is their commitment to the divinity of the Torah and the binding quality of halachah. That's what links the Ultra-Orthodox to the Modern Orthodox.

Throughout the 19th century new Judaisms have emerged—and for the first time, one could opt out of Judaism altogether. It's not really for the first time. Baruch Spinoza in the 17th century represents the first opting out of Judaism altogether, and Professor David Bruderman has a wonderful series from The Teaching Company on modern Jewish intellectual history, which covers that phenomenon (that process). But as we see these new Judaisms emerge, there is one more ancient Jewish yearning that emerges in this age of European nationalism. I am talking about Zionism, and that is the subject of our next lecture.

Lecture Twenty
Israel and Zionism

Scope:

The longing to return to the Land of Israel, a yearning that suffuses Jewish prayer and rituals, began to be fulfilled toward the end of the 19th century. The irony is that many of the early pioneers to the Land of Israel were secularists, motivated by politics rather than theology. Theodor Herzl, the father of political Zionism, believed that a Jewish state would resolve the lingering problem of antisemitism in Europe.

During the 20th century, Zionist pioneers settled the land, drained the swamps, and built an infrastructure appropriate for a modern state. The League of Nations endorsed the establishment of a Jewish state following World War I. Tragically, World War II both decimated the European Jewish population and crystallized the imperative of Jewish statehood.

Outline

I. The initial yearning to remember and return after the Babylonian exile.

    A. "If I forget you, O Jerusalem, let my right hand wither; let my tongue stick to my palate if I cease to think of you, if I do not keep Jerusalem in memory even at my happiest hour" (Ps. 137: 5–6).

    B. "Thus said the Lord: Again there shall be heard in this place, which you say is ruined, without people or beast—in the towns of Judah and the streets of Jerusalem that are desolate, without people, without inhabitants, without beast—the sound of mirth and gladness, the voice of bridegroom and bride, the voice of those who cry, 'Give thanks to the Lord of Hosts, for the Lord is good, for His kindness is everlasting!' as they bring thanksgiving offerings to the House of the Lord. For I will restore the fortunes of the land as of old—said the Lord" (Jer. 33:10–11).

II. Rabbinic mechanisms to promote the status of Jerusalem.

    A. The rebuilding of Jerusalem is featured among the petitionary prayers in the daily prayer service.

B. Returning to Jerusalem is mentioned in the Grace after Meals and in the Torah service on the Sabbath.

C. The Passover seder concludes with singing "next year in Jerusalem."

D. The seven blessings at the center of every Jewish wedding feature those verses from Jeremiah reinforcing the notion that Jerusalem belongs to the Jewish people like a bride belongs to her groom.

E. Even the glass that is broken under the wedding canopy is often associated with the destruction of Jerusalem.

III. Medieval writings on Israel.

A. My heart is in the east, and I in the uttermost west—
How can I find savor in food? How shall it be sweet to me?
How shall I render my vows and my bonds, while yet
Zion lies beneath the fetter of Edom, and I in Arab chains?
A light thing would it seem to me to leave all the good things of Spain—
Seeing how precious in my eyes to behold the dust of the desolate sanctuary. (Yehudah HaLevi, c. 1141)

B. Commenting on "You shall take possession of the land and settle in it" (Deut. 33:53), the Spanish mystical commentator Nachmanides says that this mitzvah is still in force. Citing a Talmudic discussion (b. Ketubot 110b), Nachmanides writes that if a husband wants to make *aliyah* (immigrate) to Israel, but the wife does not, she can be compelled. Even more startlingly, the husband can be compelled if the roles are reversed!

C. Both Yehudah HaLevi and Nachmanides agree that prophecy is only possible in the Land of Israel.

IV. Harbingers of political Zionism.

A. In Eastern Europe, a combination of nationalism and antisemitism motivated a small number of Jews to begin considering the possibility of reestablishing a Jewish presence in the Land of Israel.

B. As early as 1843, Rabbi Yehudah Alkalai, following the Damascus Blood Libel of 1840, called for collective return (*teshuvah*) for the third redemption.

    1. Alkalai raised funds to buy parcels of land from the Turkish sultan, who was then in control of the Land of Israel, and establish the infrastructure for a Jewish society.

    2. Alkalai also promoted the rehabilitation of the Hebrew language.

C. By 1890, the call to build and return to the Land had spread from Eastern Europe to Western Europe, particularly in the writings of Moses Hess. It had also been taken up by secularists, such as Leo Pinsker. Common to all these writers was the desire to normalize the Jews by giving back to the Jewish nation a Jewish state.

V. The Dreyfus affair.

A. In 1894, a French Jewish captain, Alfred Dreyfus, was falsely accused of selling military secrets to Germany. He was convicted and sentenced to life on Devil's Island.

B. New evidence later surfaced exculpating Dreyfus, but the military tried to suppress the evidence. Another trial again found Dreyfus guilty of espionage, even though a suicide note by the confessed traitor, Major Esterhazy, had been discovered.

C. In 1899, the French President brought Dreyfus back to Paris from Devil's Island. He was exonerated only in 1906, and the family had to wait until 1995 for the French Army to admit it had been mistaken, though without issuing an apology.

VI. Theodor Herzl (1860–1904).

A. This young man, born in Budapest and attending university in Vienna, was "emancipated," in the sense that he was a secular Jew, with little formal Jewish education, who had accepted the liberal program of emancipation.

B. After studying law and trying his hand as a playwright, Herzl decided to become a full-time writer, and, in 1890, he went to work for the *Neue Freie Presse* of Vienna. He covered the Dreyfus affair.

C. In France, the home of the French Revolution and Jewish emancipation, Herzl understood that antisemitism could not be cured through granting citizenship and secular education to the Jews. The Jews had to have a state of their own. He believed that it was in the world's best interest to assist the Jews in obtaining sovereignty.

D. In 1895, Herzl began outlining his ides and meeting with Jewish and European statesmen to further his program. He published *The Jewish State* in 1896, outlining his vision of a secular, Jewish state. Herzl was not initially dedicated to returning to the Land of Israel, only to reestablishing Jewish political sovereignty.

E. In 1897, Herzl presided over the First Zionist Congress in Basle, Switzerland. The mission was to "create for the Jewish people a home in Palestine."

    1. This would be attained by promoting Jewish agriculture and industry.

    2. Zionist associations and educational initiatives should be implemented.

    3. International cooperation should be secured.

VII. International activities.

A. The Balfour Declaration of 1917 was issued by the British Foreign Secretary after Palestine was transferred to British control at the end of World War I.

B. "His Majesty's Government view with favour the establishment in Palestine of a national home for the Jewish people, and will use its best endeavours to facilitate the achievement of this object, it being clearly understood that nothing shall be done which may prejudice the civil and religious rights of existing non-Jewish communities in Palestine, or the rights and political status enjoyed by Jews in any other country."

C. In 1922, Britain, under pressure from the Arabs, cut away three-fourths of Palestine and created a new Arab entity, Trans-Jordan.

D. The League of Nations, later in 1922, approved the Balfour Declaration and established the British Mandate, whereby Britain assumed responsibility for the implementation of the Balfour Declaration.

E. The British Peel Commission of 1937, prompted by Arab riots against Jews beginning in 1936, concluded that the remaining territory west of the Jordan River should be divided between Jews and Arabs, with the Arabs receiving Jerusalem, Bethlehem, and a corridor to the sea.

   1. The Zionists reluctantly accepted the plan.
   2. The Arab leadership summarily rejected it.

F. Continued Jewish immigration and Arab terrorism triggered the White Paper of 1939, whereby the British severely curtailed Jewish immigration on the eve of World War II and the Shoah.

VIII. Achieving the superstructure for the infrastructure.

A. On November 29, 1947, the United Nations General Assembly voted to partition Palestine into Jewish and Arab states, with Jerusalem under international sovereignty.

   1. The partition plan passed by a margin of 33 to 13, with the United States and the Soviet Union voting in favor. Britain abstained and stated it would do nothing to enforce the plan.
   2. Once again, Israel reluctantly accepted the plan.
   3. And again, the Arabs rejected it.

B. David Ben-Gurion, chairman of the Jewish Agency and the first Prime Minister of Israel, proclaimed the establishment of the State of Israel on May 14, 1948.

   1. The following day, Egypt, Syria, Trans-Jordan, Saudi Arabia, Lebanon, and Iraq sent troops against Israel.
   2. The Arabs succeeded in losing more territory to the Jews than the U.N. Partition Plan had offered them. Nevertheless, the Holy City of Jerusalem was in Jordanian control until the 1967 Six-Day War.
   3. As a result of the Arab rejection of the U.N. Partition Plan, the Arab state in Palestine was stillborn.

C. Despite wars, economic boycotts, and terrorism, Israel continues to serve as a haven for Jews throughout the world and as a democratic beacon amongst a sea of totalitarian regimes.

Essential Reading:

Diament, *Reflections on Jerusalem*.

Halpern, "Zionism," in *Contemporary Jewish Religious Thought*, pp. 1069–1076.

Hertzberg, *The Zionist Idea*.

Heschel, *Israel: An Echo of Eternity.*

Rosenak, "State of Israel," in *Contemporary Jewish Religious Thought,* pp. 909–916.

Schweid, "Land of Israel," in *Contemporary Jewish Religious Thought*, pp. 535–542.

Talmon, "Jerusalem," in *Contemporary Jewish Religious Thought*, pp. 495–504.

Supplementary Reading:

Bin-Nun, "The Obligation of Aliyah," in *Israel as a Religious Reality*, pp. 75–104.

Diament, *Zionism: The Sequel.*

Questions to Consider:

1. Given the centrality of Jerusalem and Israel over the hundreds of years of exile and dispersion, why didn't more Jews immigrate to Palestine in the early 20th century? Why don't they today?

2. At the heart of the Dreyfus affair is the suspicion of dual loyalty. Is this suspicion any less today? Is it any different with Muslims or Catholics in a predominantly Protestant culture? (How was it different between Japanese-Americans and German-Americans during World War II?)

3. The public and the media in the United States tend to be far more supportive of Israel than in Britain. Why?

4. It is sometimes said that the State of Israel was the world's guilt offering for the Shoah. Why is this not true?

Lecture Twenty—Transcript
Israel and Zionism

The topic of this lecture is Israel and Zionism. This is undoubtedly the most politically controversial of all the lectures in this course on the *Introduction to Judaism*. I have no doubts that an Englishman, or an Arab, or an American would tell this story differently about the creation of the State of Israel. I am telling this story as a committed American, and a committed Jew, and a committed Zionist. There could be other renditions of this story, within a course on history or American foreign policy, or international relations in the Middle East; but, this is the story I am presenting on Israel and Zionism in the context of an *Introduction to Judaism* class.

With that said, the whole thrust of the Hebrew Bible is getting the Jews into the Land of Israel. That is the Promised Land. It is Moses's last request or last action—God takes Moses up to Mount Nebo and shows Moses the entire Land of Israel, from north to south, and then Moses expires and is collected to his forefathers. Once the Israelites get onto the land, that's the bulk of the second section of the TaNaKH (of the historical prophets). And then, of course, the Jews are exiled from the land. Immediately, when we get to Babylonia, the first thing that we do is we pine and we cry about returning back to the Land. "*Im eshkachech Yirushalayim tishkach yemini*"

The Psalm says:

> If I forget you, O Jerusalem, let my right hand wither; let my tongue stick to my palate if I cease to think of you, if I do not keep Jerusalem in memory even at my happiest hour.

Later on, Jeremiah says:

> Thus said the LORD: Again there shall be heard in this place, which you say is ruined, without people or beast—in the towns of Judah and the streets of Jerusalem that are desolate, without people, without inhabitants, without beast—the sound of mirth and gladness, the voice of bridegroom and bride, the voice of those who cry, 'Give thanks to the LORD of Hosts, for the LORD is good, for His kindness is everlasting!' as they bring thanksgiving offerings to the House of the LORD [The Temple]. For I will restore the fortunes of the land as of old—said the LORD (Jeremiah 33:10-11).

There is this imagination that the Jews will be brought back to the Land of Israel, that the Temple will be rebuilt, that the sounds of brides and grooms will once again gladden the streets of *Yirushalayim*—of Jerusalem. That's in the Bible.

When we move to the Rabbinic period, the Rabbis also created mechanisms by which to promote the status of Jerusalem. As we have already said, the rebuilding of Jerusalem is featured among the petitionary prayers in the daily prayer service. Returning to Jerusalem is also mentioned in the Grace after Meals, as well as in the Torah service on the Sabbath, on Shabbat. The Passover seder concludes with singing *hashanah haba'ah birushalayim*—"next year in Jerusalem." In ritual ways, in liturgical ways, three times a day when we pray on the Sabbath, what we have is this leitmotif of the Jews returning to the Land of Israel. The seven blessings at the center of every Jewish wedding feature those verses from Jeremiah that I just read, reinforcing the notion that Jerusalem belongs to the Jewish people like a bride belongs to her groom.

Even the glass that is broken under the wedding canopy is often associated with the destruction of Jerusalem. Let me read to you a few Rabbinic comments about Jerusalem from the Talmud:

> Ten measures of beauty were brought down to the world. Nine were given to Jerusalem and one to the rest of the world.

This is actually a quote that relates to breaking the glass underneath the *chupah*, underneath the wedding canopy, at a Jewish wedding— or Rabbis taught:

> A person may plaster his house, but he should leave a small area bare. A person may prepare a whole banquet, but omit a single dish. A woman may put on her finest ornaments, but she should leave off just one, to remember that we live in an unredeemed world; that we are not yet back in the place where we were meant to be—Jerusalem.

The Rabbis also created a law, which, on the surface, has nothing to do with Jerusalem or Israel. It has to do with lost objects. If I lose my wallet in the street and somebody else finds it, the question is raised, "At what point can the person who found my lost wallet claim it as his or her own?" The answer to that question that the Rabbis give is when I, the original owner of the wallet, despair of ever getting the wallet in return. So, how does the person who finds the wallet know when I have despaired? It's an interesting question, and the Gemarrah deals with it. But the moral of the law in the Mishnah is, "Don't despair." Don't despair of getting back what you once had. Abraham Joshua Heschel said that despair is the cardinal sin of Judaism. And as you can see from the Bible to the Rabbinic period, the Jews never despaired of getting back to the Land of Israel.

As we move into the Middle Ages, we have the poetry of Yehudah HaLevi. It's a particularly beautiful poem that goes as follows. He is writing this in the 12th century when the Christian Crusaders are in control, or occupying Palestine. They have wrested control of Palestine temporarily from the Arab Muslims that had been there, and Yehudah HaLevi is in Muslim Spain. So, that sets the context. In the poem there is a reference to "*edom*." "*Edom*" is a Rabbinic way of talking about Christendom.

> My heart is in the east, and I in the uttermost west—
> How can I find savor in food? How shall it be sweet to me?
> How shall I render my vows and my bonds, while yet
> Zion lies beneath the fetter of Edom, and I in Arab chains?
> A light thing would it seem to me to leave all the good things of Spain—
> Seeing how precious in my eyes to behold the dust of the desolate sanctuary.

Also in Spain, but in the Christian part of Spain, we have Nachmanides (whom we have met before in this class) a couple of decades later. He is commenting on the biblical verse in *Deuteronomy* 33: "You shall take possession of the land and settle in it."

What Nachmanides says is that this mitzvah, this commandment, is still in force. There is still a live mitzvah, a live commandment of dwelling in the land and settling it. He even goes so far as to say that if the husband wants to make *aliyah* ("to make aliyah" means, literally, "to ascend"), ascending to Mount Zion, Jerusalem, but it is the customary term for immigration to Israel—so, Nachmanides says that if the husband wants to make aliyah, and the wife refuses, she can be compelled to join the husband. What is even more startling is that if the wife wants to make aliyah, and the husband refuses, he can be compelled to join the wife in making aliyah.

Both Yehudah HaLevi (our poet) and Nachmanides agree that prophecy is only possible in the Land of Israel, and both leave for the Land of Israel—by themselves, without their families—in their old age. So, what we see is that poetically, liturgically, halachically, and ritually, returning to the Land of Israel is an *idee fixe* of classical Judaism.

As we move into the modern period, there are harbingers of political Zionism. In eastern Europe, as a result of a combination of nationalism and anti-Semitism, a small number of Jews were motivated to begin considering the possibility of reestablishing a Jewish presence in the Land of Israel. No longer should it be a dream—something that we talk about liturgically and ritually, but we should actually move toward the realization of a Jewish presence in the Land of Israel.

As early as 1843, Rabbi Yehudah Alkalai, following the Damascus Blood Libel of 1840, called for collective return (teshuvah) for the third redemption (the establishment of the Third Commonwealth).

We haven't mentioned what a "blood libel" is. Here I should just mention this: There was a standard anti-Semitic accusation of ritual murder, whereby Jews would take a gentile, kill the gentile, and use the gentile's blood for ritual preparations of ritual food. We see this going back 1,000 years. In 1840, there was such an accusation in Damascus, and it is called the Damascus Blood Libel.

Rabbi Yehudah Alkalai raised funds to buy parcels of land from the Turkish sultan, who was then in control of the Land of Israel, and began to establish the infrastructure for a Jewish society. The Zionist enterprise is largely one of fund raising in order to buy property in the Land of Israel, for European Jews to settle on.

Rabbi Alkalai is also well known for promoting the rehabilitation of the Hebrew language. Hebrew, up until the 19th century, had only been used for liturgical purposes. Hebrew was not a living language. But beginning in the late 19th century, as a result of efforts by people like Yehudah Alkalai and Eleazar Ben Yehuda, Hebrew was rehabilitated or resurrected from an ancient language to a living language that now has its share of slang, cuss words, and international words as well (largely in Arabic) that can be heard on the streets of Jerusalem and all over the Land of Israel today.

By 1890, the call to build and return to the Land had spread from eastern Europe to western Europe, particularly in the writings of Moses Hess. It had also been taken up by secularists like Leo Pinsker. Common to all these writers was the desire to normalize the Jews by giving back to the Jewish nation a Jewish state.

In 1894, a French Jewish Captain, by the name of Alfred Dreyfus, was falsely accused of selling military secrets to Germany. He was convicted and sentenced to life on Devil's Island. New evidence later surfaced exonerating Dreyfus, but the military tried to suppress the evidence. Another trial again found Dreyfus guilty of espionage, even though a suicide note by the confessed traitor, a man by the name of Major Esterhazy, had been discovered. The French government ended up falling as a result of the Dreyfus Affair. In 1899, the new French President brought Dreyfus back to Paris from Devil's Island. He was only exonerated in 1906, and the family had to wait until 1995 for the French Army to admit it had been mistaken—although they made this admission without issuing a formal apology.

Now let's shift to central Europe—to Vienna, where Theodore Herzl is a young man studying law in Vienna. He decides, after trying his hand as a playwright, that he should become a journalist. He is an emancipated Jew. He is not only an acculturated Jew, but an assimilated Jew, with very little formal Jewish education, and he had completely accepted the liberal program of emancipation. He decides to become a full-time writer, so he becomes a journalist. In 1890, he went to work for the *Neue Freie Presse* of Vienna. He covered the Dreyfus Affair for this newspaper. It was in France, the home of the French Revolution and the home of Jewish emancipation, that Herzl understood that antisemitism could not be cured through granting citizenship and secular education to the Jews. The Jews had to have a state of their own. He believed that it was in the world's best interest to assist the Jews in obtaining political sovereignty in the Land of Israel.

In 1895, Herzl began outlining his ideas and meeting with Jewish and European statesmen to further his program. He published *The Jewish State* in 1896, outlining his vision of a secular, Jewish state. It should be mentioned that some Zionists were not Jewish. There were many Christian Zionists then, just as there are today, who, for religious reasons, understand that the Jews should be in the Land of

Israel in order to hasten the Second Coming of the Messiah—the Second Coming of Christ. Indeed, then (in Herzl's time), some Zionists were anti-Semites, "Yeah, it's a great idea to give the Jews their own state. Let them go to Palestine. Let them re-create the Land of Israel, and then they'll get out of our state." So, to be a Zionist, at a minimum, only meant that one supported the establishment of a Jewish state in the Land of Israel.

By the way, Herzl was not wedded to the Land of Israel. He just wanted a Jewish state—a sovereign Jewish state. By the time we get to 1897 and the First Zionist Congress in Basle, Switzerland, it was clear that there couldn't be the kind of enthusiasm worked up to create a Jewish state in Uganda, or a Jewish state in South America. Israel had to be the place where this third sovereign Jewish state would be re-created.

It was also at the First Zionist Congress in Basle in 1897 that they adopted as their insignia the Shield of David. The Shield of David was a relatively recent symbol of Judaism. What does "relatively recent" mean when we are talking about Jewish history? Just for the last couple of hundred years. When we go back 2,000 years, the Shield of David, or the Star of David, is also called the Seal of Solomon—there were six-pointed stars, there were hexagrams, there were pentagrams. Christian iconography and Christian architecture also used pentagrams and hexagrams, but by the time we get to the 17th century, we see the Shield of David, as it is now uniformly called, becoming a symbol of Judaism—especially in a lot of the new Jewish architecture that was created by Christians who were looking for a symbol for Judaism, like Christianity had its symbol of the cross.

Later on, the *Knesset* (the Israeli Parliament) adopted this insignia, the Shield of David, as part of its flag for Israel, and the color blue (the two blue strips above and beneath the Shield of David, as well as the Shield of David itself, which is blue) comes from the blue dye that—according to Jewish tradition—snails would secrete and that would then be used to dye the ritual fringes on the ritual shawl of the *tallit*.

The aims of the First Zionist Congress would be to establish this Land of Israel—to establish in the Land of Israel a state for Jews. Herzl said that, if not in 5, then in 50 years there will be a Jewish state; it is to be attained by promoting Jewish agriculture and Jewish industry—again, conforming to the goals of emancipation in broadening out Jewish vocational skills. Zionist associations and educational initiatives should be implemented. International cooperation should be secured.

In terms of international activities, by the end of World War I, we have the British coming in to Palestine, which for 400 years (from 1517 to 1917) had been ruled by the Ottoman Empire (by the Turks). So, now, the Brits are in control of Palestine. The Balfour Declaration was issued in 1917. The Balfour Declaration says:

> His Majesty's Government view with favor the establishment in Palestine of a national home for the Jewish people, and will use its best endeavors to facilitate the achievement of this object, it being clearly understood that nothing shall be done which may prejudice the civil and religious rights of existing non-Jewish communities in Palestine, or the rights and political status enjoyed by Jews in any other country.

That was the Balfour Declaration that Chaim Weizmann, who becomes Israel's first president, was able to work out with Britain shortly after the conclusion of World War I.

Five years later, in 1922, Britain, under pressure from the Arabs, cut away three-quarters of what was Palestine (everything to the east of the Jordan River) and created a new Arab entity, called Trans-Jordan. This was in order to placate the Hashimites, who were cousins of the royal family from Saudi Arabia, from Sauds.

Later, the League of Nations, in 1922 (the League of Nations was the precursor to the U.N.), approved the Balfour Declaration and established the British Mandate, whereby Britain assumed responsibility for the implementation of the Balfour Declaration.

The British Peel Commission of 1937, prompted by Arab riots against Jews (which began in 1936), concluded that the remaining territory west of the Jordan River should be divided between Jews and Arabs, with the Arabs receiving Jerusalem, Bethlehem, and a corridor to the sea. This was not at all what the Zionists had hoped. But, nevertheless, because they were offered an independent state, they reluctantly accepted the plan. The Arab leadership summarily rejected it—the first of many rejections.

Continued Jewish immigration and Arab terrorism triggered the White Paper of 1939, whereby the British severely curtailed Jewish immigration on the eve of World War II and the Shoah. David Ben-Gurion, who was the chairman of the Jewish Agency and later becomes the first Prime Minister of Israel, said, "We shall fight the war against Hitler as if there was no White Paper. And we shall fight the White Paper as if there was no war."

All in all, 26,000 Palestinian Jews fought for Britain in World War II.

At the end of World War II, we have a period of time where there is some immigration to the Land of Israel. Then, in November—on November 29, 1947—the United Nations General Assembly voted to partition Palestine into Jewish and Arab states, with Jerusalem under international sovereignty—which is not so different, actually, from the last suggestion that was touted in a peace plan between the Israelis and the Palestinians, to have Jerusalem be under divine sovereignty; but, that wasn't thought of in 1947. So, there would be a state for the Jews and a state for the Arabs in Palestine, and Jerusalem—the most contested of cities—would be under international sovereignty.

The partition plan in the U.N. passed by a margin of 33 to 13, with the United States and the Soviet Union voting in favor. Britain abstained—so much for the British mandate of establishing what it called for in the Balfour Declaration—a home for the Jewish people, a national home for the Jewish people in Palestine. And, Britain stated it would do nothing to enforce the plan. So, Britain then begins to pull out of Palestine, following this U.N. vote.

In May (May 14, 1948), David Ben-Gurion, who was the chairman of the Jewish Agency and the first Prime Minister of Israel, proclaimed the establishment of the State of Israel. In terms of the Jews' and the Arabs' posture toward that U.N. resolution, again, the amount of territory that was offered by the U.N. was significantly less than what the Zionists had dreamed of—but, it was a state, nevertheless. So, they decided to accept the U.N. resolution partitioning Palestine into a Jewish and Arab state. The Arabs, again, summarily rejected the plan.

Thus, on May 15, 1948 (the day after David Ben-Gurion's proclamation of the establishment of the State of Israel), Egypt,

©2004 The Teaching Company.

Syria, Trans-Jordan (which is now called Jordan), Saudi Arabia, Lebanon, and Iraq all sent troops against Israel to wipe out the Jews—to push them into the sea. The Arabs succeeded in losing more territory to the Jews than the U.N. Partition Plan had offered them. Nevertheless, the Holy City of Jerusalem was in Jordanian control until the 1967 6-Day War. Due to the Arab rejection of the U.N. Partition Plan, the Arab state in Palestine was stillborn, and we are now trying to negotiate a new state of Palestine for the Arabs in that land, and, remarkably, for the first time in contemporary Israeli history, both major political parties in Israel (Labor and Likud) are on record as saying that there should be an independent state for the Arabs in the Land of Israel. Now it is a process (hopefully) of working out the details.

Despite wars and economic boycotts and terrorism, Israel continues to serve as a haven for Jews throughout the world and as a democratic beacon amongst a sea of totalitarian regimes. Israel's contributions in high technology, in medical technology, in health care, agriculture, and solar energy lend a degree of credibility to what is written in Conservative and Modern Orthodox prayer books—that the State of Israel is the beginning of the flowering of redemption. This is a controversial claim—that the State of Israel is the beginning of the flowering of redemption—because, after all, the Zionists who settled the land, and who drained the swamps, and who planted the farms in the desert that made the desert bloom (in David Ben-Gurion's memorable phrase)—they were not at all motivated by messianic fervor, or by a commitment to traditional Judaism or traditional halachah. What motivated them was a desire to solve the "Jewish problem," to find a national home so that the Jews could be just like any other people.

David Ben-Gurion has a great line: that "we want to be a normal people, with cops and robbers and policemen and prostitutes, just like everybody else." Israel has an abundance of those elements in society now, so David Ben-Gurion should be happy on that score. But the idea was to become not a "light unto the nations," but a normal nation, just like everyone else. Indeed, Israel has a Declaration of Independence. Israel does not yet have a constitution. But in Israel's Declaration of Independence, God is not mentioned. There was a compromise worked out whereby the term "the Rock of Israel," *tzur yisrael,* was mentioned. Religious folks understand that

that is a reference to God, and folks that are not religious can understand it any way they wish.

But within the religious world of Conservative Judaism and Modern Orthodoxy—unlike some of the Ultra-Orthodox groups who are anti-Zionist, as we saw in the lecture where we talked about the Holocaust and some of the Ultra-Orthodox Jews understanding the Holocaust to be a punishment for Zionism—Conservative and Modern Orthodox Jews understand that redemption is not here, but redemption can't happen unless the Jewish people are back in the Land of Israel. It doesn't negate the existence of the Diaspora. Jews can still live outside the Land of Israel, but in order for the Jewish mission to be complete, the Jews need to have a nation in order to actualize that biblical model of living righteously in God's eyes—not just as individuals, but as a community and, indeed, as a nation. This is a tremendous challenge, given the neighborhood that Israel inhabits.

So, the idea that Israel is the beginning of the flowering of redemption is, indeed, optimistic, but Judaism is optimistic. The idea that history has a direction, that we can't despair (no matter how seemingly terrible the world feels), is part and parcel of this Jewish outlook.

Now that we have entered the 20th century in full steam, our next lecture brings us back home to the Judaisms of America in the 20th century.

Lecture Twenty-One
American Judaisms

Scope:

Reform Judaism's emphasis on personal autonomy complemented the American ideal of the rugged individualist. But as traditional Eastern European Jews immigrated throughout the early 20th century, they found American Reform foreign. The Conservative movement, begun in Germany, was transplanted to America and catered to the traditional sensibilities of Eastern European Jews.

It wasn't too long, however, before elements of Reform ideology married Conservative practice, and a fourth movement began to emerge—Reconstructionism. In the past few decades, Jewish Renewal has attempted to revitalize Judaism by investing traditional rituals with new meanings and by creating new halachah informed by the wisdom of the old. Most recently, Humanistic Judaism has tried to distill the ethical significance of traditional Jewish practice while avoiding any reference to the existence of God. Proper behavior, whether understood as divinely commanded or not, continues to be a hallmark of Judaism.

Outline

I. Reforms in early 19th-century America.

    A. The Reform movement began in Germany, but in America, with its tradition of rugged individualism, certain reforms sprang up without ideological underpinnings.

        1. In 1824, a small group of young Jews petitioned for minor changes in the liturgy and prayer service in Charleston, South Carolina.

        2. Their 1825 constitution argued against "a blind observance of ceremonial law, to the neglect of the essential spirit of revealed religion contained in the Law and the Prophets."

        3. This reform-minded group broke away from the main synagogue and founded its own in 1826.

        4. Services were conducted partly in English, instrumental music was allowed, and *kippot* (pl. of *kippa*, "yarmulkah") were optional. But there was still separate seating for men and women, and the Rabbi was made to declare belief in the resurrection of the dead. This was not yet a Reform temple.

5. By 1850, only two Reform temples were in existence, Har Sinai in Baltimore and Temple Emanu-El in New York City. They had mixed seating. *Tallitot* (pl. of *tallit*, "prayer shawl") and the second day of holidays were discontinued. But, even in these temples, the changes were more practical than ideological.

B. German immigration and Reform ideology.

1. From 1844 to 1860, the Jewish population in America surged from 50,000 to 200,000. In 1850, there were 14 synagogues in New York City. By 1860, there were 27. The vast majority of this immigrant wave came from Germany.

2. Isaac Mayer Wise (1819–1900) arrived from Germany in 1846 and began to spread reforms and build the institutions of American Reform Judaism, which he hoped would serve all American Jews.

   a. In 1873, Wise founded the Union of American Hebrew Congregations in Cincinnati (renamed in 2003 the Union of Reform Judaism).

   b. In 1875, he founded the first rabbinical seminary in America, Hebrew Union College, also in Cincinnati.

   c. In 1899, he founded the Central Conference of American Rabbis.

II. Reform, ethical culture, and Unitarianism.

A. One prominent Rabbi's son, Felix Adler, upon returning from the Reform seminary in Germany in the early 1870s, abdicated his Jewish particularity.

B. He advocated that Reform merge with Unitarianism, because their theology and ethics were basically the same. But the ethnic distinctions proved too difficult to overcome.

C. Adler then founded the Movement for Ethical Culture in 1876.

III. The Reform Pittsburgh Platform of 1885.

A. Judaism recognizes in all religions the attempt to grasp the Infinite One.

B. Reform accepts biblical criticism, the academic position that the Bible was written by men over hundreds of years.

C. "We accept as binding only the moral laws."

D. Laws regarding diet, purity, and dress are "altogether foreign to our present and spiritual state."

E. "We consider ourselves no longer a nation but a religious community."

F. Rabbi Emil G. Hirsch, son of Rabbi Samuel Hirsch, a German leader of Reform, endorsed the Social Gospel.

IV. The Reform movement has changed significantly since the Shoah.

A. Although there is still a commitment to individual autonomy, there is also greater respect for the role that ritual mitzvot can serve in a religious life.

B. The curriculum for rabbinical students has recently been overhauled to include significantly more traditional text study.

C. A new prayer book is being developed that is more traditional.

D. All graduate students in the Hebrew Union College spend their first year in Jerusalem as a testimony to the centrality of Israel to the Jewish people.

V. Positive-Historical Judaism/Conservative Judaism.

A. Just as Reform began in Germany, so did Conservative Judaism, but under the name Positive-Historical Judaism.

    1. Zecharias Frankel (1801–1875) tried to modernize Judaism without the excesses he perceived in Reform.

    2. He conceived of Judaism as a historical religion that unfolded progressively over time, as did Reform, but he understood this to be a positive development rather than a claim to undermine the divine authority of Jewish law.

    3. Frankel stressed the importance of Hebrew and the binding authority of Jewish law, even if individual laws were amenable to change, as they always have been throughout Jewish history.

B. Changes on the ground in the United State made many Reform temples too foreign for newly arrived Jews.

1. From 1880–1920, the Jewish population exploded from 230,000 to 3,600,000. The immigrants were almost entirely from Eastern Europe, where Reform Judaism had not made any inroads.
2. In 1883, at the banquet for the first graduating class of Hebrew Union College, non-kosher seafood was served. (This episode is referred to as the *Treyfa Banquet*.) This signaled to the attending traditional Rabbis that this seminary was flagrantly disrespectful of Jewish tradition.
3. The Conservative Movement opened its seminary in 1886 in New York City as the Jewish Theological Seminary to attract that more traditional population.
4. When Solomon Schechter arrived from England in 1902, the Jewish Theological Seminary acquired significant status.

VI. Orthodoxy as the third movement in America.

   A. Although the Etz Chaim Yeshiva opened in 1886, there wasn't a rabbinical academy until the Rabbi Isaac Elkhannan Specktor Yeshiva opened in 1897.

   B. The two *yeshivot* (pl. of *yeshiva*, "seminary") later combined to become Yeshiva University under the guidance of Bernard Revel. To this day, Yeshiva University strives to combine Torah study with secular learning.

VII. Reconstructionism.

   A. Rabbi Mordecai M. Kaplan (1881–1983), long a teacher at the Jewish Theological Seminary, was persuaded to leave the Conservative movement and found his own fourth denomination, Reconstructionism. The Reconstructionist Rabbinical College was founded in 1968.

   B. Kaplan was more aggressive about liturgical and halachic change than the Conservative movement as a whole. But he would advocate a change of tradition only if the tradition itself were problematic. Reform, by contrast, tended to drop those traditions that were no longer spiritually edifying.

   C. Like Reform, Kaplan's Reconstructionism understood halachah to be a matter of individual choice and not obligatory. Unlike Reform, Reconstructionism believed that Judaism was an evolving religious civilization and that

Jewish peoplehood was the core of that civilization. Ironically, Kaplan is similar to the Ultra-Orthodox with their insistence that peoplehood is logically prior to religion.

D. Among the most radical reforms that Kaplan espoused, and to which we will return in the final lecture, is his rejection of the Chosen People concept.

VIII. Jewish renewal.

    A. Beginning in the 1960s, Rabbi Zalman Schachter-Shalomi, reaching back to the prophetic and mystical sources of Judaism, began teaching a post-denominational Judaism that eschewed halachic doctrine.

    B. The flagship institution of this movement, Aleph, provides opportunities and training to spread this joyous approach to individual spiritual renewal that can, in turn, have healing effects on society at large.

    C. Although the movement is not halachic, its members look toward specific rituals and social activism to further their agenda of spiritual growth and world healing.

IX. Jews without God.

    A. The Society for Humanistic Judaism, organized in 1969 by Rabbi Sherwin Wine, promotes Jewish customs in a non-theistic framework.

    B. According to the American Jewish Identity Survey of 2001, Jews are the most likely religious group to describe their outlook as secular or somewhat secular, including 14 percent who could be classified as atheists or agnostics.

Essential Reading:

Cohen, "Conservative Judaism," in *Contemporary Jewish Religious Thought*, pp. 91–99.

Gurock, *American Jewish Orthodoxy*.

Kraut, "Reform Judaism and the Unitarian Challenge," in *The American Jewish Experience*, pp. 89–96.

Meyer, "German-Jewish Identity in 19th-Century America," in *The American Jewish Experience*, pp. 45–61.

———, "Reform Judaism," in *Contemporary Jewish Religious Thought*, pp. 767–772.

Schachter-Shalomi, *Paradigm Shift*.

Schulwies, "Reconstructionism," in *Contemporary Jewish Religious Thought*, pp. 755–760.

Supplementary Reading:

Gurock, *The Men and Women of Yeshiva*.

Kaplan, *Judaism as a Civilization*.

Sarna, *American Judaism*.

Waskow, *Godwrestling, Round II*.

Wine, *Judaism beyond God*.

Questions to Consider:

1. Why is it easier to be an inconsistent Conservative Jew than an inconsistent Reform Jew?

2. Given that Reform Judaism has come to recognize the centrality of the Jewish people and the importance of Israel, why don't Reform and Reconstructionism merge?

3. Given the history of Jewish thought, is it surprising that secular humanistic Jews who are atheistic or agnostic want to continue "doing" Judaism even without a firm belief in a personal God?

4. Can one be a Jewish atheist? If so, why can't one be a Jew who believes in the divinity of Jesus?

Lecture Twenty-One—Transcript
American Judaisms

With this lecture we move from the old country to the new country. This gives me an opportunity to recommend a couple of films. When I teach the *Introduction to Judaism* class at Vanderbilt, I ask my students to see two films, the first of which is *Fiddler on the Roof.* I imagine that many of you have seen *Fiddler on the Roof* before. But after having taken this class, I think you will have a better appreciation for the religious dynamics and the social dynamics that went on behind the scenes of that movie. That movie really represents the breakdown of tradition. I won't say it the way Tevye says it, but you really see the old world breaking down and the different options of going to Israel and becoming a Christian, and becoming a socialist, and reforming Judaism, and going to America—those different kinds of responses to modernity are reflected in that film. So when we make the move from the old world to the new world, we are also really taking a leap into a new land that doesn't have that kind of baggage that the old world had in terms of a negative relationship with the Jews, a history of anti-Semitism, or emancipation. There was never emancipation in the new world because Jews were (Missing word or words here?)—not that they were always treated as equals, but they didn't have the same kinds of liabilities and disadvantages in this country (even before it was the United States of America) as are characteristic of the Jews living in the nations in Europe.

We mentioned in an earlier lecture that the Jews came to this land in 1654. So, 2004 is the 350th anniversary of the Jewish arrival. There were 23 Jews. They came to New Amsterdam, and the Jews remained a very, very, very small presence in the country for at least 200 years. We'll be taking a look at some of the population figures in just a moment. There is good reason why the Jews were such a small percentage of the population and why there were so few Jews— because there weren't the kinds of opportunities and lifestyle requirements for Jews in this country, in terms of keeping Kosher, in terms of a traditional Jewish education. So, people that came to this country were already a self-selected group of individualists. Many of the immigrants to this country who were Jewish came from Germany. It was a very nice confluence of the Reform emphasis (from Germany) on personal autonomy with the emphasis in this country on rugged individualism.

So, the Jews that ended up coming to this country, at least before the Civil War (from 1760-1860, say), were already well disposed to certain changes in Judaism, and they weren't so strictly wed to the traditional forms of the ancient lands and the ways of the fathers. So, we already have a self-selected group who is ready to move into the new world. So, let's begin our story in the years leading up to the Civil War and Reconstruction, in 1824.

In Charleston, South Carolina, you've got a small and young group within a larger congregation—Congregation Beth Elohim—that is agitating for change. They are petitioning for change—minor changes, changes on the ground, practical changes—not ideological changes. That's important. The practical changes come before the ideological justifications. What did they want the changes in? In the liturgy and the prayer service, "Let's make it shorter."

A year later, in 1825, their constitution argued against "... a blind observance of ceremonial law, to the neglect of the essential spirit of revealed religion contained in the Law and the Prophets."

So this language is reminiscent of German Reform, "We don't want to be so fastidious about the ceremonial laws or ritual laws anymore. Let's get back to the spirit, not the letter, but the spirit of the Law and the Prophets, social justice, being a light unto the nations." They don't use that language, but you can see an overlap in the kinds of sensibilities expressed by this young, upstart group in South Carolina and what was going on unbeknownst to them at the same time amongst the *Wissenschaft* group (the maskilim, "the Jewish Enlightened Ones") and the founders of Reform Judaism in Germany.

The next year, in 1826, this reform-minded group broke away from the main synagogue and founded their own congregation. This really represents the kind of beginning or the emergence of a grassroots reform in this country. They would no longer tolerate the old ways of the fathers, the ancestral ways. They wanted to create something new.

What were they interested in creating? Services should be conducted partly in English, not all in Hebrew—and not just choral music, but instrumental music was allowed. *Kipot* (yarmulkahs) were optional.

"*Yarmulkah*" is the Yiddish word for a head covering. I don't like to use the word "yarmulkah" because it has a silent "r". I shy away from words with silent "r's." In Hebrew, this is called a *kipah*. (The plural is *kipot*.) So, *kipot* were optional, but there was still separate seating for men and women, which you find in Orthodox synagogues until this very day.

And the Rabbi was actually made to declare and sign a statement of his belief in the resurrection of the dead. So this is not a Reform Temple (with a capital "R"), as we might see in Germany at this point, but this is the beginning of a grassroots reform movement in this country.

By 1850, there were only two Reform Temples officially aligned in some ideological way with Reform in Germany: That was Har Sinai (the Mount Sinai Temple) in Baltimore, and Temple Emanu-El in New York City. They did have mixed seating, so there was no longer a separation of the sexes, and *tallitot* (prayer shawls) and second-day of holidays were discontinued. This is part of the ideological program of Reform Judaism.

But even in these Temples, the changes were still more practical than ideological. They fit in with some of the ideology of Reform, but they were introduced to make life easier for people—so, that there would be only one day of holidays and not two—and also to fit in to the other modes of worship by the other faith groups in New York City and Baltimore, so you don't have these identifying marks of the *kipah* and the *tallit*.

From 1844 to 1860, the American Jewish population surged from 50,000 to 200,000. In 1850, there were only 14 synagogues in New York City. By 1860, there were 27. The Christians amongst you might be saying, "Wow! That's impressive growth!" And the Jews amongst you might be saying, "That doesn't mean there was any growth, it just means that disagreements within each Temple ended up splitting each Temple. There might not be any more Jews, but the Jews who were in a single congregation couldn't agree with each other, and they just split apart." There's a little bit of truth to both of those views.

But we do know that there was this surge in population during this period, and that most of the wave of immigrants was from Germany. Why? Because after the Revolution of 1848 there were restrictive social laws directed against Jews, as well as marital restrictions; so, there were issues pushing them out of Germany, and there was also the attraction of going to the Golden *medina* (the Golden State) with lots of opportunity. So, those Jews from Germany that didn't have a particularly strong commitment to maintaining a rich Jewish lifestyle—they were more likely to come to the United States in that period, and they were associated with the Reform movement, which is really why Reform Judaism is the first and strongest denomination within the United States.

In 1846, Isaac Meyer Wise arrives from Germany. He describes himself as a Rabbi. He describes himself as a doctor. We don't really have any documents to testify to his credentials, but he assumes that role for himself and he begins to spread reforms and build the institutions of American Reform Judaism, which he hoped would serve all of America.

So, for instance, in 1873, Wise founded the Union of American Hebrew Congregations in Cincinnati. He named it the Union of American Hebrew Congregations because he believed that this union of temples or synagogues would serve the entire American Jewish population. Just last year, in 2003, the name of that union was changed in order to reflect the reality that it really only serves the Reform community; so, today, it is called the Union of Reform Judaism.

A couple of years later, in 1875, Isaac Meyer Wise founded the first Rabbinical seminary in America, Hebrew Union College, also in Cincinnati. At that time there were great hopes that Ohio would become the next New York, and Cincinnati—in particular—would become the next New York City as a result of routing the railroads through Cincinnati. But that dream never happened. So, today, you've got this incredibly rich Jewish life in Cincinnati, and it seems somewhat incongruous being in the middle of the country. That's the explanation.

In 1899, Isaac Meyer Wise founded the Central Conference of American Rabbis—a union for the Rabbis. So, whether we're talking about the congregations, or the Rabbinical school, or the Rabbinical union, Isaac Meyer Wise really created the institutions of American Reform Judaism. So, he is properly considered to be the father of American Reform.

During this building period in the late 19ᵗʰ century, one prominent Reform Rabbi sent his son, Felix Adler, back to Germany to get a proper Rabbinic education. But when Felix Adler returned from his proper Reform Jewish education as a Rabbi, he took the pulpit on one of the high holidays (I believe it was Rosh Hashanah) and he basically disavowed Jewish particularity. He said that all this stuff about God choosing the Jews doesn't make any sense, and God writing the Torah doesn't make any sense. And what he advocated later on was to have a merger between Reform Judaism and Unitarianism, since basically they have the same ideology, the same theology, and the same ethics. But the ethnic distinctions proved too difficult to overcome. For the Unitarians, they had a Christian background, and their model of a perfect ethical being was still Jesus, even if they didn't believe that Jesus was divine, Jesus was still somehow central to their religious worldview. That wasn't the case with Reform Jews. So they decided not to merge.

But Felix Adler then had no place to go. So, in 1876, Felix Adler left Reform Judaism and he founded the movement for Ethical Culture in New York City. Some of you might be familiar with that. The vast majority of adherents or congregants in the Society for Ethical Culture were disaffected Jews who no longer could buy into any version of Judaism, whether it was traditional Judaism or Reform Judaism. Nevertheless, they wanted some kind of religious expression and religious community, so they joined the Society for Ethical Culture.

The small cadre of Reform Rabbis got together in 1885 in Pittsburgh, Pennsylvania, and they created a platform that articulated to themselves, and to the general public, what Reform Judaism in this country was all about.

So, they start off by saying that Judaism recognizes in all religions the attempt to grasp the Infinite One. Immediately, the Reform Pittsburgh Platform begins with a kind of universal recognition that whether we are talking about Christianity, or Islam, or Hinduism, everybody is trying to get at that ultimate truth. It's a nice way to begin in America, with a kind of democratic statement that we are all equal in our attempt at striving toward that religious ideal.

Reform accepts biblical criticism as well as evolutionary science. This really does distinguish them from Orthodoxy, as we have talked about. The academic position of biblical criticism says that God did not dictate the Torah, but that it was written by men over hundreds of years.

Another one of their planks was that, "We accept as binding only the moral laws," so that says that what we don't accept as binding are all the ceremonial laws and all the ritual laws. Even regarding the idea of accepting as binding the moral laws, it is still left up to the individual (and the emphasis is still on individual autonomy) to decide how they express their commitments and their allegiance to those moral laws.

Here's something that we see right out of the German Reform ideology: Laws regarding diet, sexual purity, and laws of family purity and dress are "altogether foreign to our present and spiritual state." So, they're sloughing those off. "We consider ourselves no longer a nation but a religious community." So, they are trying to say that they are first and foremost Americans, of the Hebrew persuasion, or of the Jewish religion, but what is at their core is their nationality as an American.

Finally, I want to mention that Rabbi Emil G. Hirsch—who was the son of one of Reform's founders in Germany, Rabbi Samuel Hirsch—endorsed the Social Gospel from the Christian community, and he made sure that it was also part of the Platform in Pittsburgh in 1885. It said that Judaism should be committed to those acts of social justice. He's not really drawing explicitly from the social justice motifs that are found in the Hebrew prophets, but he's really borrowing from the Christian commitment to the Social Gospel that we find in the late 19th century.

Although that's how Reform Judaism begins in this country, by the end of the 19th century, I don't want you to think that that's where it has ended. Especially in the last 20 years, we have seen a dramatic swing by the Reform movement to a more traditional approach to Judaism. So, for instance, there is now a new curriculum for Rabbinical students that is much more traditional. There is a new prayer book coming out in the next couple of years that is much more traditional than the previous prayer book, *The Gates of Prayer*.

All of their Rabbinic students (and education students and cantorial students) have to spend the first year of their studies in Jerusalem, at the Reform campus in Jerusalem. That really demonstrates their commitment to the centrality of Israel and the idea of the Jewish peoplehood. David Ellenson, the new President of Hebrew Union College, is very much a traditionalist. He is very much committed to Reform ideology, but he is someone who is much more leaning towards tradition than leaning toward innovation. Similarly, some of the new leaders of the unions for the Rabbis and for the congregations are much more traditional than they have been in the past.

We now want to take a look at another denomination that emerged in the wake of Reform Judaism's articulation of its own vision. I am talking here about the Conservative movement. The Conservative movement, like Reform and like Modern Orthodoxy, began in Germany, and it really took off—as Reform did—much more in the United States than it did in its founding country of Germany.

The figure who is associated with the founding of Conservative Judaism—in Germany it was called the Positive-Historical School— was Zecharias Frankel. What he tried to do was to modernize Judaism without the excesses that he perceived from Reform Judaism. He bought into the idea that Judaism is a historical religion that unfolds progressively over time, as did Reform, but he understood this to be a positive development rather than a claim to undermine the divine authority of Jewish law. That's why he started out with the name the Positive-Historical School because, of course, Judaism is historical and has developed over time—but that merely testifies to the partnership that each generation of Rabbis has with the tradition and with God. What Reform did is say, "The Torah was written by men. It doesn't have divine, binding authority. Therefore, we can overthrow it."

Zecharias Frankel took a very different tack and said, "Okay, the Torah was written by men in their best attempt to translate God's will into a program of action to live a divine life. And we, as the inheritors of that tradition, need to be faithful—both to the tradition and to what we understand to be God's will as we strive, grapple, and struggle to lead a divine life today, in circumstances that are very different from those who wrote about the tradition (whether we're talking about in the Rabbinic period or in the biblical period."

So, Frankel stressed the importance of Hebrew and the binding authority of Jewish law, even if individual laws were amenable to change, as they always have been throughout Jewish history. So, each individual halachah (with a small "h") might be amenable to change. But the idea that the Halachah (with a capital "H") is binding on every individual Jew, that is something that Zecharias Frankel and the entire Conservative movement absolutely agrees with. Judaism is about (for the Conservative movement) a binding law.

Changes on the ground in the United States made many Reform Temples too unfamiliar—too foreign for newly arrived Jews—because from 1880 to 1920, the Jewish population exploded from less than 250,000 to more than 3.5 million Jews. These immigrants were almost entirely from eastern Europe, where Reform Judaism had not made any inroads. Therefore, when they came to this country and saw services in English, by people who weren't wearing *kipot* or *tallitot* (prayer shawls), they didn't recognize this as Jewish. So, on the ground, there was a kind of cognitive dissonance between what they had experienced in the old country as Judaism and what they were now seeing in the *treyf medina*—the *treyf* country. "*Treyf*" means "not kosher" in Yiddish. So, what they were seeing now as Judaism, it just didn't add up.

Furthermore, in 1883, you have the first graduating class of Hebrew Union College, the Reform Rabbinical Seminary. This was an event of national importance. Isaac Meyer Wise invited all the big Rabbis from New York and Baltimore, including the traditionalists, because at this point he still had grand hopes that Reform Judaism would be the Judaism of America. All these big Rabbinic dignitaries come to the banquet to celebrate the first graduating class of Hebrew Union College, and what is served? Clams on the half-shell. This is a problem because clams on the half-shell, as tasty as they may be, are not Kosher. They are *treyf*. This episode is referred to as the *Treyfa* Banquet. This signaled to the attending traditional Rabbis that Reform was flagrantly disrespectful of Jewish tradition. It's not as though there is anything immoral about—or so inconvenient about—not eating clams. You can not eat clams and still be a good human being. So, these traditionalists didn't understand why the caterer or why Isaac Meyer Wise went so far out of his or their way to include non-Kosher items on the menu, when everyone knew that these traditional Rabbis who kept Kosher would be in attendance. That was in 1883.

We've got the Pittsburgh Platform (that we've discussed) in 1885 coming out.

In 1886, the Conservative movement opened up their seminary, opened up their doors in New York City, as the Jewish Theological Seminary—in order to train Rabbis to minister to that more traditional Jewish population that was coming from eastern Europe. The beginnings of the Jewish Theological Seminary after 1886 are a little bit shaky. But in 1902, they were able to get Solomon Schechter, who was a great Jewish scholar from England. They were able to entice him to come and head up the Jewish Theological Seminary and, all of a sudden, JTS (the Jewish Theological Seminary) had a certain kind of status and credibility on the American Jewish scene.

Orthodoxy—that's the third movement in America. The Etz Chaim Yeshiva is an Orthodox yeshiva; *yeshiva* means "a place to study traditional texts"; it also means "a Rabbinic seminary." In this case, the Etz Chaim Yeshiva wasn't a Rabbinic seminary, it was just a school to study Talmud and Talmudic commentaries. That, like JTS, was opened in 1886, but there wasn't a Rabbinical academy until the Rabbi Isaac Elkhannan Specktor Yeshiva opened up one in 1897. Later on, those two *yeshivot* (the plural of yeshiva) combined to become Yeshiva University, which, until today, is the flagship institution of Modern Orthodoxy. At that point, when the two yeshivot combined under the guidance of Bernard Revel, Orthodoxy had a foothold on the American-Jewish scene. To this day, Yeshiva University is a flagship for Modern Orthodoxy, where they really do strive to combine intense Torah study, and graduate Rabbis, as well as promote high learning on a secular level.

There is a fourth denomination in Judaism. It is the smallest of the denominations and, indeed, it emerged out of the Conservative movement. I'm talking about Reconstructionism. The founder of Reconstructionism is Rabbi Mordecai Kaplan. He was born in the old country. He came to the United States as a young boy, with a brief stop in France. For decades and decades, he was a teacher at the Jewish Theological Seminary. He articulated as early as 1934 his idea that Judaism is a civilization; that was the name of the book— *Judaism As A Civilization*—that he had published, in 1934, to describe Judaism as an evolving religious civilization where peoplehood is primary. The laws are consequential to the people's attempt to bring God into their midst and to act in a godly way. They are folkways, and they don't have binding authority.

He was never altogether comfortable within the Conservative movement. He was finally persuaded to leave the Conservative movement and to establish his fourth denomination, Reconstructionism, in part by his son-in-law, Ira Eisenstein. In 1968, the Reconstructionist Rabbinical College was founded, outside of Philadelphia.

Kaplan was more aggressive about liturgical and halachic change than the Conservative movement as a whole. But, he would only advocate a change of tradition if the tradition itself were problematic. If there was something bad about not eating clams, then he would say, "then go ahead and eat clams." But he didn't eat clams, because there is nothing essentially, intrinsically immoral about abstaining from clams. It's a very different approach from Reform Judaism. Reform Judaism says, "Abstaining from clams doesn't promote my spirituality. It's not spiritually edifying, so why should I maintain this custom?" Kaplan, and the Conservative movement in general, come about that question from a different angle.

But, like Reform, Kaplan understood that the Torah is a human document; It is not a divine document. Therefore, when there are laws that need to be changed, it is fine to go ahead and change them. And the locus of authority for changing laws is the individual. You don't need to go in front of a board of Rabbis and petition.

Amongst the most radical reforms that Kaplan espoused, and to which we'll be returning in the final lecture, is his rejection of the Chosen People concept. So, that's a preview of coming attractions. We'll get back to that rejection of the Chosen People concept.

Several decades ago, in the 1960s, there was another movement—certainly not a denomination—but Jewish Renewal emerged in the 1960s. One name that is associated with Jewish Renewal is Rabbi Zalman Schachter-Shalomi. He was a traditional Rabbi—he had a traditional upbringing. He was associated with Chabad, a Hassidic group. What he did was to reach back to the prophetic and mystical sources of Judaism, and he began teaching a post-denominational Judaism that wasn't so concerned with halachic doctrine. He basically left the halachic world. He emphasized the universality of religious experience, and he was very willing to borrow certain meditative practices from eastern religions.

Jewish Renewal's flagship association is called "Aleph." It provides opportunities and training to spread this joyous approach to individual spiritual renewal that (they believe) can, in turn, have healing effects on society at large. Although the movement is not halachic, they do look toward specific rituals and social activism to further their agenda of spiritual growth and world healing.

Perhaps the most recent emergence or expression of Judaism is Jews Without God. The

Society for Humanistic Judaism was organized in 1969 by Rabbi Sherwin Wine. He promotes Jewish customs in a non-theistic, or perhaps atheistic, framework. That should strike you as bizarre, that somebody is a Rabbi and wants to continue Judaism, but doesn't believe in God. It's bizarre if you understand Judaism as a religion. But if you understand Judaism like Mordecai Kaplan did, as I've tried to explain in this course, as an evolving civilization, then it makes sense that people would want to maintain their identity—their Jewish identity—and their affiliation with the Jewish community on a cultural level or on a national level through Zionism—even if they don't have a firm spiritual, religious belief in a traditional supernatural deity.

What's more, it seems as though American Jews are particularly secular in their outlook.

According to the American Jewish Identity Survey of 2001, Jews are the most likely religious group to describe their outlook as secular or somewhat secular, including 14% who could be classified as atheists or agnostics. So, you've got 14% of the American Jewish community that doesn't have a belief in God, yet still proudly calls itself Jewish. That tells you that we've got a kind of cultural, ethnic, national component to the Jewish identity, and it's not just a religion.

I said that I introduce two movies to my *Introduction to Judaism* students at Vanderbilt. The first is *Fiddler on the Roof*. The second gets at that movement towards secularism in modernity, so I show them Woody Allen's *Crimes and Misdemeanors*. If you haven't read Dostoevsky's *Crime and Punishment*, you might not understand the riff that Woody Allen is making with his title, *Crimes and Misdemeanors*. But it's a wonderful movie to show you how one secular Jew (Woody Allen) perceives Judaism in the modern period. It is recommended.

So, what unites all these Jews—whether they're atheists, or agnostics, or Reform, or Conservative—is their search for appropriate behavior. And they are searching traditional Jewish sources, as well as their own consciences, to find appropriate behavior. As I have said before, Judaism is about deed, more than creed. Lots of different creeds exist within this family of Judaism—lots of different Judaisms, I would say. So, with that in mind, our next lecture will focus on the development of laws related to women.

Lecture Twenty-Two
Women and Jewish Law

Scope:

The underlying theme of this lecture is the development of Jewish law from the Torah to today. Our three case studies highlight issues of particular concern to women, though important to us all. We begin with a selection of laws concerning marriage and divorce, eventually arriving at the plight of the *agunah* ("anchored woman," "grass widow"). We will then look at the case of feticide in the Torah and how the laws of abortion have unfolded over the past 2,000 years in ways that defy categorization as either "pro-life" or "pro-choice." We conclude by looking at the leadership roles held by women in contemporary religious life.

Outline

I. Marriage in the Torah.

    A. The groom pays a bride price to the father of the bride.

    B. The bride also comes into the marriage with a dowry.

    C. Once married, the husband is responsible for "food, clothing, and conjugal rights" (Exod. 21:10).

II. Divorce in the Torah.

    A. If the man finds something objectionable about the woman, he has the sole prerogative to issue a writ of divorce (Deut. 24:1).

    B. She takes her dowry with her.

III. Marriage in the Rabbinic period.

    A. The Rabbis instituted a document called a *ketubah* that greatly enhanced the rights of the woman in a marriage.

        1. No longer are funds given to the father of the bride at the time of the marriage.

        2. The ketubah stipulates that a minimum amount of money will be provided to the woman on divorce or the death of the husband. Thus, we see the move from a purchase to a process of negotiation requiring the woman's consent.

     a. Deferring the financial burden of the bride price allowed poor men to marry who might otherwise not have been able to raise the money.

     b. Deferring the financial transaction until the death of the husband or divorce also has the effect of inhibiting rash divorces. Now, the husband had something to lose by divorcing his wife. This situation differs from both the biblical condition and the Roman law of the time.

B. The Rabbis also instituted an additional series of laws to protect the wife.

   1. Should the woman be taken captive, the husband must redeem her.

   2. Should the woman take ill, the husband must provide her with medical care.

   3. If she dies before her husband, her sons inherit the funds from the ketubah, as well as her dowry.

   4. If she outlives her husband, she can either maintain herself from his estate indefinitely or take her ketubah.

IV. Divorce in the Rabbinic period.

A. Unlike men, women must receive a bill of divorce before remarrying. Although monogamy is the ideal, polygyny is a biblical institution that was "temporarily suspended" for Ashkenazi Jews about 1,000 years ago but is still on the books.

B. Although technically the husband initiated the divorce, the Rabbis found several ways of protecting the woman from a recalcitrant husband to prevent women from becoming *agunot*, "straw widows."

   1. The Rabbis sometimes physically forced men to "voluntarily" issue their wives a *get*, a writ of divorce.

   2. Other times, rabbis annulled the marriage altogether, thus freeing the woman to marry another man even without a get.

V. Contemporary attempts to further fairness toward women.

A. Some rabbis have husbands sign a get at the time of the marriage that they, the rabbis, keep in their possession should the marriage effectively come to an end. Although this works well for soldiers going off to war who might be missing in action, for others, it makes a divorce too easy, given that the paperwork has been completed. (This practice actually began in the Rabbinic period.)

B. The Lieberman Clause, named after a Talmudic scholar who taught for the Conservative Movement, is written into the ketubah itself and authorizes a court to "force," through excessive monetary sanctions, a divorce.

C. The Orthodox Rabbinical Council of America and the Conservative Rabbinical Assembly use a similar strategy but with a separate document outside of the ketubah.

D. Finally, Rabbi Shlomo Riskin has recently suggested that annulment be rehabilitated in order to persuade men to stop blackmailing their wives and, if that does not succeed, to free anchored women from their recalcitrant husbands.

VI. Feticide.

A. "When men fight, and one of them pushes a pregnant woman and a miscarriage results, but no other damage ensues, the one responsible shall be fined according as the woman's husband may exact from him, the payment to be based on reckoning. But if other damage ensues, the penalty shall be life for life" (Exod. 21:22–3).

B. "If a woman is having difficulty in labor, one cuts up the fetus within her womb and extracts it limb by limb, because her life takes precedence over that of the fetus. But if the greater part is already born, one may not touch it, for one may not set aside one person's life for another" (M., Oholot 7:6).

C. In the 17th century, several rabbis permitted elective abortions based on "mother's need" and "mother's healing," which included psychological factors.

D. As a result of advances in medical technology, abortion has been permitted for those to whom the knowledge of having a Tay-Sachs baby is traumatic.

E. "Jewish law *requires* abortion when the woman's life or health—physical or mental—is threatened by the pregnancy; Jewish law *permits* abortion when the risk to the woman's life or health (again, physical or mental) is greater than that of a normal pregnancy but not so great as to constitute a clear and present danger to her" (Rabbi Elliot Dorff [Conservative], *Matters of Life and Death*, italics his).

F. "Legal permissibility is not synonymous with moral license" (Fred Rosner, *Biomedical Ethics and Jewish Law*, p. 192).

VII. Women in communal leadership roles.

    A. Throughout history, individual women have attained positions of leadership through charisma. The community recognized them as exceptions.

        1. The first woman to receive private Rabbinic ordination was Regina Jonas in 1935.

        2. Jonas was German and a graduate of the liberal seminary in Berlin. After the Nazis came to power, she was sent to Theresienstadt and, eventually, to her death at Auschwitz.

    B. In the modern period, under the influence of feminism, the Reform movement ordained Sally Priesand as a Rabbi in 1972. For the Reform movement, egalitarianism is an issue of fairness.

    C. Reconstructionists began ordaining women in 1975.

    D. For the Conservative movement, ordaining women as Rabbis was a halachic hurdle.

        1. Rabbi Joel Roth argued that, today, women are competent in legal and business issues, which had not been the case in the Rabbinic period.

        2. If women take upon themselves the responsibilities of Jewish men, then they are entitled to the rights, including ordination as a Rabbi. (Traditionally, Jewish women have been exempt from most positive, time-bound mitzvot, such as thrice-daily prayer with a quorum.)

    E. Women began being ordained in the Conservative movement in 1985.

    F. Over the last 20 years, significant strides have been made for women in Orthodoxy.

        1. There are now women's yeshivot, where women learn Talmud and halachah on very high levels.

        2. There are women's prayer groups, where women conduct services without male support.

3. One women's yeshiva in Jerusalem, Nishmat, began training halachic advisors in 1997 for legal issues specific to women.
4. A handful of women have studied and are studying for Orthodox Rabbinic ordination. There are female Rabbinic Assistants. The issue of female Rabbis is on the Orthodox table.

Essential Reading:

Dorff, *Matters of Life and Death*, pp. 28–33 and 37–42.

Feldman, *Health and Medicine in the Jewish Tradition*, pp. 55–68 and 79–90.

Hauptman, "Marriage" and "Divorce," in *Rereading the Rabbis*, pp. 60–76 and 102–129.

Wolowelsky, "Rabbis, Rebbetzins, and Halakhic Advisors," *Tradition* 36:4 (2002), pp. 54–63.

Supplementary Reading:

Biale, *Women and Jewish Law*.

Greenberg, *On Women and Judaism*.

———, *The Ordination of Women*.

Nadell, *Women Who Would Be Rabbis*.

Washofsky, "Abortion and the Halakhic Conversation," in *The Fetus and Fertility in Jewish Law*.

Questions to Consider:

1. In what ways is the ketubah similar and dissimilar to the contemporary prenuptial agreement?

2. One contemporary halachic authority, David Feldman, has coined the term "solemn hesitation" to describe Judaism's posture toward abortion. How is solemn hesitation different than the pro-life and pro-choice labels we use in American political discourse? Is it preferable?

3. What does the influence of feminism on the non-Orthodox movements tell us about the relationship between religion and society? Many religions exclude women from leadership positions for a variety of reasons. Are any justified in doing so?

Lecture Twenty-Two—Transcript
Women and Jewish Law

The subject of this lecture is "Women and Jewish Law." What we are really going to be doing throughout this lecture is looking at how certain laws have developed from the biblical period, through the Rabbinic period and the medieval period, up to the modern period. We are going to be using as our case studies laws of particular relevance to women. Men are also concerned about these issues, but I wanted to dedicate at least one of our lectures to Judaism's relationship to women.

If we go back to the Hebrew Bible itself, the role and the position of women is not always what a modern feminist might like it to be. Let me give you an example from *Exodus*, chapter 19. This is the chapter where God is talking to Moses about preparing the people for revelation, for the giving of the Decalogue, in a few days. *Exodus* 19, verse 10, says:

> The LORD says to Moses, Go to the people and warn them to stay pure today and tomorrow. Let them wash their clothes. Let them be ready for the third day. For on the third day, the LORD will come down in the sight of all the people on Mount Sinai.

Now, let's see what Moses actually says, in verse 14-15:

> Moses came down from the mountain to the people, and warned them to stay pure; and they washed their clothes. And he said to the people, Be ready for the third day. Do not go near a woman.

So, if Moses is saying, "Do not go near a woman," it seems as though he is speaking only to the men. So, does that mean that the women weren't included in the revelation of God at Mount Sinai? Part of the reason I want to focus in on laws related to women is to see how this group, "fifty percent of the kingdom" (to quote the book of *Esther*), is treated—not so much in the narrative of the Hebrew Bible, but throughout the halachah within Judaism because, in some ways, women are the "other" within Judaism. So, let's begin our examination by taking a look at the laws regarding marriage and divorce within the Torah itself.

There is a bride price, when one wants to get married, that the groom pays to the father of the bride in order to cement the relationship. The bride also comes into the marriage with a dowry. Once they are married, the husband is responsible (according to *Exodus* 21:10) for "food, clothing, and [most translations say] conjugal rights." In other words, the husband has an obligation to satisfy his wife sexually. If you are thinking about the three things that a man is responsible for when he takes a wife—food, clothing, and—the next word that falls off my tongue is "shelter." Right? "Food, clothing, and shelter," not "food, clothing, and conjugal rights." And indeed, we have a medieval commentator, Rashbam, from the 12th or 13th century in France, who says, "No, we really should understand that word as 'shelter,' not as 'conjugal rights,'" which makes it all the more interesting why the Rabbis who interpreted this word as "conjugal rights" did so, perhaps against the grain of the contextual reading. Perhaps shelter was taken for granted.

What's not taken for granted is that the husband has certain sexual obligations to his wife. Why is that so important in the biblical period and in the Rabbinic period? Because a husband can have multiple wives according to the Torah. One man can have any number of wives, but a woman can only have one husband. So, if a man is favoring his third, fourth, and fifth wives, it might mean that his first and second wives are being neglected. That's not fair to them because they have no other avenue of satisfying their own needs. So, the Rabbis made sure that anybody who took a wife would need to tend to their food, clothing—shelter is taken for granted—as well as conjugal rights.

How does divorce happen in the Torah? If a man finds something—anything—objectionable about the woman, he has the sole prerogative to issue the writ of divorce. When the woman leaves the relationship, she takes her dowry with her, and there the marriage ends.

Now let's see what innovations we find in the Rabbinic period. The Rabbis instituted a document called the *Ketubah*, which literally means "something written." *Lichtov* means "to write." But this prenuptial agreement, or this wedding contract, greatly enhanced the rights of women. No longer were funds given to the father of the bride at the time of the marriage.

The Ketubah stipulates that a minimum amount of money will be provided to the woman upon divorce or the death of the husband. Thus, we see the shift from a purchase (where, in the biblical period, the groom would pay the father of the bride) to a process of negotiation requiring the woman's consent. Also, by deferring the financial burden of the bride price—to either the death of the husband or the dissolution of the marriage—it allowed poor men to marry who might otherwise not have been able to raise the bride price. So, that's a good thing in the eyes of the Rabbis. If more men can marry, more women can be married, and they can start families earlier.

Furthermore, by deferring this financial burden, it has the effect of inhibiting rash divorces. Think about the logic there. Now the husband has something to lose by divorcing his wife. He has to pay the amount stipulated in the Ketubah. But, if, in the biblical period, a man decides to divorce his wife, she leaves. He loses nothing but the dowry that she had brought into the marriage to begin with. So this situation, interestingly enough, differs from biblical law (as we have seen), but it differs also from Roman law that was current at the time that the Rabbis made these innovations.

The Rabbis also instituted an additional series of responsibilities to protect the wife. Among them, should the woman be taken captive, the husband must redeem her. This reminds me of a scene from *Ruthless People*, when the character played by Danny DeVito finds out that his wife, played by Bette Midler, has been kidnapped. He celebrates, he laughs, he dances, he sings, he pops open a bottle of champagne. Thank goodness, somebody else has taken her off his hands. That's okay to do in Judaism, but eventually you have to redeem her, according to the stipulations of the Ketubah. You can't just leave her at the mercy of her captors.

Also, should the woman be taken ill, the husband must provide her with medical care. If she dies before her husband, her sons will inherit the funds from the Ketubah as well as her dowry. If she outlives her husband, she can either maintain herself from his estate indefinitely (so that she doesn't have to be thrown out into the cold wild), or she can take her Ketubah, and start her new life over again.

Regarding divorce in the Rabbinic period, unlike men, women must receive a bill of divorce before remarrying. If it is a man, a man doesn't have to receive a bill of divorce because he can marry as many women as he wants. But the woman can only be married to one person at a time, so she has got to receive that writ of divorce, which in Hebrew is called a *get*. She needs to receive that get in order to be eligible to marry another man.

So, monogamy is certainly the ideal in the biblical world as well as in the Rabbinic world. Is monogamy an ideal in the biblical world? I'm not sure. Let me take that back. With Moses, no one imagines that Moses was a bigamist. But if you read *Numbers*, chapter 12, it seems as though Moses had taken an additional wife, a Cushite. But we know that Moses had taken Jethro's daughter, Zipporah, as a wife, and she was a Midianite. So, Moses was a bigamist, but the Rabbis bend over backwards to read those verses in *Numbers* that describe Moses's taking a Cushite wife as Zipporah, which means that the Rabbis were very uncomfortable with Moses, their hero, being a bigamist. So, for certain in the Rabbinic period, the ideal was monogamy.

But, polygamy (a man marrying muliple wives) is a biblical institution that was "temporarily suspended" for Ashkenazi Jews (those Jews in Europe) about 1,000 years ago—but it is still on the books.

Although technically the husband initiated the divorce, the Rabbis during the Rabbinic period found ways of protecting the woman from a recalcitrant husband in order to prevent women from becoming *agunot*. Literally, agunot means "chained down," or "anchored." In English, we call them "straw widows." The Rabbis were concerned that the women would not be able to remarry unless their husbands gave them a get. So sometimes the Rabbis forced men to "voluntarily" issue their wives a get, or the writ of divorce. Other times, Rabbis annulled the marriage altogether—thus freeing the woman to marry another man even without a get.

Both of those solutions to the problem of an agunot—an anchored woman, a straw widow—were not very popular, and they were exercised less and less as we move into the Middle Ages and into the modern period. So, the Rabbinic authorities weren't willing to apply physical force to make the husband divorce the woman or to sign a get, nor were they willing to annul the marriage.

But, now we move into the contemporary world, and we look at Rabbinic mechanisms in the last 20 years that are put in place in order to further fairness towards women. Some Rabbis have husbands (or the fiancée before they get married) sign a get at the time of the marriage that they (the Rabbis) keep in their possession. Should the marriage effectively come to an end, the woman who is in a marriage that has effectively come to an end can go to the Rabbi and say, "You know what? I'm ready for a divorce. He won't give me the get. You've got the get. Please give it to me." Although this works very well for soldiers who are going off to war, who might be missing in action, and therefore you don't know if they are dead or alive, and they are not around to sign a get—for others it just makes getting a divorce too easy since all the paperwork has been completed. (This practice actually goes back to the Rabbinic period, also.)

Another attempt at making things more fair for women is the Lieberman Clause, named after a scholar (a Talmudic scholar) who taught at JTS (the Conservative seminary) for many years. The Lieberman Clause is a clause that is actually written into the Ketubah itself. It authorizes a court to "force," through monetary—through excessive monetary—sanctions, a divorce. Again, this also doesn't have the kind of binding power that would necessarily compel a man to issue his wife a get.

Another option: The Orthodox Rabbinical Council of America and the Conservative Rabbinical Assembly use a similar strategy but with a separate document outside of the Ketubah. Leave the traditional text of the Ketubah alone, and have the husband sign another document agreeing that he will pay excessive monetary sanctions in the event that the marriage has effectively come to an end—same kinds of problems that we mentioned above.

The most recent Orthodox attempt to deal with the problem of aguno*t* is one by Rabbi Shlomo Riskin, who suggested that annulment be rehabilitated in order to persuade men to stop blackmailing their wives. Blackmailing their wives! Some men, when they are in a marriage that has gone south, they tell their wives, "I'm not going to give you a ge*t*, so you can move on with your life, unless you pay me $10,000." In that kind of a circumstance, the woman is stuck. If she doesn't pay the money, she remains anchored to the man. Rabbi Riskin is familiar with this problem, and he is sympathetic to the agunot, so he wants to rehabilitate this idea of annulling the marriage, retroactively, in order to deal with those kinds of men—also, to free women from recalcitrant husbands, even if they are not trying to blackmail their wives.

So, we see in the modern period a variety of attempts in the Orthodox world and the Conservative world (those denominations who still take halachah as binding) to further fairness toward women.

Let's take a look at the issue of abortion, or feticide. The biblical text that begins our discussion is found in *Exodus*, chapter 21, verses 22 and 23:

> When men fight, and one of them pushes a pregnant woman and a miscarriage results, but no other damage ensues, the one responsible shall be fined according as the woman's husband may exact from him, the payment to be based on reckoning. But if other damage ensues [namely, if the woman dies—if the pregnant woman dies; that's the other damage that would ensue], the penalty shall be life for life.

So, what this means is that, according to the Bible, a fetus doesn't have the legal status of a full life, because, if it did, then the reckoning would be life for life. But if just a miscarriage results, and the woman doesn't die (who was pushed), then it is monetary compensation. You only have the case of life for life when you have the case of manslaughter (unintentional homicide)—when the two men are fighting, the pregnant woman is pushed and, in addition to the fetus dying, the woman dies; then, you have the case of life for life.

This informs the Jewish discussion of abortion. According to the Bible, the fetus does not have the full legal rights of a living being. Is this talking about abortion? No. This is not talking about abortion, but the Rabbis will use this case in order to inform their decisions and their discussions about abortion.

Now, let's take a look at that first layer of Jewish law, in the Mishnah.

> If a woman is having difficult in labor, one cuts up the fetus within her womb and extracts it limb by limb, because her life takes precedence over that of the fetus. But if the greater part is already born [and in other manuscripts of the Mishnah, 'if the head and shoulders' of the fetus, so it's not

a breech baby], one may not touch it, for one may not set aside one person's life for another.

So, what does this mean? That until the fetus has the majority of its body out (head and shoulders), it doesn't have the status of a full human being. Therefore, if the woman is in difficulty—*only* if the woman is in difficulty—during this labor process, then the Mishnah is very clear: You extract the fetus, even if you need to cut it up limb by limb, in order to save the woman's life. She has the full status of a living being. The fetus doesn't have the full status of a living being until the majority of its body is outside of the woman's body. But once that happens, then you try to save them both, and you do whatever you can to try to save both.

How does that law develop once the medical technology and know-how gets to be sophisticated enough to allow for elective abortions? In the 17th century, several Rabbis permitted elective abortions based on "mother's need" and "mother's healing," which included psychological factors. Here's how they did it. It says in the Mishnah, "if the woman is having difficulty in labor." The only way to justify an abortion in Judaism is if the woman is having difficulty. But, it doesn't necessarily, explicitly say that she's having physical difficulty; it might be psychological difficulty. Let me give you an example, the example that the Rabbis were dealing with. If a woman has been raped and having that child would be very difficult for her because the child would be illegitimate, then the Rabbis will sanction or tolerate an abortion. Similarly, if a woman has—in a moment of indiscretion—had an extramarital affair, or if she has committed an act of incest, similarly her product—or her child—would be illegitimate, and the Rabbis will allow her to abort such a fetus because of the psychological factors on the mother, based on their rereading of this Mishnah.

As we move into the 20th century, we have advances in medical technology. Abortion has been permitted for those for whom the knowledge of having a Tay-Sachs baby (a genetic disease that is particularly prominent within the Ashkenazi Jewish population)—if the woman knows that her baby (as a result of genetic testing) is going to have Tay-Sachs and is going to end up dying very quickly after birth, and that knowledge is traumatic to the woman, that maternal indicator (for at least one school of Rabbinic thought) will allow the woman to have an abortion.

So, let's try to wrap up this discussion of Judaism and abortion. I want to quote from a Conservative Rabbi who teaches at the University of Judaism, Rabbi Elliot Dorff. He writes that:

> Jewish law *requires* abortion when the woman's life or health—physical or mental—is threatened by the pregnancy; Jewish law *permits* abortion when the risk to the woman's life or health (again, physical or mental) is greater than that of a normal pregnancy but not so great as to constitute a clear and present danger to her.

This means that the terminology that we use in American political discourse of "pro-choice" and "pro-life" is simply inapplicable in the world of Judaism because if the woman's health is in danger, not the Rabbi, but the doctor—if her physical health is in danger—then the doctor has to make a split-second decision that her life takes precedence over the fetus's. It's not her choice. Abortion has to be allowed, but it's not the woman's choice.

Let's say that we are talking about mental anguish—psychological distress. The woman goes to the Rabbi to ask whether or not she can abort this child who is going to be a Tay-Sachs child, and the Rabbi says, "Does it really bother you that you're going to have a child that's going to end up dying?" Theoretically, the woman could say, "No. If that's God's will, to give me a child that has a degenerative disease and will relatively quickly die, then I accept that from God." In that situation, the woman isn't undergoing any distress, and the Rabbi couldn't allow her to have an abortion. But if the woman comes to the Rabbi and is pulling out her hair and says, "I just can't imagine giving birth to this creature that is going to slowly die before my eyes in such a short time." In that case, there are maternal indicators of psychological distress, and the Rabbi can allow her to have an abortion. But in neither case is it the woman's choice, so that's why these labels of "pro-choice" and "pro-life" don't quite work in Judaism.

Fred Rosner has the following sentence that I think nicely sums up the issue of Judaism and abortion, "Legal permissibility is not synonymous with moral license." Just because there is a dispensation or an allowance to have an abortion, doesn't mean that you can do that without approaching it with, in the words of one Rabbi, "solemn hesitation."

The final example of women and Jewish law that we are going to look at is women in communal leadership roles. In the biblical world there were always individuals—like Sarah, and Miriam, and Deborah, and Jael—who had charisma and were lifted up by the community to lead the community in certain situations.

And that happened in the Rabbinic period. We know of a few women who seemed to be very learned and who seemed to command the respect of the community also in the Middle Ages—but nothing institutional. It was all on an individual level. Those were the exceptions. It was generally—the rule was—that it was the men who were leaders of the community.

The first woman to receive private—not institutional, but private—Rabbinic ordination was a woman in Germany by the name of Regina Jonas. This was in 1935. She received *smicha*, or ordination, from a Reform-leaning Rabbi. Jonas was German and a graduate of the liberal seminary in Berlin. She did study, but the seminary didn't give her ordination; it was through a private, individual Rabbi. After the Nazis came to power, she was sent to Theresienstadt in Czechoslovakia, and eventually to her death at Auschwitz. So, Regina Jonas was the first woman to get private ordination.

We had to wait several decades until an institution gives women ordination, and we see that within the Reform movement, in 1972, really as a result of the feminist influence that swept over the United States as well as western Europe in the 1960s and 1970s. A woman named Sally Priesand became a Reform Rabbi. For the Reform movement, egalitarianism was an issue of fairness. If men can become Rabbis, why shouldn't women become Rabbis? Therefore, let's make women Rabbis. It was almost that simple.

The discussion was similarly simple for Reconstructionists, and they began ordaining women in 1975.

For the Conservative movement, ordaining women as Rabbis wasn't so simple. It involved a halachic hurdle because ordaining women had never been done. There were some halachic problems with it, and those halachic problems needed to be addressed. This came to a head in the 1980s. Professor Joel Roth was one of the members of the law committee for the Conservative movement, and he argued that today women are competent in legal and business issues, which had not been the case in the Rabbinic period. Very often, what a

Rabbi is asked to do is to make a judgment about a legal issue that involves business. If women don't know anything about business, then you can't expect them to be competent to make a judgment. But today, it is not the case that women are incompetent about business issues. I went to the Wharton School of Business, and half of the class was female. Women know law and women know business practices as well as men. So, that was the first part of his argument—that there is no reason now to prevent women from exercising their judicial opinion.

But there was another part of the argument. Women in Judaism don't have the same responsibilities as men, and therefore they don't have the same rights as men. Traditionally, Jewish women have been exempt from most positive, time-bound commandments, such as praying three times a day with a group. It was understood 2,000 years ago that women had other things to do, mainly to take care of their nursing babies or their children. They had responsibilities at home. So, if the commandment involved something that they had to do at a certain time, they were exempt from that because what they had to do at a certain time couldn't wait. It was time-sensitive because they had to take care of the needs of their family, but, today, women are freed—to a large extent—from those kinds of time-sensitive needs. So, if women are willing to take on those responsibilities that men have, then they can also assume the rights that men have; therefore, women can become Rabbis.

So, it was a two-part teshuvah, or Rabbinic decision: A) Women have the capability of doing it; and B) Women who take on the responsibilities of the male Jew, in terms of *davening*, or praying, three times a day, as well as all of the other commandments, then they will similarly have the rights that men have to be leaders in the community. So, women began being ordained in the Conservative movement in 1985.

Over the last 20 years, there have been incredible strides made for women in Orthodoxy as well. There aren't Orthodox institutions, like Yeshiva University, ordaining women, but there already has been an Orthodox woman, Mimi Feigelson, who was given private ordination in Israel, and she is now teaching at the University of Judaism in Los Angeles, California. In addition to that pathbreaking move, there are women's yeshivot—places for women to do serious Jewish text study and serious Talmud study on very high levels.

There are women's prayer groups where women conduct services without male support. There is one women's yeshiva in Jerusalem, Nishmat, that began in 1997 training their women to be halachic advisors for certain legal issues specific to women.

Already, we know about a handful of women who are studying for Orthodox Rabbinic ordination; although, to my knowledge, none has been ordained, with the exception of Mimi Feigelson. We have female Rabbinic Assistants today, and the issue of female Rabbis is on the Orthodox table.

Now that we've taken a look at the "other" within Judaism, our next lecture will focus on the "other" outside of Judaism—how Judaism responds to non-Jews—Christians, in particular.

Lecture Twenty-Three
Judaism and the Other

Scope:

Like most ancient law codes, the Hebrew Bible distinguishes between insiders and outsiders. Rabbinic legislation maintains that formal distinction, but sometimes, for the sake of social tranquility, erases the distinction in practice. The Rabbis also drafted a series of laws that they maintained were obligatory for all humans to fulfill in order to live righteously. These are called the *seven laws of Noah*, and one of those laws prohibits idolatry.

In the Middle Ages, there was a split between European Ashkenazi Jews and North African Sephardic Jews as to whether the Christian claim of the divinity of Jesus constituted idolatry. The positions and nuances of the medieval debate provide a fascinating case study in inter-religious accommodation. This lecture will conclude with recent developments in Jewish-Christian relations.

Outline

I. The "other" in the Torah.

   A. "You shall have one standard for stranger and citizen alike; for I the Lord am your God" (Lev. 24:22).

   B. "You shall not deduct interest from loans to your countrymen, whether in money or food or anything else that can be deducted as interest; but you may deduct interest from loans to foreigners" (Deut. 23:20–1).

   C. The distinction is whether the non-Israelite/Jew lives in Israel or not.

II. Ways of peace.

   A. Which is the greatest principle in the Torah? Rabbi Akiva answered: You shall love your neighbour as yourself (Lev. 19:18). Ben Azzai responded: God created humanity in the divine image (Gen. 5:1). (Sifra, Kedoshim 2:4.)

   B. "Our Rabbis taught: We provide support for the poor of the gentiles along with the poor of Israel, and visit the sick of the gentiles along with the sick of Israel, and bury the dead of the gentiles along with the dead of Israel in accord with the ways of peace" (b. Gittin 61a).

C. "Her ways are pleasant ways, and all her paths, peaceful" (Pro. 3:17).

III. The seven Noahide laws.

    A. God commands Noah and his family about murder and eating animals while their blood is still surging (Gen. 9).

    B. But the Rabbis, as lawyers, assumed that God could not have punished humanity with the flood unless they had been previously made aware of the laws.

    C. Thus, in the Rabbinic revision of primal history, the very first utterance of God to man in the Garden implicitly contained the following commandments that that Rabbis understood obligated all future humanity:

        1. Establish courts of laws in your communities.

        2. Do not commit blasphemy toward the Lord.

        3. Do not worship false gods or idols.

        4. Do not commit incest or adultery.

        5. Do not murder.

        6. Do not steal.

        7. Do not eat the limb from a live animal. (b. Sann. 56a)

IV. Is the Christian claim that Jesus is God idolatrous?

    A. The Jews of the Muslim world, who generally had little contact with Christians, maintained that Christianity was, indeed, idolatrous.

        1. Muslims consider the association of God with anything or anyone else to be the greatest of sins.

        2. Maimonides, although living in the Muslim world and agreeing that Christianity was idolatrous, nevertheless recognized the contributions of Christianity for helping to spread the truths and ethics of the Torah.

    B. In 12th-century France, where Jews lived with Christians, there was a different response.

        1. Rabbi Isaac made the distinction that the Christian association of Jesus with God is not prohibited for Gentiles who follow the Noahide laws (Tosafot to b. Sann. 63b).

2. In the early 14th century, Rabbi Menachem Ha-Me'iri of Provence argued that Christians were a "people restricted by ways of religion," unlike the pagans and idolaters described in the Talmud.

3. For the Ashkenazi Jews of medieval France, Christianity was a moral religion devoted to God. From the Jewish perspective, Christians were mistaken about certain theological issues related to the unity of God. However, because deed is more important than creed in Judaism, that same attitude was extended to Christianity. Intellectual differences, which characterize Jewish literature, can be tolerated as long as they do not translate into immorality.

V. Modern developments in Jewish-Christian relations.

A. The Second Vatican Council (1962–1965) recognized that God's covenant with the Jewish people remains intact.

1. The church repudiated antisemitism and the charge that Jews were collectively responsible for the crucifixion of Jesus.

2. Given that the covenant between God and the Jews is intact, there is no need for Jews to convert to Christianity to achieve salvation.

B. Beyond the Catholic world, there have also been major efforts in promoting Jewish-Christian dialogue. A recent statement (2002) by the Christian Scholars Group on Christian-Jewish Relations made the following points:

1. God's covenant with the Jewish people endures forever.

2. Jesus lived and died as a faithful Jew.

3. Ancient rivalries must not define contemporary relations.

4. Judaism is a living faith, enriched by many centuries of development.

5. Christians should not target Jews for conversion.

6. We affirm the importance of the Land of Israel for the life of the Jewish people.

7. Christians should work with Jews for the healing of the world.

C. Since the Shoah, Jews have also struggled to redefine their relationship with Christians.

1. On the level of cooperation with Christian groups concerning social and political issues of social justice, there has been widespread participation throughout the mainstream Jewish community.
2. In terms of religious dialogue, there remain elements within Orthodoxy that are either suspicious of Christian conversionary activity or convinced that nothing positive can come from such dialogue. In the words of Rabbi Joseph Soloveitchik: "Each religious community is endowed with intrinsic dignity and metaphysical worth."
3. Other Jews, including some Orthodox, are willing to engage in inter-religious dialogue. *Dabru Emet* is a recent statement by Jews on Christians and Christianity.
   a. Jews and Christians worship the same God.
   b. Jews and Christians accept the moral principles of Torah.
   c. The humanly irreconcilable difference between Jews and Christians will not be settled until God redeems the entire world, as promised in Scripture.
   d. A new relationship between Jews and Christians will not weaken Jewish practice.

Essential Reading:

Ellenson, David. "A Jewish Legal Authority Addresses Jewish-Christian Dialogue," in *American Jewish Archives Journal*, pp. 113–128.

Greenberg, Irving, "The Relationship of Judaism and Christianity," in *Quarterly Review* 4:4 (1984), pp. 4–22.

Lander, Shira, and Daniel Lehmann, "New Wine for New Wineskins" in *Religious Education* 91:4 (1996), pp. 519–528.

Sandmel, *Irreconcilable Differences?*

Supplementary Reading:

Borowitz, *Contemporary Christologies: A Jewish Response*.

Katz, *Exclusiveness and Tolerance*, chapter 10.

Pallière, *The Unknown Sanctuary*.

Signer, "Trinity, Unity, Idolatry?" in *Lesarten des judische-christlichen Dialoges*, pp. 275–284.

Questions to Consider:

1. Since the Noahide laws were written in the Talmud, in a language that non-Jews don't read, what was their purpose?

2. When considering the split of opinion concerning Christianity between the Jews of Christendom and the Jews of Islam, which factors may be responsible?

3. Most agree on the virtue of inter-religious cooperation for the purpose of healing the world. What are the dangers, from both sides, of inter-religious dialogue?

Lecture Twenty-Three—Transcript
Judaism and the Other

All ancient law codes made a distinction between the "in" group and the "out" group, and the law codes in the Hebrew Bible are no exception to that rule. But we want to take a look at how the Hebrew Bible, Rabbinic Judaism, medieval Judaism, and modern Judaism understand the relationship to the outsiders, and how that has changed over time.

So, the first biblical verse I want to take a look at is in *Leviticus* 24:22, which seems to suggest something unique in the world of the ancient Near East: "You shall have one standard for stranger and citizen alike; for I the LORD am your God."

Hmm. So does that mean that there isn't a distinction between insiders and outsiders? Not quite. Let's look at another biblical verse, this time from *Deuteronomy* 23:

> You shall not deduct interest from loans to your countrymen, whether in money or food or anything else that can be deducted as interest; but you may deduct interest from loans to foreigners.

Ah. So, here we are making a distinction—the Bible is making a distinction—between "foreigners" and "strangers." "Strangers" are what we would call "resident aliens." They are people that have come to the Land of Israel and are living amongst you, even though they are not Israelites—they are not ethnically Israelites. While "foreigners" are people from outside that may be here temporarily, and they are (unlike the resident alien, for whom you are to have the same law as you would toward another Israelite) the foreigner from Moab or from Mesopotamia—there you do have this two-tiered legal system whereby they are judged by a different set of rules, and they are extended a different set of rights than are the *Ger*, or the resident alien—the "stranger," or the native Israelite.

So, it really has to do with how long they are in the Land. So, already we see that the Torah is trying to make some accommodations to those people who weren't born in the "in" group, but have moved here (to the Land of Israel) for one reason or another.

The Rabbis talk about the "ways of peace." The Rabbis have this general category of "the ways of peace" that they get—they get that language from the book of *Proverbs*. *Proverbs* 3 talks about "her ways are pleasant and all her paths are peaceful." That's in the Torah itself; that's in the TaNaKH. The Rabbis, then, derive a series of general principles about the Torah only being for nice, gentle, pleasant ways. There is a dispute between two of the great Rabbis of the Mishnaic period—Rabbi Akiva and Ben Azzai—as to what is the greatest principle in the Torah. Rabbi Akiva says, "You shall love your neighbor as yourself." Jesus said the same thing, in the Gospels: "You shall love your neighbor as yourself." That's the greatest mitzvah, the greatest commandment, in the Torah.

Ben Azzai disagrees. Azzai says, "No. The greatest principle in the Torah is that God created all of humanity in the divine image." What's the distinction between the two?

If I were to say that in Aramaic, as a good Talmudic scholar, I would say, "What's the *nafkeminah*?" What's the practical difference? If I were to say it as a disciple of William James, "What's the cash value?" What's the practical difference between these two positions of Rabbi Akiva and Ben Azzai?

Rabbi Akiva is setting a pretty high bar for love, but it is love for your neighbor, and your neighbor, generally, is an Israelite— somebody who lives right in your neighborhood, who shares your worldview, and is part of your own ethnic group. Ben Azzai has a lower bar, right? Everyone is created in the divine image so you need to accord to each person a certain amount of dignity for having been created in the divine image. So, dignity or respect for the other is perhaps easier to extend than love, but you have to extend it to a wider base. You have to extend it to everyone.

So, this kind of tension within Rabbinic Judaism is there from the very beginning. Do we just love those people that are just like us? Or/and do we also extend respect and dignity for all of God's creation?

Another statement from the Rabbis:

> Our Rabbis taught: We provide support for the poor of the gentiles along with the poor of Israel, and visit the sick of the gentiles along with the sick of Israel, and bury the dead of the gentiles along with the dead of Israel in accord with the ways of peace.

So, those nice things that we do—things that we are not specifically commanded in the Torah to do, but it falls under the general category of loving your neighbor and ways of peace, just like we do to the Israelites, in the Rabbinic period to Jews wherever they are—we should also extend the same courtesies to the gentiles. Why? Because the Torah's ways are pleasant—the Torah's ways are to promote peace.

And, if you remember, in a previous lecture we talked about the Hebrew loan associations that popped up in this country when the eastern European immigrants first came to these shores, as a way that the veteran Jewish Americans could lend a helping hand to their brethren who were newcomers (to the greenhorns) who were just coming to this land. It turns out that many of those Hebrew free loan associations also extended credit and loaned money to gentiles.

The Rabbis were very concerned about balancing rights and responsibilities, so if the gentiles - they don't technically have rights, but we extend to them these pleasantries, and we also expect a certain level of behavior. The Rabbis created something called the Seven Noahide Laws as a kind of minimum expectation of what it means to be a righteous gentile. These seven laws are imagined by the Rabbis to have been told by God to Adam in the Garden of Eden. It's very, very important for the Rabbis that these laws are articulated to the founder of humanity (according to the biblical story), at the very beginning. Why? So that when the Flood of Noah happens, the Rabbis will feel as though the punishment of Noah's generation was justified because they broke laws that they knew about. It very much bothered the Rabbis, who were also judges (in their capacity as Rabbis), that there would be this punishment recorded in the Torah, while it wasn't explicit that the generation of Noah knew what the laws were that they were violating. So, the Rabbis—in good midrashic fashion—read the following seven laws into God's first statement to Adam in the Garden of Eden.

The seven laws are as follows. There is one positive and six negative. Just like in the Decalogue, you've got more things that we shouldn't do than we should do. It's the same in the Seven Laws of Noah. The thing that we should do: "Establish courts of law in your communities." Every society needs to be a lawful society, where people know what the laws are and there is some kind of mechanism to hold people accountable for violating the laws.

Now we have six negative commandments. "Do not commit blasphemy toward the LORD." That's what you shouldn't do toward the real God. But you also shouldn't worship "false gods or idols." So, there are two ritual laws in the Seven Laws of Noah: Don't blaspheme the LORD, and don't commit idolatry.

"Do not commit incest or adultery." That is number four. "Do not murder." "Do not steal." "Do not eat the limb from a live animal; do not rip the limb from a live animal." In other words, cruelty to animals is also a part of the Seven Laws of Noah, which some people like to think of as Judaism's version of natural law. This is what you would think of if you didn't have any kind of revealed religion. I'm not so sure, because the laws about blasphemy and idolatry, I'm not sure that a rational person would come up with those on his own.

But, in any case, according to the Talmud, according to the Rabbis, that's what a non-Jew needs to do in order to be considered righteous and achieve salvation in the world to come; to achieve a portion of the world to come; to make it to life in the next phase. That's part of the reason why Judaism isn't a proselytizing religion because there is nothing that you get out of becoming Jewish, except more responsibility. But, both Jews and non-Jews have the capability of making it into the world to come. The Jews have 613 commandments, although now that the Temple isn't around, there are fewer. (Thank goodness, I say in parentheses.) And the gentiles have seven: the Seven Laws of Noah.

But the question became (in the Middle Ages, when Jews and Christians started living in close proximity to each other—in France, in particular): Is the Christian claim of the divinity of Jesus (that Jesus is God)—is that idolatrous? Because if it is, then the Christians are idolaters, and there is a whole series of laws that go into effect in order to separate the Jews from the Christians, because the Mishnah has a whole tractate called "Idol Worship"—*avodah zarah*, which talks about the relationships between the Jews and the pagan Romans, who were the idolaters of the Mishnaic period. The idolaters of the Mishnaic period, at least as presented in Rabbinic literature—they weren't just worshipping other gods; they were immoral. They engaged in sexual practices that the Rabbis considered immoral, and they engaged in ritual sacrifices of human beings, which the Rabbis considered immoral. So, in order to separate the two communities, the Rabbis said, "You can't do any business with idolaters three days before or three days after the days that they have their holy days or their sacrifices because you don't want to be financing them for doing immoral things." So, if you now transfer that to medieval France—that would mean that the Jews could never do business with the Christians because three days before and three days after their Sabbath—that's the entire week. So, there were economic implications to how the Christians should be viewed.

That is perhaps a cynical explanation. A less cynical explanation is that as a result of rubbing elbows with Christians, the Jews saw a different kind of religious practice. There is nothing intrinsically, inherently immoral about Christianity. They have a different way of relating to their God, of offering prayer, and understanding the triune nature of God. But it is not necessarily immoral in the way that the Roman pagans were necessarily immoral in the Rabbinic eyes.

This is also a very interesting case study of comparative religious sociology. In the Muslim world, where you don't have too many Christians (I'm talking about North Africa and the Middle East), for the Muslims, Christianity is idolatry. *Shirk* is what the Muslims called that kind of association, and it is the cardinal sin. Associating anything with Allah is a terrible transgression for the Muslims. In the Jewish communities in Muslim lands, they similarly agreed with the Muslims that what Christianity was all about, or what was involved with Christianity, was idolatry. And they didn't have any sociological need to see Christians as anything other than idolaters because it didn't affect their economic life. So, for Maimonides and the Jewish community in the Sephardic world, in North Africa and the Middle East (in the Muslim world), they continued to see the Christian community as idolaters, even though, in Maimonides's code—the *Mishneh Torah* that he wrote in 1180—he acknowledges that the Christians have also helped to extend the morals and the virtues that are presented in the Hebrew Bible all across the world. So, he recognizes and appreciates the contributions to world morality that Christians have engaged in. But, nevertheless, their understanding of Jesus as "fully human and fully God" for Maimonides and the rest of the Muslim world, is idolatry.

Not so, not so for the Jews in Ashkenaz (the Ashkenazi Jews). They had good economic reasons as well as sociological reasons to reinterpret what idolatry was. And so, in the 12th century, Rabbi

Isaac made the distinction that the Christian association (or *shituf*) of Jesus with God is not prohibited for gentiles who follow the Noahide laws. It is not flat-out idolatry. It is associating something with God. Again, is it because the Jews saw that the Christians weren't immoral idolaters? Or, having a more cynical reading, is it because of the economic implications of considering French Catholics, the whole French world, the whole Ashkenazi world from France and Germany, to be idolaters, and therefore there wouldn't be any business or commercial interactions between the Jewish community and that idolatrous community?

So, we already have in the 12th century a statement that Christianity is not idolatrous because of their association of Jesus with God. But, even more, in the early 14th century, we have Rabbi Menachem Ha-Me'iri of Provence (in what is today France); he argued that Christians were a "people restricted by ways of religion," unlike the pagans and idolaters described in the Talmud. So, it's not only that what the Christians were doing with the Trinity wasn't technically idolatry as the Talmud had defined it, it was association—something different. But, the Christian people—they've got a good religion. They are restricted by morals. It is even more than saying that it's not idolatrous. There is a positive statement that comes from the Rabbinic establishment in the 14th century, toward Christians.

What are they saying? From the Jewish perspective, Christians are mistaken about certain theological issues regarding Jesus and the unity of God. It's an intellectual mistake. It's an intellectual mistake, but it is not a moral failing. Just like Rabbi Akiva and Ben Azzai can disagree, and Maimonides and Nachmanides can disagree, the Jews were willing to extend that same generosity to Christians. "Okay. We have an intellectual disagreement about the nature of God—whether God is one or whether God is triune. But as long as the 'cash value' of that difference doesn't come out to acts of immorality, you know what? We are very willing, if not happy, to live in your midst because Christianity is a religion that is constrained by morals and morality."

In the modern period, I want to talk about a few developments in Jewish-Christian relations. Let's start with Catholicism and Judaism. The Second Vatican Council, which ran from 1962 to 1965, recognizes that God's covenant with the Jewish people remains intact. Traditionally, we have an Old Testament and a New

Testament. Now the Catholics are more sensitive about their vocabulary, about their terminology of the books as well, because they have come to understand that God's covenant with the Jews didn't expire when Jesus came onto the scene to offer a new covenant. Now there are two covenants; it's not that one has stopped and the other one has picked up, but Judaism continues to be a living relationship with God, between God and the Jewish people, and Christianity is another expression of that relationship between God and the Jewish people—and here it is a very nice metaphorical parallel. We talked about how, in the Hebrew Bible, a man can marry multiple women, and we also talked about how the relationship between God and the Jewish people is compared to a wedding. So, just like a man can have multiple wives, God can have multiple relationships and multiple covenants with different people. That seems to be the new model that's emerging between Jews and Christians.

Furthermore, the church in the Second Vatican Council repudiated anti-Semitism and the charge that the Jews were collectively responsible for the crucifixion of Jesus. So, since the covenant between God and the Jews is intact, there's no need for Jews to convert to Christianity to achieve salvation. This had long been a historical sore point for Jews because, historically, the Christian community has forced—or tried to force or persuade—Jews to convert. I will tell you that as a result of living for three years in Nashville, I have been the object of proselytizing activity, and it's uncomfortable, although I appreciate the motive: to save my eternal soul—I do appreciate that. On a personal level, it strikes me as obnoxious that someone thinks that I need to be saved—that my religion and that my relationship with God isn't sufficient for that end.

Beyond the Catholic world, there have also been major efforts at promoting a Jewish-Christian dialogue. A recent statement by the Christian Scholars Group on Christian-Jewish Relations offers the following points:

- "God's covenant with the Jewish people endures forever."

- "Jesus lived and died as a faithful Jew." (That's something that, historically, was not well recognized, and it is very much recognized now within many church communities.)

- "Ancient rivalries must not define contemporary relations." (It is true, and we should not try to sweep under the rug that relations between Christians and Jews have, historically, been filled with bloodshed and animosity. We can recognize that but not let it determine our future relationship.)

- "Judaism is a living faith, enriched by many centuries of development." (This is a surprising point that needs to be made. It is surprising that this point needs to be made. But many Christians have the understanding that Judaism was synonymous with the religion of the Old Testament. And there wasn't a sensitivity—just like the New Testament came after the Old Testament, or after the Hebrew Bible, Rabbinic Judaism also has a more progressive and modern [relatively speaking] understanding, that just like Christianity continued to develop, so too did Rabbinic Judaism.)

- Furthermore, the fifth point in this statement by the Christian Scholars Group on Christian-Jewish Relations is that "Christians should not target Jews for conversion."

- They also affirm the importance of the Land of Israel for the life of the Jewish people.

- Finally, "Christians should work with Jews for the healing of the world."

I don't want to leave people with the impression that all of the activity in the modern period has been from Christianity to Judaism. There have also been some Jewish statements recently of accommodation and rapprochement between the Jewish community and the Christians. Especially since the Shoah (the Holocaust), Jews have struggled to redefine their relationship with Christians.

On the level of co-operation with Christian groups concerning social and political issues—issues of social justice—there has been widespread participation throughout the mainstream Jewish community. I should emphasize that I think that Reform Judaism has done the best job of partnering with Christian churches and congregations in order to promote deeds of social justice. Reconstructionist Judaism is also aggressive in that direction; less so, but somewhat, the Conservative movement, and more so recently. They have tried to get together in interfaith groups in order to build ramps for disabled people who need ramps in order to be able to go into buildings, and other such issues of social justice. The Orthodox, I believe, have been the slowest in coming on board to this idea of Jewish-Christian co-operation on issues of social justice, but there is no official, explicit Orthodox resistance to that. It's just that, on the Orthodox agenda, there are other things that take priority.

But there is official resistance to interfaith dialogue. So, we need to make the distinction between Jewish-Christian dialogue and Jewish-Christian co-operation on issues of social justice. Many in the Jewish community—and not just in the Orthodox world—are, in my opinion, justifiably suspicious that part of what is going on in the motivation for Christians to engage in Jewish-Christian dialogue or interfaith dialogue, is a conversionary motive. So, there is a certain reluctance to engage in interfaith dialogue.

Within the Orthodox community, I think that suspicion and resistance is perhaps most pronounced, but you've got a leader of the Modern Orthodox world, Rabbi Joseph Soloveitchik, who has the following to say, "Each religious community is endowed with intrinsic dignity and metaphysical worth."

What he means by that is that we really don't have anything to talk about. I can read about what you believe, and you can read about what I believe, but to try to change our faiths in any significant or substantive way as a result of a dialogue, diminishes or depreciates the intrinsic dignity and metaphysical worth of our religions. We don't want to say that Christianity is metaphysically unworthy, or doesn't have intrinsic dignity. Please don't say that about Judaism. Let's continue to develop our own religions, but not necessarily in co-operation. We have our own irreconcilable understandings of the way that God requires us to be in this world. So, even though there is a conservative (with a small "c") reluctance to engage in interfaith dialogue, it doesn't also amount to a condemnation of Christianity in any way.

Other Jews, including some Orthodox, are willing to engage in inter-religious dialogue. *Dabru Emet* is a recent statement by Jews on Christians and Christianity. They say the following:

"Jews and Christians worship the same God." (That is an important point, and recently Muslims have also made that point. The Jews, and Christians, and Muslims—we all worship the same God. So, that's a good place to start from in any kind of interfaith dialogue. We might express our worship differently, and we might disagree intellectually with how one another worships that God, but at least if we can start from the common ground of worshipping the same God, that's already a huge step.)

Number two: "Jews and Christians accept the moral principles of Torah." (That's phrased very delicately. It's not that the moral laws are obligatory. We accept the moral principles of the Torah—both Jews and Christians. "Love your neighbor as yourself." All of those wonderful moral maxims of *Leviticus* 19, for instance: not cursing the deaf; not placing a stumblingblock before the blind. We want to emphasize what we have in common without ignoring or without minimizing what separates the Jews from Christians, or Judaism from Christianity.)

Number three in this statement by Jews (*Dabru Emet*): "The humanly irreconcilable difference between Jews and Christians will not be settled until God redeems the entire world as promised in Scripture." (That's something that Jews and Christians can agree about. There is going to be redemption. Whether it's going to be redemption number one or Jesus's Second Coming is something that we won't know until it happens, and then we can point fingers and say, "Ah, I was right. You were wrong," or "You were right. I was wrong,"—however it goes. But we both agree that redemption is coming, so let's focus on working toward redemption.)

And the fourth point is: "A new relationship between Jews and Christians will not weaken Jewish practice." (This addresses the Jewish concern, the Jewish suspicion, that there is some kind of proselytizing motive in any interfaith dialogue. No. Not at all. It shouldn't diminish our commitment to the Judaism as we understand it should be practiced, whether that's in the Orthodox variety, or Conservative, or Reconstructionist, or Reform.

That third point—that we look forward to redemption—that really feeds into the whole program of working together toward redemption, which grows out of this interfaith dialogue.

Okay. Our next and final lecture will take us from Jewish perceptions of the "other" to Jewish perceptions of ourselves. Are Jews the Chosen People?

Lecture Twenty-Four
The Chosen People?

Scope:

The claim of being chosen by God has been both a source of pride and puzzlement. The Talmud records many Rabbis who expressed discomfort with the idea, although it became canonized in the liturgy. In the mystical streams of medieval Judaism, chosenness takes on something of a racial cast. The philosophical tradition, on the other hand, avoids any such understandings of chosenness by turning the idea on its head—the Jews chose God. In the modern period, Reconstructionism does away with the status altogether. But it is more characteristic of Judaism to reinterpret than to reject; thus, we will look at some modern interpretations of this ancient claim.

Outline

I. Biblical foundations for the relationship.

    A. "For you are a people consecrated to the Lord your God: of all the peoples on earth the Lord your God chose you to be his treasured people" (Deut. 7:6).

    B. "Now then, if you will obey Me faithfully and keep My covenant, you shall be my treasured possession among all the peoples" (Exod. 19:5).

        1. The word *segulah* designates the special treasure of the king. Jewish commentaries vacillate between emphasizing its aspect as superior versus its aspect as unique.

        2. Is the status conditional upon performance of the commandments or permanent?

    C. "You alone have I singled out of all the families of the earth—That is why I will call you to account for all your iniquities" (Amos 3:2).

    D. "To Me, O Israelites, you are just like the Ethiopians—declares the Lord. True, I brought Israel up from the land of Egypt, But also the Philistines from Caphtor and the Arameans from Kir" (Amos 9:7).

        1. In the TaNaKH, a man can have multiple wives, but a woman can have only one husband.

2. There is a parallel with God. Israel, symbolizing the female, can only have a relationship with the Lord. But the Lord can enjoy relationships with many peoples.

3. The metaphor of marriage to describe the relationship between Israel and God is highlighted in the prophetic book of Hosea. These verses are said by those who wrap *tefillin* (phylacteries) daily, as well as under the *chuppah* (wedding canopy) at the time of marriage: "And I will espouse you forever: I will espouse you with righteousness and justice, and with goodness and mercy, and I will espouse you with faithfulness" (Hosea 2:21–2).

II. Rabbinic discomfort with chosenness despite its canonization in the liturgy.

A. God offered the Torah to many other nations whom, upon inquiring of the contents, decided to forego the relationship with God and not commit themselves to such a restrictive lifestyle. When, finally, God scraped the bottom of the barrel and offered the Torah to the Israelites, they immediately accepted without even asking about the contents (see Sifre Dt. 343).

B. "Every single utterance that went forth from God was split up into 70 languages" (b. Shabbat 88b).

1. Israel was not God's first choice.

2. Revelation is universal and all have the potential to translate God's message into their own language or form of expression.

III. Medieval racialism and rationalism.

A. The biblical language of treasure and the Rabbinic endorsement of the idea of God having chosen the Jews led some medievals of a mystical bent to assume that there was something essentially different about Jews than non-Jews (see also Ezra 9:2).

1. Yehuda HaLevi was the first to articulate this in his 12th-century book *Kuzari*.

   a. For HaLevi, only Jews could be prophets.

   b. Also, there was something essentially superior about the Land of Israel compared to all other lands. Thus,

Israel and Israelites were on the top of the holiness hierarchy.

2. The *Zohar*, in the 13th century, develops the idea that Jews and non-Jews have different souls.

3. In the mystical stream of Judaism, there are still sects, such as Lubavitch/HaBaD, which adhere to an essential difference between Jewish and non-Jewish souls.

B. Moses Maimonides inverts election.

    1. Maimonides turns Abraham into a philosopher who recognized by himself that the one true God is responsible for the motion of the celestial sphere.

    2. When he began spreading the word that idolatry was false, he aroused the ire of the king of the Ur of the Chaldees, who sought to kill him.

    3. He fled to Haran. "He then began to proclaim to the whole world with great power and to instruct the people that the entire universe had but one creator and that it was right to worship Him. He went from city to city and from kingdom to kingdom, calling and gathering together the inhabitants of the world until he arrived in the land of Canaan" (Maimonides, *Laws of Idolatry*, 1:3).

        a. In Genesis 12:1, God calls out to Abram and tells him to leave his home.

        b. In Maimonides's account, Abram flees Ur and ends up in Canaan, not because of a divine call, but because Abram exercises his intellect, sees the philosophical errors of his countrymen, and strives to enlighten them.

IV. Modern expressions of chosenness.

    A. The Reform Movement, as we have seen, emphasizes the notion of mission found in Isaiah.

    B. The Ultra-Orthodox emphasize a division of labor whereby Jews were chosen for a life of mitzvot and Torah study. But the contributions of Gentiles to worldly affairs, science, and technology are no less important.

    C. "The people of Israel were not the chosen people but were commanded to be the chosen people. … The Jewish people had no intrinsic uniqueness. Its uniqueness rather consists in the demand laid on it. The people may or may not heed this demand. Therefore its fate is not guaranteed" (Yeshayahu Leibowitz).

    1. Leibowitz, like Maimonides and the rationalist school, eschews any hint of racialism.

    2. He emphasizes both the idea of duty and the idea that the relationship is contingent upon Israel fulfilling its duty, which Leibowitz understands to be the mitzvot.

V. Mordecai Kaplan and the rejection of chosenness.

    A. On the theological level, how can God chose anyone? We moderns no longer believe in a God who acts like a glorified human being.

    B. On a psychological level, for Jews to consider themselves chosen might induce a certain smugness and complacency. Moreover, the need to have asserted such a claim in the first place smacks of an inferiority complex that should be overcome in modernity.

    C. On a sociological level, such a claim may foster resentment and antisemitism.

    D. Finally, the idea of a chosen people is anti-democratic. It's just not fair to the others who were not chosen.

VI. "Have we not all one Father? Did not one God create us? Why do we break faith with one another, profaning the covenant of our ancestors?" (Malachi 2:10).

VII. "The Lord spoke those words—those and no more" (Deut. 5:19).

    A. "The Lord spoke those words and did not stop" (b. Sann. 17a and RaSHI).

    B. Rabbi Menachem Mendel of Kotsk (1787–1819) said, "The giving of the Torah took place at Shavuot; but the receiving of the Torah takes place every day. The giving of the Torah was the same for everyone; but the receiving of the Torah is different for everyone according to his capacity."

Essential Reading:

Atlan, "Chosen People," in *Contemporary Jewish Religious Thought*, pp. 55–59.

Kaplan, *Dynamic Judaism*, pp. 189–196.

Leibowitz, *Judaism, Human Values, and the Jewish State*, chapter 7 and pp. 120–122.

Silber, "Invention of a Tradition," in *The Uses of Tradition*, pp. 62–66.

Supplementary Reading:

Eisen, *The Chosen People in America*.

Ha-Levi, *Kuzari*.

Maimonides, *Mishneh Torah, Laws of Idolatry*, chapter 1.

Questions to Consider:

1. Should the ambiguities in the biblical verses about chosenness be harmonized or explained as different voices representing different theological visions?

2. Given that the Rabbis incorporated the notion of chosenness into the liturgy for Sabbath and holidays, why would any Rabbis have expressed discomfort with the idea?

3. We have seen examples of selecting, interpreting, and repudiating a central religious idea within Judaism. Are there any religious ideas for which these strategies are inapplicable?

4. What about for other religions? Are there some religious tenets that are so central that they must be preserved precisely as they appear in the original texts? What if there are inconsistencies, as there are with chosenness and as we have with certain details in the four Gospels, which require selection or emphasis?

The Chosen People?

In the early part of the 20th century, a British wag named William Norman Ewer said the following:

> How odd of God
> To choose the Jews.

We're going to be exploring that idea in this final lecture and offering several retorts to Mr. Ewer. So, as is our custom, let us begin with some biblical verses that get at this idea.

Deuteronomy 7:6 says:

> For you are a people consecrated to the Lord your God: of all the peoples on earth the LORD your God chose you to be his treasured people.

Seems pretty clear. Of all the people on the earth, God chose the Jews to be his treasured people. Now let's take a look at another verse, this time from the book of *Exodus* 19:5:

> Now then, if you will obey Me faithfully and keep My covenant, you shall be my treasured possession among all the peoples.

The word in question in these two verses is the Hebrew word *segulah*, which designates the special treasure, or the special property, of the King. Jewish commentaries on these verses vacillate between emphasizing that word's aspect as "superior" (because it's the King's treasure) versus its aspect as unique (it's not anyone else's treasure; it's just the King's treasure). And that really gives you the groundwork for understanding some of the tension in this word segulah and the idea of the Chosen People. Does it mean that the Jews are superior as the Chosen People? Or are they just unique, and separate, and special as a result of being differentiated from all other peoples?

Also, as I emphasized in that verse from *Exodus*, is the status conditional upon performance of the commandments, or is it a permanent status?

Let's take a look at another verse, this time not from the Pentateuch, but from the Prophets—from the prophet Amos:

> You alone have I singled out of all the families of the earth—That is why I will call you to account for all your iniquities.

Ah! So that explains it. That explains why Jews have received more than their fair share of punishment. It's because we are in this special relationship to God. "You alone have I singled out of all the families of the earth." So, it is not a relationship that bequeaths upon the Jews (according to this verse in *Amos*) any particular merit or any advantage. On the contrary, this explains why the Jews have been punished for their transgressions more than other nations have been punished for their transgressions. It sets up a kind of double standard. I should point out that this is a double standard that God can apply, as opposed to CNN applying a double standard to the behavior of the Jews or Israel. But there is another verse in *Amos* that gives us a little tension here, and that is in *Amos* 9:7:

> To Me, O Israelites, you are just like the Ethiopians—declares the LORD. True, I brought Israel up from the land of Egypt, but also the Philistines from Caphtor and the Arameans from Kir.

So, in the same book, six chapters later, *Amos* says that, in God's eyes, Israel is just like everybody else. So, within the Hebrew Bible itself, we've got different understandings of what it means to be the Chosen People, and even whether or not Israel has this kind of unique designation.

We have talked before about the metaphor of marriage corresponding to the relationship between God and the Jewish people, and the corollary that just like a man can have multiple wives, God, similarly (as *Amos* says), has multiple relationships with the different nations. In one of the other prophetic books, the book of *Hosea*, that marriage metaphor is highlighted. There are some verses from the book of *Hosea* that are repeated daily by traditional men (and now some traditional women as well) who wrap *tefillin* (the phylacteries that traditional Jews place on their foreheads and on their bicep), and in the process of wrapping them around (you wrap the leather cord seven times around your forearm), and you recite the following verses from *Hosea*:

And I will espouse you forever: I will espouse you with righteousness and justice, and with goodness and mercy, and I will espouse you with faithfulness.

And what's so interesting about this is that if you think of the etymology of the word "religion," it means, "to bind again." That root "lig" like "ligament" is something that binds bone to cartilage. So, as we are binding ourselves with tefillin, it is a ritual act that concretizes the etymology of the word "religion." We are binding ourselves to God every day, in this act of love, by saying these words of love that are then repeated by the groom at the moment of his wedding underneath the chupah, underneath the marriage canopy. So, we leave the biblical world with an understanding that there is this sacred relationship; there is this special relationship between God and the Jewish people. We are the *am segulah*—the treasured people, the Chosen People, but does that mean that we are special and different? Or does that mean that we are superior?

When we move into the Rabbinic period, what needs to be said immediately is that the concept of the Chosen People was adopted by the Rabbis and canonized within the liturgy, so that on every Shabbat and for every holiday, the Jews say to themselves that we are the Chosen People. How they understand what it means to be the Chosen People is up for interpretation—but the idea of the Jews being the Chosen People is canonized by the Rabbis in their liturgy.

Nevertheless, there were some Rabbis who were uncomfortable with the idea, and we have a few Rabbinic statements that display that discomfort. One of my favorite pieces of aggadah is the following. We have the image of God coming to one of the ancient peoples, let's say the Moabites, and God says, "Hey, You Moabites! You guys interested in my book, the Torah?" And the Moabites say, "Well, I don't know. Tell me about it. What's in your book, the Torah?" And God says, "Well, among other things it says, 'Do not murder.'" And the Moabites say, "Whoa, whoa, whoa! We're not going to sign on to 'Do not murder.' We're all about murder. We love to murder. We are a bloodthirsty people. Sorry. Go shop your Torah someplace else." So God goes, "Okay." So he walks around to another ancient Near Eastern group, say the Perizzites. And the Perizzites say, similarly, "Tell me what's in your Torah." And God says, "Well, amongst other things, it says, 'Do not commit adultery.'" And the Perizzites say, "Sorry, that's not for us. We love to commit adultery. Adultery is what we live for. Try shopping your Torah someplace else." And the aggadah has God trying to get all these other ancient Near Eastern nations to agree to accept the Torah, and for one reason or another, all of these ancient Near Eastern nations say, "No thank you. It's not for us. We don't want those kinds of laws." Finally, the aggadah says that God comes to the Israelites. He's scraping the bottom of the barrel. It's his last choice. God goes to the Israelites and says, "Would you like my Torah?" And the Israelites respond, "We will do and then we will understand." *Na'aseh v'nishmah* They don't ask any questions about what is in it. They just say, "Yes."

Another piece of Rabbinic aggadah, from the Talmud, this time, "Every single utterance that went forth from God was split up into 70 languages."

Let me say it again, "Every single utterance that went forth from God was split up into 70 languages."

This means at Mount Sinai when God revealed God's will to the Jewish people, it wasn't only to the Jewish people—but everyone heard, all over the world, in their own language. Seventy is the Rabbinic way of saying "universal." So, all the 70 nations of the world heard it in their own language. So, when I first saw this piece of aggadah, I thought of an episode from *Star Trek*, where the *USS Enterprise* had ventured into this area where there was a higher intelligence, and there was a message given by this form of higher intelligence, this higher being. And I heard it as well as Captain Kirk heard it, in English, but Mr. Spock heard it in Vulcan, and Chekov heard it in Russian, and Lieutenant Uhura heard it in Swahili—and we finally figure out that this intelligence is speaking in a way that everyone can understand.

What do these two pieces of Rabbinic lore tell us? That the Rabbis were uncomfortable with being selected, so they created the first piece of aggadah to say that the Israelites were the last ones that God wanted to give the Torah to, but, nevertheless, we were the only ones that accepted the Torah.

Then, the second aggadah about every single utterance that went forth from God was split up into 70 languages, is a very universalistic teaching that God's message is available and is accessible to everyone in their own language or form of expression. I don't think that we need to read the word "language" there literally, as Hebrew, Spanish, French, or English. It can also be the person's mother tongue, the person's language—their form of expression.

So, although the idea of the Chosen People was canonized by the Rabbis, there are many *aggadot* (the plural of aggadah) that reflect a kind of discomfort that somehow the Jews were chosen for this, separate from other people.

Let's now move into the Middle Ages and see how this idea of the Chosen People unfolds. The Biblical language of segulah (of treasure) and the Rabbinic endorsement of the idea of God having chosen the Jews led some medievals (particularly those of a mystical bent) to assume that there was something essentially different about Jews than non-Jews—that there was something ontologically superior. "Ontologically" means "in our very essence as human beings."

This goes back to a description of Jews that we find in *Ezra*, chapter nine. Somehow the Jews contain *zerah kadosh* (a holy seed), and this distinguishes us in essence (intrinsically) from non-Jews. This is something of a racialist description of the Jewish people, and it explains—or the medievals use this idea of a *zerah kadosh* (a holy seed) to explain to themselves—either why God chose the Jews, or, as a result of having been chosen, the Jews were endowed with a kind of superior DNA—so that, in our *kishkas*, in our guts, Jews were different than others.

Yehuda HaLevi (whose poem I read several lectures ago) was the first to articulate this idea in his 12th-century book, the *Kuzari*. For Ha-Levi, only Jews could be prophets. Also, there was something essentially superior about the Land of Israel compared to other lands. Yehuda Ha-Levi was a Neo-Platonist, and if we remember part of what Neo-Platonism is about, there are these different levels. So, in this hierarchy of different levels, Israel and the Israelites were on the top of the holiness hierarchy.

Generations later, in the *Zohar*, in the 13th century (also from Spain), develops the idea that Jews and non-Jews have different souls. So, within the mystical stream of Judaism there developed this idea that a Jewish soul was more than—and superior to—a non-Jewish soul. It is repugnant for me to say, but, nevertheless, it is part of the Jewish tradition, and I think it needs to be exposed for what it is. Also, I feel committed to exposing it for what it is because there are Jews today who belong to the mystical trends within Judaism (I'm thinking here particularly of Chabad) who still adhere to this idea that there is some kind of essential difference between Jewish and non-Jewish souls.

Let's now leave the mystical world and come to the rationalist, Aritsotelian/Maimonidean world, to see what Maimonides does with this idea of the Chosen People. In the Mishneh Torah, in Maimonides's law code, he describes the process by which Abraham comes to the understanding that there is only one God in the world. Maimonides turns Abraham into a philosopher who recognized, by himself, that the one true God is responsible for the motion of the celestial sphere, and that we shouldn't be engaged in astrological practices, and worshipping the stars, and the moon, and the sun— but, that there is just one God who is in charge of all the celestial rotations.

When Abraham began spreading the word that idolatry was false, he aroused the ire of the King of the Ur of the Chaldees (according to Maimonides), and the king sought to kill him. Why? Because Abraham was upsetting the political/economic order. He was getting people up in arms. So, Maimonides imagines that the king wanted him killed, rather than to disturb the peace. So, what does Maimonides have Abraham do? Abraham flees to Haran. Now I'm quoting Maimonides:

> He [Abraham] then began to proclaim to the whole world with great power and to instruct the people that the entire universe had but one creator and that it was right to worship Him. He went from city to city and from kingdom to kingdom, calling and gathering together the inhabitants of the world till he arrived in the land of Canaan.

For those of you who have *Genesis*, chapter 12, verse 1, memorized, you'll start scratching your head because that's not what *Genesis* 12:1 says. *Genesis* 12:1 says that God called out to Abraham (to Avram; this was before his name change) and tells him to leave his home, and that Abraham moves from Ur of the Chaldees to the land of Canaan at God's initiative.

But what does Maimonides do? Maimonides reverses it. Maimonides has Abraham leaving Ur of the Chaldees and going to Canaan of his own initiative. Why? Because he has figured out—because he is a philosopher, like Maimonides. For Maimonides, by the way, all of the Jewish prophets are philosophers. They are necessarily philosophers, and Abraham is no exception. He is the first philosopher to figure out the errors of his countrymen through the use of his intellect, and he strives to enlighten them by spreading the word, by spreading the good news.

So, here we have one response to our British wag, Mr. Ewer. This is not my own creation. This is out and about in the world.

> Not news.
> Not odd.
> The Jews chose God.

In other words, it wasn't God choosing the Jews, it was the Jews choosing God. Here, Maimonides represents Abraham figuring this out on his own.

As we move into the modern period, we have already seen certain reinterpretations of this idea of chosenness. The Reform movement emphasizes the notion of mission found in *Isaiah*, that the Jews should be a "light unto the nations," that we should spread the truths of ethical monotheism, without having to proselytize, but by just being role models; that was the Reform response, or reinterpretation of what it means to be the Chosen People. But, Reform Judaism kept that language. They still understand that they are the Chosen People, and for the Sabbath and the holidays, the idea of being the Chosen People is rehearsed in the liturgy.

The Ultra-Orthodox also keep the idea of being the Chosen People, but they understand it; they interpret it in the modern era slightly differently—very differently—than we have seen in the past. They emphasize a division of labor whereby it is true that the Jews were the Chosen People, but they were chosen to serve God through the study of Torah, while the gentiles were also chosen, but not to serve God through the study of Torah, but to engage in worldly affairs, and science, and technology. As we saw when we discussed the Ultra-Orthodox, those endeavors of the gentiles are no less worthwhile than studying Torah, but the Ultra-Orthodox emphasize the distinction aspect of am segulah, that, "Yeah, the Jews were chosen for this; the gentiles were chosen for that; but, no value distinctions are placed upon those."

There is an Israeli gadfly (he passed away about 10 years ago) by the name of Yeshayahu Leibowitz. He was known as a very controversial figure in the State of Israel. Immediately after the 6-Day War, when Israel acquired the Holy City of Jerusalem and the West Bank of the Jordan River, Leibowitz went on record as saying, "We need to give that land back immediately, with all the Palestinians. It will be an albatross around our neck if we don't separate ourselves from those people immediately." It turned out that he was something of a prophet, but the way in which he said it aroused the ire of many Israelis.

He had this to say about the notion of the Chosen People, also picking up on an element of its biblical formulation that, up until this point in Jewish history, had lain dormant.

> The people of Israel were not the chosen people but were commanded to be the chosen people. … The Jewish people has no intrinsic uniqueness. Its uniqueness rather consists in the demand laid on it. The people may or may not heed this demand. Therefore its fate is not guaranteed.

Yeshayahu Leibowitz, like Maimonides (who was his hero within the world of Judaism) and the entire rationalist school, eschews any hint of racialism. Indeed, the idea of being the Chosen People is not a *fait accompli*; the Jews have to earn it. It goes back to that verse in *Exodus* where "if you obey my commandments, then you will be a chosen people." This is a charge for the Jewish people to behave in a righteous way, and Yeshayahu Leibowitz was constantly prodding and poking the Jews to improve their behavior. For Leibowitz, what it meant to be part of the Chosen People, or to have earned that designation, was to fulfill the commandments.

There is another aspect of the interpretation in the modern period of the Chosen People that we must discuss. That is the rejection or repudiation of chosenness by Mordecai Kaplan and the Reconstructionist movement. If, today, you were to open up a Reconstructionist prayer book, you would not find any reference to the Jews being the Chosen People. What they have done is inserted other words where "chosen people" appears in a traditional prayer book, in order to maintain a traditional rhythm, so that you can still sing it to the same tune, as it were. But Mordecai Kaplan was very invested in having the liturgy accurately—and with intellectual honesty—reflect his ideology. So, those parts of the traditional liturgy that no longer make sense (like the resurrection of the dead, for instance)—Reform Judaism got rid of that, and Reconstructionist Judaism got rid of that idea of the resurrection of the dead; that didn't seem to be anything that a modern, rational person could agree to anymore. While Reform just reinterpreted the idea of the Chosen People, Mordecai Kaplan and the Reconstructionist movement rejected it altogether. And Kaplan had four reasons for rejecting it.

On the theological level, how can God chose anyone? We moderns no longer believe in a God who acts like a glorified human being and can select one over something else. So, Kaplan didn't believe that on a theological level the idea of a Chosen People made any sense. (Nor, I will add, did Baruch Spinoza. Kaplan wasn't the first person to raise this question.)

Two: On a psychological level, for Jews to consider themselves chosen might induce a certain smugness, complacency, or arrogance, and the need to have asserted such a claim in the first place smacks of an inferiority complex (according to Kaplan) that should be overcome in modernity. Why would you need to say that God chose us over all the other people unless you're feeling like, "God chose everybody else, and what about us?" So, you make the opposite claim to compensate for your ego deficiency. Kaplan said that, in the modern world we no longer need to have that kind of complex, although he understood how it could have come about sociologically and historically, especially once the Jews were exiled by the Romans, and the emphasis on Jews being the Chosen People compensates for them no longer having a homeland and no longer having a Temple in which they would conduct their worship services.

One final response to our British wag, Mr. Ewer, comes from Leo Rosten, a Yiddishist, who responds to Ewer. Remember what Ewer said:

> How odd of God
> To choose the Jews.

So Leo Rosten's retort is:

> Not odd of God.
> The *goyim* annoy Him.

Goyim is a Yiddish word that means "gentiles." Actually, in Hebrew, it just means "nations," but in Yiddish it is often a derogatory term used to describe non-Jews, the gentile world. And Leo Rosten's retort to Ewer I think exemplifies exactly what Mordecai Kaplan is talking about. In order for us to feel like we are superior, we create this Chosen People idea, and to justify it, "Well, look how the goyim act. Look at what they have done to the Jews, and look at what they continue to do to themselves." So, psychologically, Kaplan wants to eliminate that element of the Chosen People complex. So, we've got a problem on the theological level. We've got a problem on the psychological level.

Third, there's a problem on the sociological level with the idea of the Chosen People because such a claim may foster resentment and anti-Semitism. And, indeed, throughout history, very often, before Jews have been killed or persecuted, there has been the taunt issued by their tormentors, "Ah, you're the Chosen People? Let me show you what you've been chosen for." So, this claim of being superior also arouses anti-Semitism from non-Jews.

The fourth and final reason that Mordecai Kaplan offers for repudiating the Chosen People idea, rather than reinterpreting it, is that the Chosen People idea is anti-democratic. We are living in a democracy in the United States of America, and it's just not fair to those other peoples who were not chosen. God doesn't act like that on a theological level. On a psychological level it's no good. On a sociological level it's no good. And, finally, it's anti-democratic. Mordecai Kaplan founds the first Judaism that is native to America. Remember, Reform and Conservative Judaism were transplanted from Germany. So, Reconstructionist Judaism is the American Judaism, and, as such, it is democratic—seeing God's image in all of God's creatures, and not singling out the Jewish people for any special treatment or designation.

There is a quote from *Malachi*:

> Have we not all one Father? Did not one God create us? Why do we break faith with one another, profaning the covenant of our ancestors?

I saw this quote when I first went to the Reform Temple in Nashville. They have a mosaic by Ben Shaun, with that verse from *Malachi* underneath it. It emphasizes this idea that we are all God's children, and we should be responding to each other as siblings, and not warring siblings or rival siblings, but recognizing that we all have "one Father." That puts the idea of the Chosen People into a different context—into a different frame.

Let me give you one more Rabbinic quote. There is a verse in *Deuteronomy* 5:19 that says: "The LORD spoke those words. Those and no more."

That's right after the reiteration of the Decalogue (the Ten Commandments). So, it says God spoke those words. Those and no more. The way the Rabbis read that verse—which was later canonized as the normative Jewish understanding by RaSHI, who was the medieval biblical commentator *par excellence*—was to see that verb "and no more," and to re-punctuate the vowels underneath the three consonants (*yodh, sin, pe*) and to read it as: "And the LORD spoke those words and did not stop."

God's word continued to come from God—just the opposite of what the plain sense means, it is true, but without adding any letters or subtracting any letters. Just with reconfiguring the points under the letters (the vowels) the Rabbis came up with this idea that God's revelation never ceases.

A Hassidic Rabbi, Rabbi Menachem Mendel of Kotsk, in the 19th century (in the early 19th century) said:

> The giving of the Torah took place at *Shavuot*. But the receiving of the Torah takes place every day. The giving of the Torah was the same for everyone. But the receiving of the Torah is different for everyone according to his capacity.

The name *Yisrael* means "one who struggles with God." We find that with Jacob struggling with the angel who is representing God. For all of us who claim to be spiritual heirs of Yisrael, we are charged with the struggle of receiving the Torah and responding to it according to our own individual capacity—in our own language and our own form of expression.

The story of Judaism is the story of the struggle to respond appropriately to the gracious love, the harsh justice, and the all-pervading unity to which our lives and this grand universe testify.

The Judaisms we've examined in this course reflect the ongoing struggles of the Jewish people—from their ancient life as a sovereign nation, to the travails of exile; to the opportunities of acculturation in modernity; and finally, to the reestablishment of the State of Israel. Hearing God's words anew—receiving Torah every day—has meant reinterpreting the tradition, creatively rereading the words of the past—whether they relate to core ideas like notions of evil and the Chosen People, or mitzvot such as the prohibition of idolatry, or the laws of marriage and divorce. Even the basis for reinterpreting the tradition, the claim that God's words do not cease, is itself a rereading of Torah.

I'm Shai Cherry. Thank you for joining me in The Teaching Company's *Introduction to Judaism*.

Maps

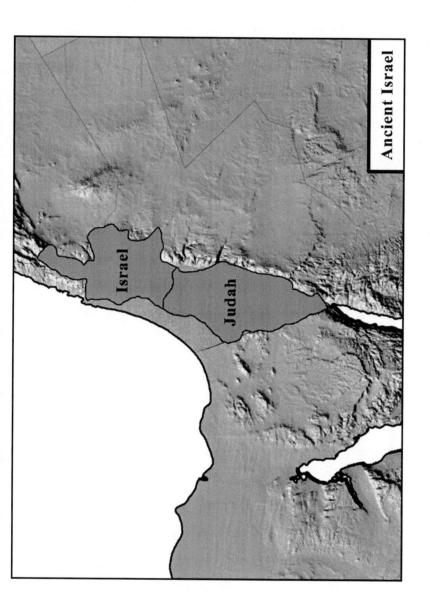

Ancient Israel

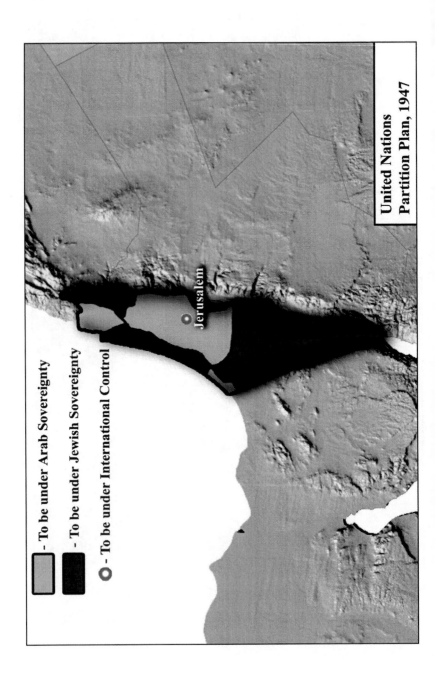

United Nations Partition Plan, 1947

- To be under Arab Sovereignty
- To be under Jewish Sovereignty
- To be under International Control

Jerusalem

©2004 The Teaching Company.

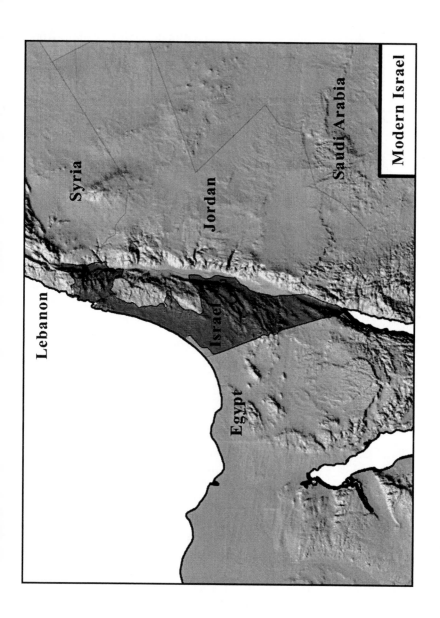

Modern Israel

Timeline

Biblical Period

c. 2000 B.C.E. ....Abraham and Sarah migrating from Ur to Canaan.

c. 1250 ....Moses leads the Israelites from slavery in Egypt.

c. 1200 ....Joshua leads the Israelites in battle against the Canaanites.

1020 ....Saul is anointed the first king of Israel.

1000 ....David becomes the second king of Israel. Jerusalem is capital city.

961 ....Solomon, David's son, builds the Temple in Jerusalem.

922 ....Solomon dies and the kingdom splits: Israel in the north and Judea in the south.

721 ....Assyria destroys Israel and exiles population. Ten Lost Tribes.

597 ....Babylonia conquers Judah.

586 ....Temple is destroyed and Judeans are exiled, en masse, to Babylonia.

539 ....King Cyrus of Persia conquers Babylon.

516 ....Second Temple is dedicated in Jerusalem.

458 ....Ezra leads a group of Jews back to Jerusalem.

Hellenistic Period

333 ....Alexander the Great conquers Judah and brings in Hellenistic culture.

200	Land of Israel passes from the Egyptians to the Syrians.
168–164	Hasmoneans/Maccabees win war against Syrians and Hellenized Jews.
63 B.C.E.	Rome enters Judea.
66 C.E.	Great Revolt against Roman rule.
70	Second Temple is destroyed.
74	Massada.

Rabbinic Period

132–135	Hadrianic persecutions and Bar Kochva Revolt.
c. 220	Redaction of Mishnah by Judah the Patriarch.
313	Emperor Constantine legalizes Christianity.
c. 450	Redaction of Jerusalem Talmud.
c. 550	Redaction of Babylonian Talmud.
7th century	Rise and spread of Islam.

Medieval Period

10th century	Rise of Jewish philosophy.
1180	Maimonides's *Mishneh Torah* (code of law).
1190	Maimonides's *Guide of the Perplexed*.
12th century	Crusades.
12th century	Rise of Jewish mysticism/Kabbalah.
Late 13th century	*Zohar*.
14th century	Rabbi Menachem Ha-Me'iri of Provence writes that Christians are

not to be classified as pagans or idolaters.

1492 ....Christians conquer Spain from Muslims and exile the Jews.

16th century.................................Rise of Lurianic Kabbalah in Tzfat.

Early Modern Period

1654 ....First group of Jews arrives in New Amsterdam.

18th century.................................Rise and spread of Hassidism in Eastern Europe.

1782 ....Edict of Tolerance in Lower Austria.

1789 ....French Revolution.

1790 ....Jews given political rights in France.

19th century.................................Haskalah (Jewish Enlightenment) begins in Western Europe and slowly spreads to Eastern Europe.

1818 ....Hamburg Temple begins reforming its services.

1824 ....A small group petitions for liturgical reforms in Charleston, S.C.

1840 ....Damascus Blood Libel.

Modern Period

1853 ....Rabbi Samson Raphael Hirsch opens up a school in Frankfurt, Germany, that combines Jewish and secular studies.

1873 ....Hebrew Union College (Reform seminary) founded in Cincinnati.

1876 ....Felix Adler founds Ethical Culture Society.

1885 ....Pittsburgh Platform of Reform Judaism.

1886	Jewish Theological Seminary (Conservative) founded in New York City.
1894	Dreyfus affair.
1896	Theodor Herzl writes *The Jewish State*.
1897	First Zionist Congress in Switzerland.
1897	Rabbi Isaac Elkhannan Specktor Yeshiva (Orthodox) founded in New York City.
1917	Balfour Declaration.
1922	League of Nations gives Britain a mandate to establish a national home for the Jewish people in Palestine.
1939	Britain effectively terminates immigration to Palestine on the eve of World War II.
1939–1945	*Shoah*: Six million Jews systematically murdered in Nazi Europe.
1947	United Nations partitions the western portion of Palestine into Arab and Jewish states. Jews reluctantly accept. Arabs reject.
1948	Prime Minister David Ben-Gurion declares the establishment of the State of Israel.
1962–1965	Second Vatican Council.
1967	Six-Day War. Israel acquires the Old City of Jerusalem.
1968	Reconstructionist Rabbinical College founded.

1969 ....Society for Humanistic Judaism organized.

1972 ....Reform ordains first female rabbi.

1975 ....Reconstructionists begin ordaining women.

1985 ....Conservative movement begins ordaining women.

1997 ....A women's *yeshiva* in Jerusalem begins training *halachic* advisors.

Glossary

aggadah: Non-legal material, lit. "telling."

aguna/agunot (lit. "anchored"): Straw widows, women who are incapable of marriage because their husbands refuse to give them a *get*, a writ of divorce.

aliyah (lit. "ascent"): Immigration to Israel.

amidah: Central prayer in Rabbinic prayer service, lit. "standing."

Apocrypha: Such books as First and Second Maccabees were excluded from the TaNaKH, but included in the Christian Bible.

Ashkenazi: Jews from Germany (Ashkenaz) and surrounding European countries, particularly Poland, Ukraine, and Russia. The vast majority of Jews in the United States are of Ashkenazi descent.

Assyrians: Destroyed the northern kingdom of Israel in 721 B.C.E.

avodah: Worship or service.

ba'al teshuvah: Penitent or one who has returned.

Babylonian Talmud (b.): Edited in Babylon around 550.

bal tashchit: Prohibition against wastefulness.

Bar Kochva Revolt: Revolt against Rome from 132–135 C.E.

British Mandate: Established by the League of Nations in 1922 to implement the Balfour Declaration's promise of providing a national home for Jews in Palestine.

Chalutzim: Pioneers who settled the Land of Israel.

chametz: Leaven, forbidden on Pesach.

Channukah: Winter holiday celebrating the military triumph of the Macabbees. Literally, "dedication."

Channukiah: A nine-branched candelabra especially for Channukah.

cheshbon nefesh: Soul-searching.

Chol hamoed: Intermediate days of the week-long festivals of Sukkot and Passover.

chuppah: Wedding canopy.

Conservative Judaism: Begun in 19th-century Germany, but finds greater acceptance among Eastern European immigrants to America. Motto is tradition and change. *Halachah* is binding, though subject to modifications.

ein sof: Without end, infinity. In Kabbalah, the realm of God to which we have no access.

Elul: Babylonian/Hebrew name for the sixth month.

Emancipation: The granting of Jews citizenship and political rights in 19th-century Western Europe.

Essenes: Second Temple sect that was ascetic and apocalyptic. One group lived by the Dead Sea.

Free loan societies: Established in late-19th century to help Eastern European Jews transition to America.

gehena: The Rabbinic name for Hell.

Gemara: The larger part of the Talmud that analyzes the Mishnah and brings related legal and non-legal material. *Gemara* is Aramaic for "learning."

gematria (gamma-tria): Letters corresponding to numbers.

Geonim: Medieval Jewish leaders in Babylonia.

get: A writ of divorce.

gilgul: Rolling over, reincarnation.

G'milut chasadim: Deeds of loving kindness.

Gnosticism: Dualistic theology with gods of good and evil.

Great Revolt: Jewish revolt against Rome, 66–70 C.E.

Hagaddah: The Rabbinic "script" for retelling the Exodus from Egypt.

Halachah: Jewish law, lit. "the way."

haredi: Contemporary term meaning "quaking" to describe all Ultra-Orthodox (Mitnagdim and Hassidic) Jews.

Haskalah: Jewish enlightenment, 19th century, beginning in Western Europe.

Hasmoneans (Maccabees): *Maccabee* means a "hammer," and it is also the first letters of the words: *Mi Kmocha B'elim YHWH*, "Who is like YHWH among the gods" (Exod. 15:11).

hassid: Follower of a *tzaddik*.

Hassidism: Religious renewal movement in 18th-century Eastern Europe emphasizing devotional posture and prayer.

Hebrew Union College: Reform seminary founded in Cincinnati in 1875.

heichalot: Palaces, a genre of mystical literature in the Rabbinic period.

Holocaust: Wholly burnt offering to God (see Lev. 1). See Shoah.

Jerusalem Talmud (y.): Edited in the Land of Israel around 450.

karaites: Medieval heretics who rejected Rabbinic tradition.

kavannah: Intention, consciousness, awareness.

ketubah: Jewish marriage contract, similar to a prenuptial agreement, protecting the wife's interests in the event of divorce or the death of her husband. Often ornately decorated.

kiddush l'vana: Blessing of the waxing moon.

kippa: *Yarmulkah*, skull cap.

kitniot: "Small stuff," such as rice, beans, and peas; Ashkenazi Jews avoid these on Pesach.

LaG b'Omer: The 33rd day of the Omer. Celebrated with bonfires and outdoor activities.

letzaref: To purify, to join.

Maccabees: See Hasmoneans.

Mashiach: "Anointed," Gr. "Christos." A divinely appointed human being who will preside over the ingathering of the exiled Jews and the reestablishment of Jewish political sovereignty in the Land of Israel.

Maskilim: Proponents of the Haskalah.

matzah: Unleavened bread.

menorah: Seven-branched candelabra (Exod. 25:31–40).

menuchah: Tranquility, the special rest that God created on day seven.

merkavah: Chariot, a genre of mystical literature from the Rabbinic period.

mezuzah (pl. ***mezuzot***): Biblical word for doorpost that today refers to the parchment that Jews are commanded to place on their doorposts (see Deut. 6:9).

midrash: An idea linked to a biblical verse, lit. to "seek," "inquire," or "weave."

mishnah (m.): Codex of Jewish law and earliest Rabbinic literature, lit. "learning." Compiled by Judah the Prince, circa 220 C.E.

Mitnagdim: Opponents of Hassidism who stressed centrality of Talmud Torah.

mitzvah (pl. ***mitzvot***): Commandment/s.

Nazarenes: Early followers of Jesus of Nazareth who believed he was the messiah.

Noahide laws: Laws that Rabbis say are incumbent upon Gentiles: establishing courts; not committing murder, idolatry, blasphemy, adultery, or thievery; and not tearing a limb from a living animal.

Olam haba: The coming world. Can either refer to existence after death or this world in the messianic era.

omer: Sheaf of barley; 49-day period between Pesach and Shavuot.

payot (*payos*): Corners, sidelocks.

Peel Commission, 1937: Partitioned Palestine west of the Jordan into Jewish and Arab states. Zionists accepted the partition; Arabs rejected it.

pesach: Pass over or protect/have mercy.

Pharisees: Had an oral tradition to interpret the Torah. They are the spiritual ancestors of the Rabbis.

Ploni Almoni: The Hebrew version of Joe Shmoe, any anonymous person.

Purim: Holiday celebrating the survival of the Jews outside of Israel, lit., "lots."

Reconstructionist Judaism: Views Judaism as a civilization with religion as one component. *Halachah* is not binding, though Reconstructionists tend to be more traditional than Reform Jews.

Reform Judaism: Begun in 19th-century Germany, but flourishes in America. Rejects binding nature of *halachah* and emphasizes individual piety.

Rosh chodesh: New moon, lit., "head of the month."

Rosh Hashanah: Jewish New Year (lit., "Head of the Year"), Tishrei 1.

Sadducees: Second Temple sect that denied oral tradition and, hence, resurrection.

Second Vatican Council (1962–1965): Recognized that God's covenant with the Jewish people remains intact.

seder: "Order," word used to describe the Pesach meal and the retelling of the Exodus. There are two *s'darim* (pl. for *seder*) outside of Israel.

Sefaradim: Jews exiled from Spain (Sefarad) who moved to some European countries, such as Holland and Bulgaria. The term also commonly refers to Jews from North Africa and the Middle East.

Segulah: Royal treasure.

Sfira: A station in the unfolding or emanation of the godhead.

shames (Yiddish) or **shamash** (Hebrew): The "servant" that lights the other candles.

Shavuot (lit. "weeks"): Pentecost.

Shchinah: The 10th *sefirah* and divine presence that is the door between the supernal world and the physical world.

shefa: Overflow of divine blessings.

Sheol: The biblical term for the place where everyone goes when they die.

Shmini Atzeret: Holiday that ends Sukkot, Tishrei 22.

Shoah: Catastrophe, refers to the Holocaust.

shofar: Ram's horn that is blown on Rosh Hashanah.

Simchat Torah: Joy of Torah, Tishrei 22 in Israel and Tishrei 23 in the Diaspora.

sinat hinam: Baseless hatred or gratuitous nastiness, the cause (according to the Rabbis) of the destruction of the Second Temple.

sitra achra: Other side, evil forces in the Kabbalah.

Sukkot: Tabernacles/huts, Tishrei 15.

tallit: Prayer shawl.

Talmud (lit. "learning"): Mishnah + Gemara.

Talmud Torah: Studying Torah (in its widest sense).

TaNaKH: Torah, Nevi'im (Prophets), Ketuvim (writings).

Tefillin: Phylacteries.

Ten Lost Tribes: When the Assyrians conquered the northern kingdom of Israel in 721 B.C.E., they scattered the inhabitants all over the kingdom.

teshuvah: Return and respond. Often translated as repentance.

theodicy: Justifying God, that is, reconciling the seeming lack of justice in this world with divine power and providence.

tikkun: Mystical concept of repairing the broken vessels; now used to describe acts of social justice.

Tikkun leyl Shavuot: All-night study session on Shavuot.

Tisha b'Av: Ninth of Hebrew month of Av, commemorates the destruction of the Temples.

Tishrei: Babylonian/Hebrew name for the seventh month.

Torah: Teaching or instruction, often refers to the Pentateuch.

Treyfa (unkosher) **Banquet**: in 1883 at the first graduating class of Hebrew Union College.

tsimtsum: Withdrawal, divine self-restraint.

Tu b'Av: The 15th of the Hebrew month of Av, Jewish Valentine's Day.

Tu b'Shvat: The 15th of the Hebrew month of Shvat, New Year for the Trees.

tza'ar b'alei chayim: Prohibition against causing distress to animals.

Tzaddik: Leader of a Hassidic group.

tzedakah: Righteousness, often translated as "charity."

Ushpizin: Mystical Sukkot guests: Abraham, Isaac, Jacob, Joseph, Moses, Aaron, and David.

White Paper (1939): Severely restricted Jewish immigration on the eve of World War II and the Shoah.

Yahrzeit (Yiddish): Anniversary of death.

yesh m'ayin: Creation out of nothing.

Yom Ha'atzmaut: Israeli Independence Day.

Yom Hashoah v'Hagvurah: The Day of Catastrophe and Heroism, otherwise known as Holocaust Remembrance Day.

Yom Hazikaron: Israeli Memorial Day.

Yom Kippur: Day of Atonement, Tishrei 10.

Yom Yerushalayim: Jerusalem Day.

Zionism: Political movement beginning in late-19th century to reestablish a Jewish state in the Land of Israel.

Biographical Notes

Adler, Felix (1851–1933). The son of prominent Reform Rabbi Samuel Adler. Growing up in America, the younger Adler finished his rabbinic and secular education in Germany. On his return, he advocated abandoning the particularistic elements of Judaism to focus exclusively on universal ethics. In 1876, Adler founded the New York Society for Ethical Culture.

Akiva, son of Joseph (50–135 C.E.). One of the leading figures of Rabbinic Judaism in the decades after the destruction of the Second Temple. In some ways, "Judaism" could just as easily be named "Akivaism." He was largely responsible for the traditions recorded in the Mishnah. He was also believed to engage in mystical practices. He maintained that the most important principle in the Torah was to show love to your neighbor, although he simultaneously held that study was greater than deeds. He promoted the Rabbinic doctrine that the entire Torah was given by God at Mount Sinai. Akiva was flayed to death by the Romans toward the end of the Bar Kochva Revolt.

Ba'al Shem Tov, Israel (1700–1760). The inspiration for Hassidism, a religious renewal movement that swept through Eastern Europe from 1750 through the 19th century. The Ba'al Shem Tov maintained that the study of Talmud was not the exclusive way to serve God. One could serve God through all commandments and all human activities as long as one's awareness was so directed. He had a small group of followers who spread his teachings throughout Eastern Europe. These *tzaddikim*, or righteous ones, lent their own style and personality to the message of the Ba'al Shem Tov.

Bar Kochva, Shimon (d. 135 C.E.). The military leader of the final rebellion against the Romans in the Land of Israel that began in 132. Although Rabbi Akiva believed him to be the messiah, Bar Kochva made no such claim. Bar Kochva based himself in the south of the country, where documents and coins have been unearthed testifying to his reign.

Dreyfus, Alfred (1859–1935). An assimilated Jew and captain in the French Army. He was falsely convicted of treason in 1895. Dreyfus was demoted and sent to Devil's Island off the coast of South America. His brother worked tirelessly to exonerate him. Finally, in 1906, a court of appeals pronounced his innocence. In the interim, his case garnered international attention. One of the reporters covering the initial trial was Theodor Herzl, who was inspired to question whether assimilation was a viable solution for European Jews. Herzl subsequently outlined his vision of a Jewish national independence.

Frankel, Zecharias (1801–1875). The founder of Conservative Judaism in Germany. At the time, it was called "Positive Historical Judaism." The original name reflects the idea that Judaism is a historical religion unfolding over time and that historical unfolding is positive because it allows Jewish law to maintain its relevance in each generation. Frankel accepted certain reforms but was dedicated to the binding nature of Jewish law as a whole. He was also opposed to the linguistic acculturation of Reform and insisted on preserving Hebrew in the prayer services. In 1854, he was named the director of a rabbinical seminary (Juedisch-Theologisches Seminar), which became the model for modern seminaries that combine critical scholarship and traditional Jewish study.

Geiger, Abraham (1810–1874). A founding father of the Reform movement in Germany. Geiger was also one of the outstanding scholars from the second generation of Jewish studies. He applied his scholarly research, which emphasized the human authorship of the Torah and demonstrated the progressive nature of Jewish law, to the reforms he hoped to institute in his own day. He served as a pulpit rabbi for 35 years and was instrumental in the establishment of the first Reform rabbinical seminary in Berlin in 1870.

Herzl, Theodor (1860–1904). Best remembered as the father of political Zionism. He was an assimilated Jew from Budapest who was educated in Vienna. He served as a reporter for the trial of Alfred Dreyfus and became convinced that the only solution for the Jewish problem in Europe was a national home. He wrote *The Jewish State* in 1896 and presided over the First Zionist Congress in Basel, Switzerland, in 1897. There, he said that in 50 years, a Jewish state would exist in Palestine. His words proved prophetic.

Heschel, Abraham Joshua (1905–1972). A scion of a Hassidic dynasty and one of the leading Jewish theologians in the United States in the 20th century. He was twice invited to the White House to speak on issues of social justice and was a friend and ally of Dr. Martin Luther King, Jr. His scholarship touched on every facet of

Jewish thought, *The Sabbath* and *God in Search of Man* are representative of his style and religious thought.

Hirsch, Emil G. (1851–1923). The son of a prominent Reform ideologue, Rabbi Samuel Hirsch. Upon returning from Germany with ordination and a doctorate, the younger Hirsch served as an editor of the *Jewish Encyclopedia*, professor of Rabbinics at the University of Chicago, and a congregational Rabbi. He was responsible for bringing the Social Gospel into Reform Judaism and featuring it in the 1885 Pittsburgh Platform.

Hirsch, Samson Raphael (1808–1888). Considered to be the father of Modern (or Neo-) Orthodoxy. He was a staunch opponent of Reform and its acceptance of biblical criticism. Hirsch advocated certain "external" reforms dealing with dress, language, and even education, but he was steadfast in his opposition to *halachic* change. Although he could not tolerate changes to the traditional liturgy calling for the reestablishment of a Jewish state, he did believe that one should demonstrate patriotism toward the country of one's citizenship. Hirsch opened the first Jewish day school in 1853 that combined Jewish and secular studies.

Judah the Prince, Rabbi (c. 135 C.E.–c. 219). Redacted the Mishnah, the first literary work of Rabbinic Judaism. He was both an outstanding scholar and the political leader of the community, representing Jewish interests to Rome. In Rabbinic literature, he is often simply referred to as "Rabbi." He led the Sannhedrin, the supreme Jewish legislative and judicial body, from Tzippori and Bet She'arim. He is buried in Bet She'arim in northern Israel in a restored archaeological site.

Kaplan, Mordecai (1881–1983). Taught at the Conservative Jewish Theological Seminary for more than half a century. Kaplan is also the founder of the fourth denomination in American Jewish life, Reconstructionism. Kaplan maintained that traditional Judaism gets a vote, not a veto, on how contemporary Jews express their Jewish commitments. Kaplan promoted the idea that Judaism is a civilization and American Jews should strive to live in both the Jewish and American civilizations Toward that end, Kaplan was an early supporter of the idea of Jewish community centers, where Jews could congregate for purposes other than religion. On matters religious, Kaplan was a forceful advocate of updating traditional rituals and ideas where possible and abandoning those that could not be updated, such as the idea of the chosen people.

Kook, Avraham Yitzchak HaCohen (1865–1935). The first Ashkenazi chief Rabbi of Palestine. Born to a Hassidic mother and a Mitnagdic father, Rav Kook combined Talmudic and *halachic* scholarship with the mysticism of the Kabbalah. Rav Kook's inspirational writings, poetry, and works of *halachah* served as the ideological foundation for many religious Zionists. He is widely perceived to be a bridge between the religious and secular worlds because he expressed admiration for the secular Zionists who were doing God's work, albeit unknowingly. His son, Tzvi Yehudah Kook, has become a central figure in the Israeli settler movement, which sees the State of Israel as the beginning of messianic redemption. A good digest of his writings can be found in *The Lights of Penitence*.

Leibowitz, Yeshayahu (1903–1994). One of the most controversial figures in Israel until his death. Although deeply committed to *halachah*, he nevertheless felt that Jewish law had to adapt to the new reality of a Jewish state. Leibowitz considered himself to be a disciple of Maimonides and the rationalism that the latter represented. On the question of chosen-ness, Leibowitz denies that the Jews were chosen. He reconceptualizes the traditional notion by arguing that Jews were commanded to be the chosen people, and the Jews may or may not respond to that divine demand. But, for Leibowitz, as for all Jewish rationalists, there is no intrinsic difference between Jews and Gentiles.

Luria, Isaac (1534–1572). Also known as the Holy Lion. He led a group of Kabbalists in Tzfat in the north of the Land of Israel. Luria developed the Kabbalah he inherited into a far more elaborate system involving four different worlds within the supernal realm. He also innovated a creation myth that involves *tsimtsum*, or divine withdrawal to create a space that is not divine in order to create the world. In the subsequent process of creation, there was a shattering of vessels containing divine energy; our task is to repair (*tikkun*) those shattered vessels through the performance of the commandments with the proper intention. Lurianic Kabbalah was influential for centuries.

Maimonides, Moses (1138–1204). Also known as RaMBaM (Rabbi Moses ben Maimon); born in Spain and lived in Egypt. Maimonides was a doctor to the sultan and for the Jewish community of Fostat, Old Cairo. His two greatest works are the *Mishneh Torah* (1180), a comprehensive summation of Rabbinic law, and the *Guide of the Perplexed* (1190), a text that brings together Rabbinic Judaism and Aristotelian philosophy. Maimonides was a controversial writer, and the true meaning of his *Guide* is still hotly debated. Maimonides's influence on both the development of *halachah* and Jewish philosophy cannot be overestimated. Although it is possible to disagree with the RaMBaM, one cannot ignore him.

Nachmanides, Moses (1194–1270). Also known as RaMBaN (Rabbi Moses ben Nachman); lived in Gerona, Spain, north of Barcelona, and died in the Land of Israel. RaMBaN is the earliest biblical commentator to include Kabbalistic hints. Like RaMBaM, with whom he frequently disagreed, RaMBaN was a doctor. He was also a Talmudist and leader of the Jewish community. He represented the Jews in disputations with the Christian community in 1263, his account of which has been dramatized in *The Disputation*, a BBC production. Shortly after his participation in the disputation, he left for the Land of Israel.

RaSHI, Rabbi Shlomo son of Isaac (1040–1105). Born in Troyes, France, and is most well known for his running commentary on the Talmud and TaNaKH. In his commentary on the TaNaKH, he usually selected and condensed earlier Rabbinic understandings of the text. His commentary was the first published Jewish work, even before the TaNaKH itself. His commentary is studied along with the TaNaKH in traditional communities down to today.

Schachter-Shalomi, Zalman (b. 1924). Born in Poland, educated in Vienna, and escaped the Nazis in 1941 by immigrating to the United States. Although ordained as a rabbi with the Chassidic sect HaBaD, Schachter-Shalomi fell away from the movement and received his Ph.D. from the Reform seminary Hebrew Union College. Schachter-Shalomi, since the 1960s, has been a leader in the Jewish Renewal movement. He combines a thoroughly traditional education with a modern outlook on religion. He emphasizes the importance of ecology, as well as promoting a personal relationship with God through joyous prayer, song, and dance.

Schneersohn, Menachem Mendel (1904–1994). The latest messianic figure in Judaism. Rebbe Schneersohn lead the Lubavitch movement (HaBaD) in America for decades following World War II and oversaw its impressive growth in ranks and Jewish outreach activity. In the early 1990s, there was intense speculation in the Lubavitch community about the messianic status of the Rebbe, which Schneersohn himself did nothing to quiet. When he died, the Lubavitch movement was split between those who maintain that he was/is the messiah and those who do not. Schneersohn, having no sons, left the Lubavitch community without an heir apparent.

Shimon son of Yochai, Rabbi (c. 2nd century C.E.) was one of the leading students of Rabbi Akiva. After Akiva's death, he fled to Babylonia. He is the reputed author of the *Zohar*, the major text of medieval Kabbalah. His *yahrtzeit* ("anniversary of death") is celebrated on LaG b'Omer by thousands making pilgrimage to his reputed gravesite on Mount Meron in northern Israel.

Sofer, Moses (1762–1839). Also known as the Hatam Sofer. He served a community in Hungary and was the most important traditional Jewish scholar in central Europe for the first four decades of the 19th century. Although more flexible in practice, Sofer expressed scorn for the Reform movement and its adherents. He promoted the notion that any innovation was forbidden and that Jews should be particularly careful to retain cultural aspects of their identity, including traditional names, the use of Yiddish, and distinctive garb. Sofer became the figurehead for later generations of Jews who became known as Ultra-Orthodox and are particularly incensed by the acculturation of the Modern Orthodox.

Soloveitchik, Joseph Dov (1903–1993). Born in Lithuania into the Brisk Rabbinic dynasty. A child prodigy, Soloveitchik went to Germany to receive a Ph.D. in religious philosophy. On immigrating to the United States, he taught Talmud for decades at Yeshiva University in New York City and founded the Orthodox day school Maimonides, outside of Boston. He was arguably the leading Torah figure in the United States in the second half of the 20th century. Rav Soloveitchik combined profound Torah knowledge and secular erudition. Thousands of his students refer to him simply as "the Rav" or "the Teacher." *Halachic Man* is a prime example of his dialectical thought.

Tzvi, Shabbatai (1626–1676). A charismatic leader who proclaimed himself messiah in 1665. Although there were other false messiahs in Jewish history, Shabbatai Tzvi was the most popular. Some of his followers remained convinced of his messianic status even after he converted to Islam, under the threat of death by the Turkish sultan, in 1666. Shabbatai Tzvi's teachings combined elements of Jewish mysticism, the call to penance, and violations of *halachah*. The dashed messianic hopes placed on Shabbatai Tzvi precipitated skepticism toward messianism as well as Kabbalah.

Wise, Isaac Mayer (1819–1900). The father of American Reform Judaism. He arrived from Germany in 1846 and went on to found the Union of American Hebrew Congregations (renamed Union of Reform Judaism in 2003), Hebrew Union College, and the Central Conference of American Rabbis. He was the editor of the Jewish newspaper *The Israelite* (later named *The American Israelite*) and the German-Jewish newspaper *Die Deborah*. Wise was not a radical reformer, though he did introduce mixed seating and rejected the use of traditional head coverings and prayer shawls for men in the Temple.

Yochanan ben Zakkai was one of the leading sages at the time of the destruction of the Second Temple (70 C.E.). According to Rabbinic lore, he was spirited out of Jerusalem in the final stages of the Roman siege. He secured permission from Rome to establish what became the seed of Rabbinic Judaism at Yavneh.

Bibliography

Note: I have used the following texts successfully in both undergraduate and adult education settings.

Barnavi, Eli. *An Historical Atlas of the Jewish People.* New York: Schocken, 2003. Barnavi edits a glossy coffee-table book that provides maps and photos with a condensed historical review from the Bible to today.

Berkovits, Eliezer. *Not in Heaven: The Nature and Function of Halakha.* New York: Ktav Publishing House, 1983. Beginning with the theory of *halachic* development, Berkovits then uses the issue of a straw widow to discuss *halachic* change.

Berlin, Adele, and Marc Zvi Brettler, eds. *The Jewish Study Bible.* Oxford: Oxford University Press, 2004. This recently published gem brings together the New Jewish Publication Society translation of the TANAKH with brief essays related to the Bible and biblical interpretation.

Cohen, Arthur, and Paul Mendes-Flohr, eds. *Contemporary Jewish Religious Thought.* New York: The Free Press, 1987. This text is an anthology of essays by many different authors on Jewish subjects from antisemitism to Zionism.

Green, Arthur. *EHYEH: A Kabbalah for Tomorrow.* Woodstock, VT: Jewish Lights Publishing, 2002. Green offers a modern approach to integrating the wisdom of the Kabbalah for contemporary seekers.

Heschel, Abraham Joshua. *God in Search of Man.* New York: Farrar, Straus and Giroux, 1951.

———. *The Sabbath.* New York: Farrar, Straus and Giroux, 1975. Heschel, a scion of a Hassidic dynasty, was one of the leading Jewish theologians in 20th-century America.

Holtz, Barry, ed. *Back to the Sources: Reading the Classic Jewish Texts.* New York: Summit Books, 1984. Holtz solicits essays from leading scholars on the different genres of Jewish literature from the Torah to Hassidism.

Olitzky, Kerry M., and Daniel Judson. *The Rituals and Practices of a Jewish Life.* Woodstock, VT: Jewish Lights Publishing, 2002. This book is particularly recommended for those looking to explore the fundamentals of Jewish practice.

Steinsaltz, Adin. *The Essential Talmud.* New York: Basic Books, 1976. This book provides the nuts and bolts of Talmud.

Waskow, Arthur, *Seasons of Our Joy: A Modern Guide to the Jewish Holidays.* Boston: Beacon Press, 1982. There's no more user-friendly book with which to tour the Jewish calendar.

Note: The following texts have been cited in the Essential Readings and Supplementary Readings sections for the individual lectures. Articles are not included in this list. Full citations for articles are provided after each lecture.

Agnon, S.Y. *Days of Awe.* New York: Schocken Books, 1995. A wonderful collection of traditional comments on Rosh Hashanah and Yom Kippur.

Anderson, Gary A. *The Genesis of Perfection: Adam and Eve in Jewish and Christian Imagination.* Louisville: Westminster John Knox Press, 2001.

Barr, James. "Adam: Single Man, or All Humanity?" in *Hesed va-emet*, eds. Jodi Magness and Seymour Gitin. Atlanta: Scholars Press, 1998.

Ben-Amos, Dan. "Israel ben Eliezer, the Baal Shem Tov," in *Judaism in Practice*, ed. Lawrence Fine. Princeton: Princeton University Press, 2001. A short profile of the founding figure of Hassidism.

Berger, David. *The Rebbe, the Messiah, and the Scandal of Orthodox Indifference.* Portland, OR: Littman Library of Jewish Civilization, 2001.

Berkovits, Eliezer. *Faith after the Holocaust.* New York, KTAV Publishing House, 1973.

Biale, Rachel. *Women and Jewish Law.* New York: Schocken Books, 1984.

Bickerman, Elias Joseph. *The Jews in the Greek Age.* Cambridge, MA: Harvard University Press, 1988.

———. *The Maccabees.* New York: Schocken, 1947.

Bin-Nun, "The Obligation of *Aliyah*," in *Israel as a Religious Reality*, ed. Chaim I. Waxman. Northvale, NJ: Jason Aronson, 1994.

Bleich, David J. "Judaism and Animal Experimentation," in *Judaism and Environmental Ethics*, ed. Martin D. Yaffe. Lanham, MD: Lexington Books, 2001.

Bokser, Baruch M. *Origins of the Seder*. Berkeley: University of California Press, 1984.

Borowitz, Eugene. *Contemporary Christologies: A Jewish Response*. New York: Paulist Press, 1980.

Borowitz, Eugene B., and Frances Weinman Schwartz. *Jewish Moral Virtues*. Philadelphia: Jewish Publication Society, 1999. A lovely extension of Judaism's ethical literature.

Boyarin, Daniel. *Carnal Israel*. Berkeley: University of California Press, 1993. Boyarin examines several issues of gender and sexuality in early Rabbinic Judaism.

Buber, Martin. *Hasidism and Modern Man*. New York: Horizon Press, 1958.

———.*Tales of the Hasidim*. New York: Schocken Books, 1947.

Caplan, Eric. *From Ideology to Liturgy: Reconstructionist Worship and American Liberal Judaism*. Cincinnati, OH: Hebrew Union College Press, 2002.

Cohen, Hermann. *Religion of Reason: Out of the Sources of Judaism*. New York: F. Ungar Pub., 1972. Cohen was a leading figure in 19th-century German Jewish philosophy.

Cohen, Naomi Wiener. *Encounter with Emancipation: The German Jews in the United States, 1830–1914*. Philadelphia, PA: Jewish Publication Society, 1984.

Cohen, Shaye J. D. *From the Maccabees to the Mishnah*. Philadelphia: Westminster Press, 1987. Cohen offers a readable history of the formative period of Rabbinic Judaism.

———. "Judaism to the Mishnah," in *Christianity and Rabbinic Judaism: A Parallel History of Their Origins and Early Development*, pp. 195–223. Washington, DC: Biblical Archaeology Society, 1992.

Dan, Joseph. *Ancient Jewish Mysticism*. Tel Aviv: MOD Books, 1993. A short introduction to the genres and topics of ancient Jewish mysticism.

Diament, Carol, ed. *Zionism: The Sequel*. New York: Hadassah, 1998. A literary collection of reflections on Jerusalem.

Dishon, David, and Noam Zion. *A Different Night Haggadah*. Jerusalem: Shalom Hartman Institute, 1997. A wonderful new Haggadah.

Dorff, Elliot N. *Matters of Life and Death: A Jewish Approach to Modern Medical Ethics*. Philadelphia : Jewish Publication Society, 1998.

Eisen, Arnold M. *The Chosen People in America: A Study in Jewish Religious Ideology*. Bloomington: Indiana University Press, 1983.

Elbogen, Ismar. *Jewish Liturgy: A Comprehensive History*. New York: Jewish Theological Seminary of America, 1993.

Elon, Ari. "The Torah as Love Goddess," in *Essential Papers on Talmud*, ed. Michael Chernick, pp. 463–476. New York: NYU Press, 1995.

Elon, Ari, Naomi Mara Hyman, and Arthur Waskow, eds. *Trees, Earth, and Torah: A Tu b'Shvat Anthology*. Philadelphia: Jewish Publication Society, 2000.

Feiner, Shmuel. *The Jewish Enlightenment*. Philadelphia: University of Pennsylvania Press, 2002.

Feldman, David M. *Health and Medicine in the Jewish Tradition*. New York: Crossroad, 1986.

Fine, Lawrence, ed. *Essential Papers on Kabbalah*. New York: New York University Press, 1995.

Fishkoff, Sue. *The Rebbe's Army: Inside the World of Chabad-Lubavitch*. New York: Schocken Books, 2003.

Fox, Marvin. *Interpreting Maimonides*. Chicago: University of Chicago Press, 1990.

Fredriksen, Paula, and A. Reinhartz, eds. *Jesus, Judaism, and Christian Anti-Judaism: Reading the New Testament after the Holocaust*. Louisville: Westminster/John Knox Press, 2002.

Friedlander, Albert H., ed. *Out of the Whirlwind: A Reader of Holocaust Literature*. New York: UAHC Press, 1999.

Friedman, Richard E. *Who Wrote the Bible?* San Francisco: Harper San Francisco, 1987. An entertaining introduction to modern biblical criticism.

Fromm, Erich. "The Sabbath Rituals," in *The Forgotten Language*. New York: Grove Press, 1957. Fromm, author of *The Art of Loving*, combines psychology and traditional Jewish wisdom.

Gillman, Neil. *The Death of Death: Resurrection and Immortality in Jewish Thought*. Woodstock, VT: Jewish Lights, 1997.

Goldenberg, "Law and Spirit in Talmudic Religion," in *Jewish Spirituality*, Vol. I, ed. Arthur Green, pp. 232–252. New York: Crossroad, 1994.

Goodman, Philip, ed. *A Hannuka Anthology*. Philadelphia: Jewish Publication Society, 1976.

———, ed. *The Passover Anthology*. Philadelphia: Jewish Publication Society, 1961.

———, ed. *A Purim Anthology*. Philadelphia: Jewish Publication Society, 1949.

———, ed. *The Rosh Hashanah Anthology*. Philadelphia: Jewish Publication Society, 1970.

———, ed. *The Shavuot Anthology*. Philadelphia: Jewish Publication Society, 1974.

———, ed. *The Sukkot and Simchat Torah Anthology*. Philadelphia: Jewish Publication Society of America, 1973.

———, ed. *The Yom Kippur Anthology*. Philadelphia: Jewish Publication Society, 1992.

Greenberg, Blu. *On Women and Judaism*. Philadelphia: Jewish Publication Society of America, 1981.

Greenberg, Irving. *The Jewish Way: Living the Holidays*. Northvale, NJ: J. Aronson, 1998.

Greenberg, Simon, ed. *The Ordination of Women as Rabbis*. New York: Jewish Theological Seminary, 1988.

Gurock, Jeffrey S. *American Jewish Orthodoxy in Historical Perspective* Hoboken, NJ: Ktav Publishing House, 1996.

———. *The Men and Women of Yeshiva: Higher Education, Orthodoxy, and American Judaism*. New York: Columbia University Press, 1988.

Halivni, David Weiss. *Midrash, Mishnah, and Gemara: The Jewish Predilection for Justified Law*. Cambridge, MA: Harvard University Press, 1986.

Hartman, David. *A Living Covenant*. Woodstock, VT: Jewish Lights, 1998. Hartman is one of the leading religious philosophers in Israel today. He looks at the early texts of Rabbinic Judaism to understand what type of person the Rabbis sought to develop.

Hauptman, Judith. *Rereading the Rabbis: A Woman's Voice*. Boulder, CO: Westview Press, 1998. Hauptman gives us fresh readings of Rabbinic texts related to women. Her treatment shows *halachic* flexibility in action.

Hertzberg, Arthur. *The Zionist Idea.* Philadelphia: Jewish Publication Society, 1997.

Heschel, Abraham Joshua. *Israel: An Echo of Eternity.* New York: Farrar, Straus and Giroux, 1969. A Jewish history of Israel.

———. *Man's Quest for God: Studies in Prayer and Symbolism.* Santa Fe, NM: Aurora Press, 1998.

———. *A Passion for Truth.* New York: Farrar, Straus and Giroux, 1973. Heschel combines a study of the Ba'al Shem Tov, the Kotzker Rebbe, and Kierkegaard.

Hirsch, Samson Raphael. *Nineteen Letters.* Jerusalem: Feldheim Publishers, 1969. Letters that Hirsch, the founder of Modern Orthodoxy, wrote to a young man having religious doubts.

Hoffman, Lawrence A. *The Canonization of the Synagogue Service.* Notre Dame, IN: University of Notre Dame Press, 1979.

———. "How the Amidah Began," in *My People's Prayer Book: The Amidah* (Vol. II), ed. Lawrence A. Hoffman, pp. 17–36. Woodstock, VT: Jewish Lights, 1997.

———, ed. *My People's Prayer Book: Shabbat at Home* (Vol. VII). Woodstock, VT: Jewish Lights, 1997.

———. *The Way into Jewish Prayer.* Woodstock, VT: Jewish Lights, 2000.

Idel, Moshe. *Kabbalah: New Perspectives.* New Haven: Yale University Press, 1988.

———. *Messianic Mystics.* New Haven: Yale University Press, 1998.

Jaffee, Martin S. *Early Judaism.* Upper Saddle River, NJ: Prentice Hall, 1997.

Josephus, Flavius. *Wars of the Jews.* New York: E.P. Dutton & Co., 1929. This classic covers the period before and after the Great Revolt, 66–70 C.E.

Kadushin, Max. *Worship and Ethics: A Study in Rabbinic Judaism.* Westport, CT: Greenwood Press, 1978.

Kalechofsky, Roberta. *Hagaddah for the Liberated Lamb.* Marblehead, MA: Micah Publications, 1985.

Kaplan, Mordecai M. *Dynamic Judaism: The Essential Writings of Mordecai M. Kaplan.* New York: Schocken Books, Reconstructionist Press, 1985. A broad collection of the writings from the founder of Reconstructionist Judaism.

————. *Judaism as a Civilization.* Philadelphia: Jewish Publication Society, 1934.

Katz, Jacob. *Exclusiveness and Tolerance: Studies in Jewish-Gentile Relations in Medieval and Modern Times.* New York: Schocken Books, 1962.

————. *Out of the Ghetto: The Social Background of Jewish Emancipation, 1770–1870.* New York: Schocken Books, 1978.

Ki Tov, Eliyahu, ed. *The Book of Our Heritage*, Vol. I, pp. 192–197. New York: Feldheim Publishers, 1997. Ki Tov offers a traditional encyclopedia of Jewish practice and thought in three short volumes.

Klein, Isaac. *A Guide to Jewish Religious Practice.* New York: Jewish Theological Seminary, 1992.

Knohl, Israel. *The Divine Symphony: The Bible's Many Voices.* Philadelphia: The Jewish Publication Society, 2003. This text demonstrates that the style of preserving different voices that we see in the Talmud has its roots in the Bible itself.

Kook, Abraham Isaac. *Lights of Penitence.* New York: Paulist Press, 1978. Inspirational reading anytime, but traditionally read between Rosh Hashanah and Yom Kippur.

Kraut, Benny. "Reform Judaism and the Unitarian Challenge," in *The American Jewish Experience*, ed. Jonathan D. Sarna. New York: Holmes and Meier, 1986.

Kugel, James L. "Hatred and Revenge," in *In Potiphar's House: The Interpretive Life of Biblical Texts*, pp. 214–246. Cambridge, MA: Harvard University Press, 1994 (reprint).

————. *The Bible as It Was.* Cambridge, MA: Belknap Press of Harvard University Press, 1997. A full presentation of early interpretations of the Torah.

Kula, Irwin, and Vanessa L. Ochs. *The Book of Jewish Sacred Practices.* Woodstock, VT: Jewish Lights Publishing, 2001.

Lamm, Norman. *Shema.* Philadelphia: Jewish Publication Society, 1998. Lamm offers a tour of Jewish interpretations of a few biblical verses which become central components of the Rabbinic liturgy.

Leibowitz, Yeshayahu. *Judaism, Human Values, and the Jewish State*, ed. Eliezer Goldman; trans. Eliezer Goldman and Yoram Navon, Zvi Jacobson, Gershon Levi, and Raphael Levy. Cambridge: Harvard University Press, 1992. Leibowitz was a prominent personality in Israeli political and religious life. This collection of his writings gives English readers a sense of this controversial figure.

Levenson, Jon Douglas. *The Hebrew Bible, The Old Testament, and Historical Criticism.* Louisville: Westminster/John Knox Press, 1993.

Levine, Lee I. *The Ancient Synagogue: The First Thousand Years.* New Haven: Yale University Press, 2000.

———. "Judaism from the Destruction of Jerusalem to the End of the Second Jewish Revolt," in *Christianity and Rabbinic Judaism: A Parallel History of Their Origins and Early Development.* Washington, DC: Biblical Archaeology Society, 1992.

Levy, Ze'ev. "Ethical Issues of Animal Welfare in Jewish Thought," in *Judaism and Environmental Ethics*, ed. Martin D. Yaffe. Lanham, MD: Lexington Books, 2001.

Loewenberg, Frank. *From Charity to Social Justice: The Emergence of Communal Institutions for the Support of the Poor in Ancient Judaism.* New Brunswick: Transaction Publishers, 2001.

Maimonides, Moses. *Guide of the Perplexed.* Chicago: University of Chicago, 1963.

———. *Introduction to Perek Chelek*, in *Pirkei Avot*, ed. Eliyahu Touger. New York: Moznaim Publishing, 1994. Maimonides treats issues involved with the coming world and the messiah in this short text.

———. *Mishneh Torah*, ed. Rabbi Eliyahu Touger. New York: Moznaim Publishers, 1994.

Matt, Daniel. "Adorning the 'Bride' on the Feast of Weeks," in *Judaism in Practice*, ed. Lawrence Fine. Princeton: Princeton University Press, 2001.

———. "Ayin: The Concept of Nothingness in Jewish Mysticism," in *Essential Reflections on Jerusalem,* ed. Carol Diament. New York, Hadassah, 1995.

———. "The Mystic and the Mizwot," in *Jewish Spirituality*, Vol. I, ed. Arthur Green. New York: Crossroad, 1994.

Meyer, Michael A. "German-Jewish Identity in 19th-Century America," in *The American Jewish Experience*, ed. Jonathan D. Sarna. New York: Holmes and Meier, 1986.

———. *Response to Modernity: A History of the Reform Movement in Judaism*. Detroit: Wayne State University Press, 1995.

Nadell, Pamela S. *Women Who Would Be Rabbis: A History of Women's Ordination, 1889–1985*. Boston: Beacon Press, 1998.

Neusner, Jacob. "Varieties of Judaism in the Formative Age," in *Jewish Spirituality*, Vol. I, ed. Arthur Green. New York: Crossroad, 1987.

Pallière, Aimé. *The Unknown Sanctuary: A Pilgrimage from Rome to Israel*, translated from the French by Louise Waterman Wise. New York: Bloch, 1928. A Christian student of Elijah Benamozegh spreads the teaching of the Seven Noahide laws.

Petuchowski, Jakob J. "Spirituality," in *Open Thou Mine Eyes*, ed. Herman J. Blumberg, Hoboken, Ktav Publishing, 1992.

———. *Studies in Modern Theology and Prayer*. Eds. Elizabeth R. Petuchowski, Jakob J., and Aaron M. Petuchowski. Philadelphia: Jewish Publication Society, 1998. One of the great scholars and theologians of the 20th century.

Rosenberg, Bernhard H., and Fred Heuman, eds. *Theological and Halakhic Reflections on the Holocaust*. New York: Rabbinical Council of America, 1992.

Rosenberg, Shalom. *Good and Evil in Jewish Thought*. Tel Aviv: MOD Books, 1989.

Rosenbloom, Noah H. *Tradition in an Age of Reform: The Religious Philosophy of Samson Raphael Hirsch*. Philadelphia: Jewish Publication Society of America, 1976.

Rosenzweig, Franz. *On Jewish Learning*. Madison, WI: University of Wisconsin Press, 2002. Included in this small text is correspondence between Rosenzweig and Martin Buber that clarifies their different understandings of revelation.

Roth, John K., and Berenbaum, Michael, eds. *Holocaust: Religious and Philosophical Implications*. New York: Paragon House, 1989.

Sandmel, David F., Rosann M. Catalano, Christopher M. Leighton, eds. *Irreconcilable Differences? A Learning Resource for Jews and Christians*. Boulder, CO: Westview Press, 2001.

Saperstein, Marc. *Essential Papers on Messianic Movements and Personalities in Jewish History.* New York: New York University Press, 1992.

Sarna, Jonathan D. *American Judaism: A History.* New Haven: Yale University Press, 2004.

Sarna, Nahum M. *Songs of the Heart: On the Books of Psalms: Exploring the Prayers of Ancient Israel.* New York: Schocken Books, 1993.

Schachter-Shalomi, Zalman. *Paradigm Shift.* Northvale, NJ: Aronson Publishers, 2000. A brief exploration into the thought of the founder of Jewish Renewal.

Schechter, Solomon. *Aspects of Rabbinic Theology.* Woodstock, VT: Jewish Lights Publishing, 1993.

Schiffman, Lawrence H. *From Text to Tradition: A History of Second Temple and Rabbinic Judaism.* Hoboken, NJ: Ktav Publishing House, 1991.

Scholem, Gershom Gerhard. *Kabbalah.* New York: Quadrangle/New York Times Book Co., 1974.

———. *Major Trends in Jewish Mysticism.* New York, Schocken Books, 1961.

———. "The Messianic Idea in Judaism," in *The Messianic Idea in Judaism and Other Essays.* New York: Schocken Books, 1971.

———. *On the Mystical Shape of the Godhead.* Trans. Joachim Neugroschel. New York: Schocken Books, 1991.

———. *Sabbatai Sevi: The Mystical Messiah.* London: Routledge & K. Paul, 1973. Scholem is the father of the academic study of Jewish mysticism.

Schwartz, Elon. "Bal Tashchit," in *Judaism and Environmental Ethics*, ed. Martin D. Yaffe. Lanham, MD: Lexington Books, 2001.

Schwartz, Richard H. *Judaism and Vegetarianism.* New York: Lantern Books, 2001.

Shanks, Herschel, ed. *Ancient Israel.* Washington, DC: Biblical Archaeology Society, 1988.

Signer, Michael A. "Trinity, Unity, Idolatry?" in *Lesarten des judische-christlichen Dialoges.* Bern: Lang, 2002.

Silber, Michael. "The Emergence of Ultra-Orthodoxy," in *The Uses of Tradition*, ed. Jack Wertheimer. New York: Jewish Theological Seminary of America, 1992.

Soloveitchik, Joseph Dov. *Worship of the Heart: Essays on Jewish Prayer.* Ed. Shalom Carmy. Hoboken, NJ: Ktav Publishing, 2003.

Spitz, Elie Kaplan. *Does the Soul Survive?* Woodstock, VT: Jewish Lights Publishing, 2000.

Tishby, Isaiah. *Wisdom of the Zohar*. Washington: The Littman Library of Jewish Civilization, 1991. This extensive collection contains academic introductions to many of the topics covered by the *Zohar* followed by heavily annotated *Zohar* passages.

Urbach, Ephraim. *The Sages: Their Concepts and Beliefs.* Trans. Israel Abrahams. Cambridge, MA: Harvard University Press, 1987. A dense treatment of Rabbinic thought.

Washofsky, Mark. "Abortion and the Halakhic Conversation," in *The Fetus and Fertility in Jewish Law*, eds. Walter Jacob and Moshe Zemer. Pittsburgh: Rodef Shalom Press, 1995.

Waskow, Arthur. *Godwrestling, Round II.* Woodstock, VT: Jewish Lights Publishing, 1996. Waskow is one of the contemporary leaders in the Jewish Renewal movement.

Wine, Sherwin T. *Judaism beyond God: A Radical New Way to Be Jewish.* Farmington Hills, MI: Society for Humanistic Judaism, 1985.

Wolfson, Ron. *The Shabbat Seder.* Woodstock, VT: Jewish Lights Publishing, 1996.

Internet Sources:

Internet Jewish History Sourcebook: http://www.fordham.edu/halsall/jewish/jewishsbook.html#The%20Emergence%20of%20Judaism

Second Temple and Talmudic Era Judaisms: http://www.hum.huji.ac.il/dinur/Internetresources/historyresources/second_temple_and_talmudic_era.htm

Jewish Virtual Library: http://www.us-israel.org/index.html

On Maimonides's eight levels of tzedakah: http://www.mechon-mamre.org/jewfaq/tzedakah.htm

For a portal into all things Jewish: http://www.shamash.org

Notes